WOMEN & RISK

*How to Master
Your Fears and Do What
You Never Thought
You Could Do*

ALSO BY NICKY MARONE

How to Father a Successful Daughter

WOMEN & RISK

How to Master Your Fears and Do What You Never Thought You Could Do

NICKY MARONE

ST. MARTIN'S PRESS

New York

Design by Janet Tingey

Library of Congress Cataloging-in-Publication Data

Marone, Nicky.
    Women and risk : how to master your fears and do what you never thought you could do / Nicky Marone.
      p. cm.
    Includes bibliographical references and index.
    ISBN 0-312-07115-9
    1. Women—Psychology. 2. Self-realization. I. Title.
HQ1206.M3443   1992
155.6'33—dc20   91-36383
                                              CIP

First Edition: February 1992

10 9 8 7 6 5 4 3 2 1

For my mother, Maxine,
a risk-takin' woman and the last of the red-hot mommas.

CONTENTS

PART III
A SIX-STEP PLAN FOR MASTERY

ACKNOWLEDGMENTS

A book is a collaborative effort. It is with deep gratitude and love that I wish to acknowledge the following people, without whom it never could have happened:

Debbye Naber for her unrelenting loyalty, patience, and support during some of the most trying circumstances of my life; for seeing me through that critical first year as I struggled with self-doubt and too much material; for all her readings and acumen during the various ramshackle stages of the manuscript; and for her brains, her unfailing marksmanlike wit, and her love of the language.

Kristen Yount for all those phone calls she really didn't have time for; for her ability to ask just the right question at just the right time; for her keen and penetrating insight into both me and the nature of writing; and for her undying, high-spirited love of fun and adventure.

Bob Pasternak for teaching me how to cut through illusion; for opening my eyes to the possibilities within and without; for his wisdom, his generosity, and his commitment to something (or should I say nothing?) bigger than himself.

My editor, Hope Dellon, for giving me the privilege and opportunity to share the ideas presented herein and for the care with which she read the manuscript.

My assistant, Lisa Stein, for putting up with my detail-oriented mentality and for being a fierce young woman.

My agent, Sandy Dijkstra, for her hard work in whipping what started out as a confusing mess into a proper proposal and for her ability to spot potential in the tiny seed of an idea.

PREFACE

Few of us would describe ourselves as helpless. We pay the bills, take care of our families, meet our commitments. We are responsible, adult women.

Yet many of us also live a secret life, which, like the dark side of the moon, is kept hidden from others. It is in this secret life that we understand the meaning of helplessness. It is in this secret life that we can be held in the grip of repetitive and destructive behavior patterns. We may hold steadfastly to unhealthy love relationships; we may struggle endlessly with eating disorders or substance abuse; we may panic needlessly at the unforeseen changes in our lives. Depression stalks some of us like a samurai. Many of us scrupulously avoid risk or challenge in any areas but the ones in which we have already succeeded, fearing the process of learning a new task. Even after achieving most of our goals, many of us remain plagued by the secret self-doubts of low self-esteem.

We labor under a negative force in our lives we can't quite name, a force that depletes us of energy and denies us our right to meet life's challenges with a sense of excitement and joy. We bear an unnecessary burden, which undermines our ability to take risks and act in our own best interests. In other words, we suffer from a condition shared by many women in our society—a condition known as learned helplessness. Learned helplessness is a debilitating breakdown in our belief system that can produce serious behavior disorders. Fortunately this style of behavior can be *unlearned*, but, left untreated, it can ruin a life that would otherwise be happy and fulfilling.

The study of learned helplessness has unearthed many intriguing insights, but one is particularly noteworthy: Our common-sense explanations of human motivation and perseverance do not, in fact, explain human motivation and perseverance. For example, common sense suggests that intelligence and ability would be critical factors influencing whether an individual seeks or avoid challenges, persists or withdraws in the face of difficulty, and develops skills adequately and effectively. Research, however, shows that this is not necessarily the case, particularly among females. In studies where confusion is experimentally induced, boys of low ability are *facilitated* by their confusion; that is, they try harder. Girls of high ability, on the other hand, are the group most *debilitated* by confusion; that is, they give up.

These self-defeating patterns remain active in adult gender studies as well. When women are asked to predict their performance level on a new task, they consistently underestimate their actual performance. Males consistently overestimate theirs. On later tests, even after women have succeeded at the task and men have failed at it, these different expectations of future success do not change. Finally, if given the opportunity to avoid the task, women will typically opt out.

If, then, our competence does not predict our likeliness to seek out challenges and persist in the face of difficulty, what does? The short answer is our beliefs, or how we explain life events to ourselves. In other words, the critical factors influencing persistence and motivation are the ways we *construe* the situation, *interpret* the events, and *process* the information.

For example, I may fail at a task for a number of reasons. I may have had inadequate sleep or preparation. My boss or some other authority figure involved in the project may not have been cooperative. Perhaps I chose an inopportune moment to present my ideas. I may have misjudged what was required of me. Distracting personal problems may have depleted my energy level for that day. A whole variety of explanations is possible.

But if I believe (construe) that my failure is proof that I lack intelligence and ability, if I believe that *I* am a failure because my project failed, and if I believe that all my future attempts will fail as well, then I can be said to have acquired a helpless style.

Learned helplessness, then, reveals deficiencies at the most basic of levels: a lack of belief in one's own self-efficacy and intelligence.

Behind this deceptively simple explanation lies a complex set of self-defeating and interacting responses, choices, and behaviors (which will be examined in depth later). It is a style of behavior that psychologists consider "maladaptive."

Bear in mind that the word *maladaptive* is a scientific term and, as such, is far too clinical to capture the grim realities of learned helplessness or the terrible toll it takes on a woman's life. When you consider, for example, that the capacity to adapt is the human being's greatest advantage in the evolutionary game plan, any condition that diminishes this adaptive capacity, whether psychological or physical, proves to be a serious, possibly tragic, deficit. The subtle nature of learned helplessness makes it insidious to any individual, but its congruence with our culture's view of femininity places a double whammy on women.

Current research shows that this style of behavior systematically sabotages the very core of an individual's ability to cope with the rigorous demands of living in the world today. Learned helplessness corrodes self-esteem, blocks ambition, short-circuits motivation, and contributes to depression and panic disorders. People who suffer from learned helplessness are less likely to respond adaptively to change and more likely to avoid challenge and risk. They show low persistence in the face of obstacles and difficulties, exhibit deficiencies in strategic planning, and are often unable to assess the causes of both their failures *and* their successes.

THE JOY OF MASTERY

The opposite of learned helplessness is mastery behavior. People who have learned to be mastery-oriented are highly adaptive to new situations, are stimulated by the challenges of change, are persistent in the face of adversity, and seem to enjoy exerting effort in pursuit of a goal. They think strategically when faced with an obstacle and apply unique, creative solutions to their problems. Most importantly, they enjoy doing it!

The range of behavior from learned helplessness to mastery is a vast and uncharted terrain, particular to each individual who undertakes the journey. The price of helplessness can range from producing minor inconveniences, to obscuring one's vision of major opportunities, to blinding one to dangerous or abusive situations. Mastery behavior can span the same range, from learning to operate one's VCR, to quitting a dead-end job, to dumping the no-good louse who beats you up.

The important aspect here is that mastery-oriented individuals do more than just cope. They create reality and alter the world to fit their conception of it. For the benefit of us all, they demonstrate in living color that the world will yield to the creative and focused application of a committed psyche.

It is possible for an individual to occupy several positions on the mastery scale *simultaneously*, depending on the number and intensity of the challenges she confronts at any one time or the area of her life affected. For example, a highly competent, aggressive, executive woman may become weak-kneed and pale at the thought of a white-water river-rafting trip because of a lack of belief in her own athletic prowess. So, while she is mastery-oriented in one realm of her life, she may still be quite helpless in another. (Luckily, when she chooses to overcome this fear, or faulty belief, the skills she has acquired through confronting the risks and challenges of executive life will serve her on the rafting trip as well.)

Becoming mastery-oriented requires not only belief and commitment but *time*. It is a process. If we are not there yet, it means we are still on our way. As educational psychologist Peter Winograd puts it, "Failure is a state, not a trait." In other words, what may appear as a failure at one point in time turns out, when viewed from a later vantage point, to be part of a larger process—one step on the road to a goal not *yet* achieved.

This is not just another book about risk taking. It is about verifiable antidotes to learned helplessness, about the paradox of learning to take risks *in order* to learn mastery and using fear to change who you are and who you will become. It does not guarantee success, nor does it suggest that when they roll the final credits, you will be happy and secure. Maybe you will, maybe you won't. No one knows. That's the scary part. It is also the exhilarating part. Either way, it is vital to take those risks because there's no way you can keep avoiding them and still achieve your goals.

This book examines the difference between those who, through no fault of their own, have learned helplessness and those who have acquired mastery behavior. Those with learned helplessness will avoid and fear risk, thereby ultimately avoiding and fearing life itself, which is fraught with risk. Those who are mastery-oriented embrace both life's terror and its counterpart, life's ecstasy.

With these realities in sharp focus throughout this book, we can begin the process of taking risks and replacing the self-defeating behaviors of learned helplessness with the life-giving, self-affirming traits of mastery behavior.

WOMEN & RISK

*How to Master
Your Fears and Do What
You Never Thought
You Could Do*

PART I

*Understanding the Problem:
Stories From the Front*

CHAPTER 1

The Cherished Illusion: Women and Helplessness

Life is a gymnasium for the soul.
—ZEN SAYING

The attractive redhead in the second seat of the fourth row had been staring at me intently throughout my presentation. She wore that hyperalert expression that generally signals a desire to speak, but remained conspicuously silent during the formal discussion period that followed. Now, having joined a group of women gathered informally after the workshop to talk, she opened up.

"This workshop has really been an intense, even uncomfortable experience for me," she said. "I am a currently single, overeducated working woman. I take care of myself, pay the bills, and take out the garbage, if you know what I mean. I would never have described myself as someone with learned helplessness, but as you were listing the symptoms, I suddenly realized that a lot of them apply to me."

"In what way?" I asked, wanting to hear her story.

"You've undoubtedly heard the expression 'Publish or perish.' Well, as a university professor I can tell you it's true. Acquiring tenure means publishing in the academic journals on a regular basis.

"My tenure review was scheduled for last fall. It was imperative that I submit articles during the spring and summer, especially because I was behind. (My committee requires two articles per year.) Anyway, I'm embarrassed to say that, instead of writing, I lay around watching old Bob Newhart reruns and eating entire boxes of Ritz crackers at one sitting. Major deadlines passed, basically because I *still* don't believe in my own ability to perform up to academic standards."

The other women nodded in silent and compassionate understanding.

"Up until today I thought of it as simple procrastination and hated myself for being so lazy. Now I realize there were more complicated forces at work."

"What happened with your tenure?" I asked.

"I didn't get it. Instead, I got a reprimand from the dean. He allowed me one more year to get it together because he knows I'm a good teacher, but being a good teacher isn't enough. I was hired primarily to do research. It's publish or perish, and I'm afraid I may perish."

The woman standing behind her piped up.

"My story is a little different, but it's the same idea. I have a similar problem with finances, trying to figure out what to do with a large sum of money I have inherited. For some strange reason, this has thrown me completely off guard. I make responsible decisions all the time about my family and on the job, but this decision has completely immobilized me. Maybe it's because I am recently divorced and all the big money decisions were usually handled by my husband.

"Anyway, I hate to admit this, but I have let that money sit in a savings account for two years, earning a paltry five percent interest, instead of investing it and earning a lot more. I know I'm losing money, and a lot of it, but I just can't seem to make the decision. I'm hoping that the information you gave us at the workshop today will help me analyze what's really going on inside. I think I'm beginning to see why I'm not acting in my own best interest. Maybe now I can get past this inertia and take some action."

"Talk about inertia!" interjected an athletic-looking woman. "I put off graduate school for eleven years, all because I was convinced I couldn't pass the math portion of the Graduate Record Exam required for entrance into the business program. I didn't do anything constructive to correct this deficit, you understand, like hire a tutor. I just stewed about it and felt like a failure for ten years. I refused even to try."

"So, did you finally go?" asked another woman.

"Yeah. I woke up one day as a single parent with three kids and no child support. I realized it was graduate school or poverty. It took that kind of extreme situation, though, to start me moving through my own self-doubts."

"How did you do?"

"You won't believe this," she replied with an ironic smile. "I got a higher score on the math portion than I did on the verbal!"

As everyone shook their heads in silent camaraderie, another woman spoke up.

"I consider myself a responsible adult. I even pride myself on being something of a gutsy broad. But when you were outlining the helpless-behavior style, I thought, 'My God, *I* do that!' Not all the time, of course, but under certain conditions. Like anything having to do with the car, for instance. I completely abdicate responsibility. I won't even listen to the mechanic's explanation of what needs to be done. I just tell him to call my boyfriend and let him make the decision.

"Well, that's fine, as long as I have a boyfriend. A couple of months ago, he and I were having a lot of trouble. We weren't getting along and I wanted out in the worst way, but I kept thinking, 'Who will I get to take care of my car?' "

This comment elicited a burst of laughter from the group. Their all-too-familiar recognition of her predicament barely hides the panic lying just below the surface.

By now I have become accustomed to these groups of women who gather following my "Overcoming Learned Helplessness" workshop. The workshop was originally designed for corporations whose work forces had to cope with corporate buyouts, hostile takeovers, down-sizing, employee insecurity, depletion of morale, and so on. The audience always includes an equal number of men.

What has intrigued me over the years is that, although men are always present at these workshops, they are never the ones to gather at the end, eager to talk in more detail about the issues. (This is *not* the case, however, following my workshops on "Stimulating Creative Thinking." There, it is primarily men who gather to ask questions.)

Anxious to understand this marked divergence of interest, I began monitoring the responses of men and women as I presented the material. I found that men and women have disparate reactions, not only to the information but even to the term *learned helplessness*. When women are initially exposed to the term, there is an im-mediate, gut-level recognition of its meaning without the need for

an explanation. Women simply nod their heads and smile know-
ingly. All types of women do this, even the most successful professional women in the audience, whom the stereotype paints as
anything but "helpless."

Men, on the other hand, react with puzzled expressions and raise
their hands to ask for clarification. They just don't get it. There is
very little in their life experience that enables them to identify with
the condition or even relate to the term. Don't misunderstand me.
I am not saying men can't suffer from learned helplessness. Rather,
they are not granted permission by the culture to use it as a viable
alternative to coping with risk and challenge and therefore do not
recognize it in themselves as readily as do women.

This gender grouping that spontaneously and inevitably forms at
the end of each workshop reinforces other research that shows that
a critical breakdown of will to master difficult and risky situations
remains at the core of the *female* experience. After interviewing and
talking to scores of women, I have come to the further conclusion
that learned helplessness affects women across the socioeconomic
spectrum. This realization prompted me to write this book for and
about women.

I do not intend to imply that only women suffer from learned
helplessness. While some men carry the same self-defeating belief
systems that women do, generally they do not do so in the same
numbers or to the same degree as women. As we will see, men are
much more likely to exhibit the traits of mastery behavior when
faced with a challenge and much less willing to believe they are
inferior, at fault, or personally responsible for every failure or setback
they encounter.

Whether they are career professionals or career homemakers,
women exhibit more bravado and less mastery behavior of the kind
that men exhibit—the kind that shows confidence in their ability
to produce desired results, however risky or dangerous they might
be. This confidence in one's ability to influence outcomes, to produce desired results, is known as self-efficacy. When we lack belief
in self-efficacy, we have acquired learned helplessness. For many
of us, just behind the mask of self-assurance there are enough self-
doubts to immobilize us in times of crisis or risk, or even in everyday
decision making.

Because of a complex interplay between biology and culture,

women continue to believe in their "right" to be rescued from risky or dangerous circumstances. Society colludes to reinforce this belief, albeit more subtly than twenty years ago. There are circumstances with which women are simply not expected to cope. Fighting off physical intimidation or attack, fixing defective machinery, hooking up a winch to pull ourselves out of a snow drift, getting up on the roof to check out wind damage, climbing an old oak tree to cut out the dead branches, checking on something that went bump in the night—all these are things men will usually do for us. For the most part we are glad of it. Ultimately, though, this underlying belief in our "right to be rescued" enables us (or should I say disables us?) to embrace a belief that helplessness is a viable option.

TERROR AND ECSTASY

For many of us it is fear that begets the most intense feeling of help-lessness. Fear of being alone, fear of being attached; fear of failure, fear of success; fear of change, fear of monotony; fear of living, fear of dying; the list is as endless as there are individuals in the world.

The very first step on the long road to overcoming learned help-lessness is the commitment to overcoming fear itself. We must confront the fear of fear, or its palpable presence will always and irrevocably stand in each new bend of the road, grinning and win-ning, paralyzing us on our journey to the transformation of self.

Recently a friend said to me after a long conversation about a nagging problem in her life, "If only I could see the future. If only I knew what was going to happen." Basically what she was saying was, "If only I didn't have to take a risk, if only I didn't have to feel fear." She might just as well have said, "If only I didn't have to be human."

Ask any psychic reader, fortune-teller, or channeler the gender of most of his or her clientele, and the unhesitating answer will be women. Why are women the ones with such a burning need to know what's going to happen? Why don't men run off to psychics for glimpses of the future in the numbers that women do?

Many New Age feminists of the magical-mystical variety will argue that women are more in tune with and attuned to "other worlds," more open to the intervention of the sacred and magical in their lives, more accepting of other ways of "knowing" and therefore more likely to seek them out. I think this is perfectly possible and I often subscribe to it myself. I also think there is an additional explanation.

First, inherent in the practice of consulting psychics is the belief that events are destined to happen in a predetermined way and that if we just knew more about that way, we could prepare for it. The link here with learned helplessness is obvious. If events and outcomes are predestined, then we have no control over them. In other words, *our actions do not affect the final outcome of events*—the very definition of learned helplessness.

If you think about it, the main reason people consult psychics about specific problems is that they feel a lack of control over the outcome. This helplessness makes them fearful and insecure, so they endeavor to determine the outcome ahead of time. When we believe our own actions will be effective in solving a problem, we are less likely to turn to a psychic to give us the answer and tell us what to do.

Not only do we feel frightened of that uncertainty but, as women, we often doubt our ability to handle the final outcome of events, whatever that outcome may be. Interestingly, men, who have no more information to go on than we do (and probably less), seem to trust themselves to handle whatever happens and so are less likely to seek the pronouncements of "seers."

Often when women go to therapists, they can be heard saying, "What should I be learning?" or "What should I be doing?" Instead of taking personal responsibility, they ask someone else to tell them what to do, someone else to interpret reality for them, someone else to take away the fear and risk involved in *not* knowing what they are "supposed" to be doing. It is another attempt to flee from the unpredictability inherent in authentic living.

The truth they wish to escape from is that being human requires acceptance of the mystery. We have no choice, really, but to make most of our decisions in an existential void with only a limited set of perceptions as our guides. We have no choice but to accept the unnerving truth that life is scary; that for as long as a heart is beating, it is vulnerable to suffering and death; and that even under the best of circumstances *we do not know what is going to happen next.*

Now, we can either let this depress and frighten us into a flight from risk taking altogether (which is really a flight from life itself, since avoidance of risk is only an illusion) *or* we can prepare ourselves down on terra firma as best we can and then take to the air, developing the behaviors that will empower us to soar with the truth we cannot avoid in the first place. There is only one destination for us all. The journey is inward, and it is a solo flight. For although we may be unable to control the actions of others or the events unfolding around us, we have a magnificent array of thought-choices that create our internal landscape. When the thoughts we choose compose pictures that terrify us, an appropriate emotion follows, and we may perish. When the thoughts we choose fashion pictures that thrill and ennoble us, a different but equally appropriate emotion follows, and we arrive in a new and exotic territory. Immobilizing terror or rip-roaring exhilaration, the interpretation is ours.

As Tom Robbins said in *Even Cowgirls Get the Blues,* "All a person can do in this life is to gather about her her integrity, her imagination and her individuality and with these ever with her, out front and in sharp focus, leap into the dance of experience."[1]

Now, for some of you all this talk about leaping into the dance of experience makes you want to leap into the safety of your bed with the covers pulled over your head. Before you do, consider the following story:

My life was changed by the utterance of a one-syllable word. Only two letters, but I have not perceived or lived my life the same way since.

It began when a friend invited me to go skiing with her. I made up excuses, but she persisted, coaxing and persuading, all to no avail. I could stall indefinitely and I knew it.

Finally she said, "You are thirty-three years old, a Colorado native with access to the most magnificent slopes this or any other planet has to offer, and you've never been skiing! I've been trying to get you to go for the last three winters. What's the problem?"

"Nothing, really," I would lie, "I'll go skiing with you, I promise. It's just that I'm so busy, I don't have the time."

"For four years? Come on, Marone, something else is going on here."

What was going on was that I was stricken with fear. Careening down mountains at high speeds completely out of control and directly in the paths of others who appeared to be equally out of control was not my idea of fun. A sport that appeared to offer little more than scenery coupled with an opportunity for pain and disability was a sport I could do without.

I had been a dancer since the age of four, and though I possessed a sense of balance and coordination, I was sure these would immediately desert me when confronted with a 12,000-foot peak covered with snow. Furthermore, I could hear my mother's voice in the background of my brain, "What if you fall down and break your leg? Then you can't dance anymore."

Finally one day, after yet another feeble excuse on my part, my friend said, "All right, I've had it. *Why* won't you go skiing?"

I paused, considering whether to be truthful.

"I'm scared," I replied quietly.

Then came that one-syllable word I told you about that destroyed my comforting myths, discredited my belief system, and left me exposed and accountable.

"So?"

At first it just didn't compute.

"What?"

"I said, *So?*"

"What do you mean?"

"I mean that being scared is not a justification for not doing it. In fact it's even more of a reason *to* do it."

"Yeah, but . . ."

"Don't yeah-but me," she retorted impatiently. "That's what people say to justify a lack of courage." Then, more quietly this time, "Look, don't you know that everyone is scared the first time they go skiing?"

I didn't know that.

"It's true. Either they are scared of taking a bad spill and killing themselves or they are scared of falling off the lift and making an ass of themselves. You would have to be a little crazy not to be scared. The point is, they go anyway. It's the most important reason to do anything. If you let one fear stop you, how many other fears will you allow, *are you allowing*, to stop you from doing what you want to do?"

It's not that this was such new information. Of course I had heard it before—grabbing the gusto, only going 'round once, and all that. But I believed, in my little coward's heart, that people who grabbed the gusto never experienced fear. Therefore, my fear was a perfectly plausible reason to avoid anything. I had foolproof justification to mollycoddle myself, and I liked it that way.

I don't mind telling you I didn't appreciate someone who called herself my friend insinuating that my beliefs were all wrong. Even more irritating was her implication that the time had come for my transformation.

Just for your information, I didn't break my leg. I did fall off the chair lift, though, and spent most of the day spread-eagled in the snow. Yet on the drive back from the resort I was exultant as I munched on a well-earned granola bar and reflected on my day. "I adore skiing!" I proclaimed to my friend. But how could I adore skiing when after only one day I hadn't really experienced it yet? Then it hit me: It wasn't the skiing I adored but *myself*. Skiing was just the vehicle to teach me.

Perhaps that is the hidden lesson fear tries to teach us, the secret gift it has to bestow; that is, when we refuse to be helpless in the face of it, we learn to love ourselves with a newly acquired definition of who we are and what we can do. Our achievements, our experiences, our very lives are determined by what we believe are our limitations—and it is fear and helplessness that set those limitations.

I have become one of those obnoxious people you run into around the beginning of November who gush excitedly with the anticipation of ski season, who wax poetic about the Zen of schussing down a slope, powder flying, hair blowing, wind stinging. And I still adore myself every time I go, because, you know what? I'm still scared. Every time. It never gets any easier for me. A 12,000-foot mountain is an awesome presence to contend with. That's the whole point. Each time I stand at the top and look down, I am resonating like a tuning fork to the terror and ecstasy of the moment, and believe me, I stand there a long time. But now I understand the transformational power of the mountain, and I embrace it. For as the Zen master would say, "The obstacle *is* the path."

NO MORE BAILING OUT

Ultimately, it is no more than an insidious and seductive trap to be given permission by oneself or one's culture to quit, to bail out if things get risky or dangerous. It is debilitating and illusory, but it is an illusion we women cherish. We *want* to believe that certain situations are so frightening or overwhelming that we can't be expected to perform, that we have the "right" to be rescued.

Therein lies the trap of this cherished illusion: that any experience that becomes too painful, difficult, risky, or dangerous immediately qualifies for possible inclusion in the "I can't be expected to cope" category. Once we have permission to do so, it is entirely too tempting to run away whenever the going gets rough. Unfortunately this approach does not coincide with the realities of life. Life rarely sends in the troops when we need them. Life demands that we cope.

Just when we think we have it all together, just when we feel that nothing can shake our firm and hard-won foundation of mature self-reliance, that old rogue Life will test us once again. The temptation to hide beneath the protective covering of helplessness is an ever-present one, as I was to learn, soon after becoming a warrior of the ski slopes.

In the midst of the most productive period of my adulthood, when all my efforts were about to be crowned with the intoxicating promise of reward, just as I was preparing for a ten-city promotional tour of my first book, finally feeling I had control of my life, just when I felt at my most powerful and authentic best, my soul received the workout of its life. Without warning I was drafted into a battle with a cosmic trickster that swindled me of my belief in a benevolent force and left me helpless and floundering in a dark universe. Before my eyes schizophrenia metamorphosed the person I loved into a terrifying stranger—someone I did not know, could not predict, and most lamentable of all, could not trust.

The first sign of my descent into helplessness came the night Ben (my lover, my confidant, my friend) began babbling like an AM radio announcer gone berserk. Normally he was a humble and quiet guy, a one-syllable communicator, brilliant but unassuming. One of the kindest individuals I had ever known, his awareness of others and sensitivity to their needs were ennobling just to be near. He took no notice of his own physical beauty. To me he was a cross between Gary Cooper and Gandhi.

This night, however, he was jabbering a string of unconnected thoughts. A deluge of dissociated ideas poured from his mouth, unbidden, unstoppable, almost as if from another being. He would ask me a question, but before I could answer, he would careen off on another dissociation. By four A.M. I was begging him to shut up. Even then he was unable to stop, compelled by his delusional state to protect us from "the conspiracy." Eyes staring and unhinged, he explained to me that he had been singled out to receive vital information that would save mankind.

That a monstrous aberration had overtaken someone I loved produced such a feeling of helplessness and vertigo in me that I could not begin to grasp its impact, but the harbingers of peril were already encircling us. In the short period of four days his condition worsened, and events escalated into sheer nauseating pandemonium.

After bolting from a moving car, hurling furniture through a window, roaming from house to house lost and incoherent, he arrived on my doorstep alternately growling and whimpering, first seething with hostility, then convulsing with fear, finally collapsing on my kitchen floor, inconsolable, clutching my waist and crying out in spasms of panic and confusion, begging me to "let the wolf out." I held him in my arms and wept with the most profound grief I have ever known.

Before I did battle with the forces of chaos known as mental illness, I believed that, no matter how dire the circumstances, one is never so helpless that there is not some action to be taken that would *control* a situation. That was before I watched a brilliant and beautiful man spontaneously combust before my eyes. That was before I encountered the supreme anarchy, the ultimate bout with the meaninglessness of life known as schizophrenia. Only war must be more absurd.

Once he was in the hospital, I entered a period I can only describe as flat. In the process of shoring up an irreparably damaged belief in the essential goodness of life, I found myself utterly without emotion—no ups, no downs, no sleep—just a watchful being, lying in the dark. I held my body like someone whose ribs were broken. Cloistered in a tiny room in the middle of my house that received almost no light, I climbed into bed and stayed there for two months. I didn't change the sheets. I didn't open the drapes.

As the nights ground by without sleep or surcease of pain, a great apprehension began to take hold. Convinced that I would be unable to manage the promotional tour, that I simply no longer possessed the energy or confidence required, I remained suspended in a twilight limbo of fear and indecision.

Paradoxically *my* struggle with Ben's disease was inexorably teaching *me* helplessness. Stunned by the bleak reality of mental illness, by its contempt for human will, my reservoirs of mastery behavior were depleted. I, who had enjoyed being strong and independent, who had emerged triumphant over a 12,000-foot mountain, now found myself passive, fearful, and irresolute. I couldn't stop thinking about Dante's quote written on the gates of Hell: "Abandon Hope All Ye Who Enter Here." I thought it should be engraved on the portals of the hospital's locked psychiatric unit. It took many months before I was to learn the lesson that was waiting there.

> Before enlightenment,
> > one chops the wood and carries the water.
> After enlightenment,
> > one chops the wood and carries the water.
> —ZEN SAYING

I went through the promotional tour on automatic pilot. I spent three weeks alone and grieving in hotel rooms and airport terminals. Without a decent night's sleep and never knowing what city I was in when I awoke, I began each day disoriented. Jet lag had delayed my period, torturing me with a cavalcade of symptoms and leaving me bloated, fatigued, depressed, constipated, and bitchy. The bags under my eyes were large enough to be checked in as additional luggage. I never stopped thinking about Ben.

Waiting for connecting flights at O'Hare, I reviewed my overseas plans. I was to fly to Frankfurt, catch another flight to a smaller city (whose name I didn't know) somewhere in Germany, where I would be greeted by my contact (whose name I also didn't know) and taken to a destination somewhere in the Bavarian Alps.

In the boarding area my attention was temporarily distracted by a well-groomed, perfectly accessoried woman demurely holding onto the arm of her expensively suited husband. I hated her. Her status as a married woman with an emotionally healthy and professionally successful husband made me sick with envy. Her composure left me forlorn. *She* isn't going to get worn out and disheveled lugging her bags through this endless terminal, because she has someone to care for her. I thought enviously, *Why can't I have what she has?*

Just then the man at the ticket counter announced boarding. So far so good. We were leaving in plenty of time. Aboard the plane I resumed my surveillance of the Composed Wife, toward whom I had felt such venom. Predictably, her husband was the one grappling with the luggage while she carefully situated herself, taking her time to smooth out her skirt and adjust her seatbelt so as not to wrinkle her silk blouse. It was clearly her husband's duty to review the itinerary, secure her comfort, and anticipate any problems. He was doing so admirably.

Unexpectedly the pilot announced that our departure would be delayed for over an hour due to weather. As he apologized for any connection problems, I felt the inner fabric of my strength begin to fray. I would miss my connection in Frankfurt. I would arrive in some little town in Germany with no bags, no one to meet me, and no idea of where I was supposed to be. Despite my despair and fatigue, despite my fear and loneliness, yet another ordeal requiring emotional strength was just beginning. I yanked myself from my seat and lurched to the rest room.

Slamming the door, I exploded into violent tears. Why does this have to happen to me? What did I do to deserve such a concentration of pain? Why isn't there someone to help me handle all of this? Why am I not granted the safety and comfort of a strong, stable man to lean on in my fatigue and distress, like the Composed Wife? Why isn't the one I love there to cheer me on and provide loving support? Surely there has to be a limit to what maturity and competence can handle. I simply can't be expected to cope!

It may seem that watching a loved one slide hopelessly into mental illness just when life demanded I run a marathon of confidence justified my right to helplessness, that anyone would have broken under similar circumstances. To some, it may even seem inhumane to expect a person in my situation not to fall apart. But, gentle reader, I ask you to consider, how would surrendering to helplessness have served me? Would it have miraculously provided a rescuer, restored Ben's mental health, or notified my German contacts of my interrupted travel plans?

I didn't bail out, literally or figuratively, because I couldn't. I was aboard a jetliner and, like it or not, ready or not, I was winging my way to Germany. Period. There were no escape hatches. That unbending, immutable, hateful reality contained a hidden gift, a secret opportunity. It forced me to dig down to my toenails and draw on a strength I didn't even want to find.

Now, I thank God I *didn't* have the choice, for I would have undoubtedly surrendered to the overpowering illusion (and oh, how seductive it was) that my situation justified reneging on my contractual obligations. I most certainly would have jeopardized an excellent relationship with my publisher. I might have invited legal action and severe financial penalties. I might never have published again.

The point is, even when circumstances seem to justify a slide into helplessness, this response does not serve us. Each time we choose helplessness, even when it is justified, we elect a self-defeating response to life's challenges.

As painful and unwelcome as it may be, the truth is we must develop the *will* to master our situation, indeed, any situation. For even when external reality inflicts genuine helplessness, even when wallowing in self-pity is fully justified, we can still choose a means of control—*the refusal to internalize defeat.* Whether we are engaged in a life-or-death struggle that threatens to deal the finishing blow or are simply schlepping the bags, chopping the wood, and carrying the water, we must learn to rely on ourselves. The cavalry isn't coming, the Marines won't land, the white knight is busy. Cherishing helplessness is cherishing an illusion. By understanding *how* the beliefs of a helpless style undermine our ability to cope with risk and change, and by substituting mastery behaviors, we begin the process of exchanging helplessness for hope.

CHAPTER 2

Conditioned for Defeat?

When we are constantly re-creating our basic patterns of behavior and thought, we never have to leap into fresh air or
onto fresh ground.

— CHOGYAM TRUNGPA
Shambhala

Let's start with the bad news. Learned helplessness ensnares a
woman in a tangled web of paralyzing beliefs, emotions, and behaviors. She consistently doubts herself even when she performs at
consistently high levels. Superior achievement in one area of her
life does not necessarily translate into high self-esteem or promote
self-confidence in other areas. Criticism can so immobilize her with
its implication of inferiority (which she already believes anyway)
that she may scrupulously avoid new challenges, risks, or changes
that involve possible confusion or even the potential for negative
criticism. Fear and self-doubt short-circuit her attempts at change.
Worst of all, she eventually becomes blind to genuine opportunities
to transform the areas of her life that make her unhappy. Learned
helplessness becomes the grim reaper of her dreams.

Furthermore, she may even find herself in the strange predicament of arguing for her limitations because, in some situations and
under some circumstances, helplessness can appear to pay off. Let's
face it, what woman hasn't pretended to be helpless at some point
in her life, either as a way of getting rescued from having to take a
risk or as a way of getting attention and love. If we are honest, most
of us will have to admit to occasional episodes of helplessness tactics.
They can be very subtle indeed. Two of my workshop participants
offered good examples.

"I hate to admit this, but maybe it will help someone else," said a petite blonde who had been sitting so quietly that I assumed she was bored.

"The way I got helpless was to get pregnant. Every time my last child was old enough for me to go back to school and finish my doctorate, I would get pregnant again. I did this four times. It was just so easy because no one gave me any grief about it.

"Both my parents and my husband wanted me to go back to school, although for different reasons. My parents wanted me to fulfill the promise of my early potential when I had been a bio-chemistry major doing some new research. My father, especially, who was also a scientist, was very disappointed that I never finished my degree. My husband wanted me to get the doctorate so that I could help him earn a living for our family.

"The minute they would hear I was pregnant, though, the issue was always dropped. Everyone just assumed my fate was sealed for another four or five years.

"What is interesting," she continued, "is that I didn't really recognize that I was acquiesing to helplessness. I suppose on some level I did, but I just didn't think about it. Now that I am older, I realize that I was afraid of the competition in graduate school, especially the hard sciences, and motherhood was such a convenient way to avoid facing it."

Now, gentle reader, we have waded into some churning waters, so please don't misunderstand me. I do not mean to imply that all pregnancies are "helpless acts" nor to slight the risks inherent in giving birth itself. However, if you recognize yourself as a woman who gets pregnant *to avoid other risks*, it is imperative to acknowledge that you are doing so.

Another example of the subtle choice-to-be-helpless was presented by a young premed student whom I'll call Elyce.

"Kevin, my boyfriend, likes intelligence in a woman, but he hates it when a woman does what he calls 'shoving her competence down his throat,' " she told me. "He thinks it's masculine and it turns him off, so I play a more helpless role when I'm with him.

"I think the reason is because medical school is really hard, and the more helpless I act at home, the more sympathy I get from Kevin. If I act competent, I don't get any. When I act helpless, he tells me that I may be a big, bad surgeon some day but that I'm just his little honey-bunny at night.

"It's the feeling of being loved that I'm after. Medical school is lonely and hard, especially for a woman, and I get tired of being competent all day. I know it sounds dumb, but I don't think I could make it if I had to be mastery-oriented all the time."

It doesn't sound dumb to me, and I'll bet it doesn't sound dumb to you either. As women we often cherish the notion of being taken care of and relinquish it only with great reluctance and misgiving. Furthermore, as Elyce pointed out, appearing helpless can be one way to get nurturing from men who express their love by protecting and rescuing.

Therefore I am not here to judge this young woman's decision to appear helpless, nor to imply that we must all be competent Masters of the Universe at all times. Frankly, sobbing into a crumpled wad of toilet paper I found in the bathroom aboard the jetliner to Germany, I would have gladly handed over my Masters of the Universe Membership Card on a silver platter if it would have conjured up just one big, strong man to call me his little honey-bunny and rescue me from my dire circumstances.

So, my point is not judgment. My point is, even if we love coming home to a he-man who makes all the decisions and wraps us in a cocoon of safety, even if we are willing to create the illusion of helplessness to feel feminine, get love, and avoid risks, the danger is that we will inadvertently come to believe in the illusion of helplessness we have created. At that point we may be in trouble, because once having chosen to adopt the belief system of learned helplessness, we are vulnerable to a whole series of personal and professional prices that will have to be paid.

That's the bad news.

The good news is that learned helplessness (hereinafter referred to as LH) is a learned behavior and as such can be *unlearned*. Strange as it may seem, LH can be transformed into its exact opposite, mastery-oriented behavior. I cannot stress enough how important it is to remember this potential for transformation. Because women tend to float in the felt experience of their realities, and because this chapter provides an overview of the symptoms of LH, it is possible to identify too strongly with the symptoms, get stuck in the quagmire of that felt experience, and resign oneself to living with LH.

Therefore, regardless of how strongly the symptoms may resonate within you, it is critical to engage your *thinking* faculties. Tell yourself that you are gathering information in preparation for change. Remind yourself that learning to recognize the symptoms of LH is only the first step on your long but exhilarating journey to transformation.

Bearing this in mind, perhaps the best way to clarify the crippling nature of LH is to present the research of the man who coined the term *learned helplessness.*

In 1966 Martin Seligman, a researcher in clinical psychology at the University of Pennsylvania, devised a unique experiment.* It began with an oversized cage divided in half by a partition. One side of this cage contained a light bulb, a lever, a floor that could be electrified, and a door. The other side was empty. Seligman placed a dog on the side of the cage with the light bulb, which was activated ten seconds before the electrification of the floor. Obviously the electrical shock caused the dog pain and discomfort. The dog's behavior was then carefully monitored.

First, the shock provoked the dogs to flail about the cage until they accidentally tripped the lever, causing the center partition to fly open and allowing them to escape to safety on the other side. The dogs very quickly learned to trip the lever with their paws the instant the light was activated, thus enabling them to avoid the ensuing shock altogether. In other words, the dogs learned they had some control, some effect on their environment. The dogs believed there was indeed a connection between their efforts and the final outcome of events.

Next the researchers disconnected the lever and the door. As a result the light came on with the accompanying electrical charge, but the dogs had no means of escaping the discomfort, since the lever had been disconnected. The dogs simply whimpered and suffered.

In the final phase of the study the connection between the lever and the door was reestablished. By this time, however, the dogs had ceased their efforts to operate the lever. They no longer even attempted escape. Even when the researchers demonstrated for the dogs that they had regained the opportunity to control their environment (the lever and the door), these dogs simply would not

---

* I wish to convey my personal apologies to animal-rights advocates reading this material. This research is not of the truly gruesome variety, but it does involve animal suffering. I am sensitive to the animal-rights issue myself, and if there were another way to relate the details of this research, I would certainly do so. Unfortunately there is not.

attempt the escape to safety. Despite numerous efforts on the part of the researchers to motivate the dogs to try the lever again, the dogs refused. They were said to have acquired *a belief that there was no connection between their actions and the final outcome of events.* They were said to have acquired "learned helplessness."[1]

The notion that an animal can acquire a "belief" may sound ludicrous, but in fact these dogs believed they were helpless. Even pain, perhaps nature's greatest motivator, failed to spur the dogs to renew their attempts at escape. The dogs' belief in their own help-lessness eclipsed even their misery, and they simply surrendered to the suffering.

This study revealed two important components of LH: first, that it is a *belief* so potent that it can supersede reality; and second, that this belief creates an associated syndrome—something appropriately called opportunity blindness.[2] In other words, even when a fresh opportunity to affect one's environment presents itself, the individual is often incapable of perceiving it, just as the dogs were incapable of perceiving their new opportunities.

A fascinating example of opportunity blindness can be seen in the training of Indian elephants for work. The animal is fettered to a steel post with a heavy-gauge iron chain encircling one of his front legs. Naturally the elephant struggles to free himself, tugging against the chain with all his massive strength, but to no avail. After a time the animal becomes convinced of his inability to break the chain. Thereafter his trainer can substitute a rope for the iron chain and hold the animal just as securely in place. Even though the circum-stances have changed and the elephant's strength could snap the rope like a flimsy thread, he no longer believes his actions can affect his circumstances and he no longer attempts to break his bondage. The elephant has accepted his helplessness and is blind to oppor-tunities for escape.

The correlation with human behavior is obvious, and I won't belabor the point. Bear in mind, however, that most of us fail to assimilate on a gut level just how dominant, thorough, and insidious this process of learning helplessness can be.

Many of us, for example, wonder why abused women do not escape their tormentors when an opportunity to do so clearly presents itself. Because such women do not flee, they are chastised for their failure to act. Some literature even implies that they enjoy the "sweet suffering" of their beatings. The study of LH teaches us that other factors may be at work. These women have been beaten into a system of beliefs that utterly blinds them to their opportunities for escape. Like the tethered elephant, such women have been subdued, "blinded" if you will.

When we think of those poor suffering dogs, exposed to a painful current, able to escape but not believing it possible, we come closer to understanding not only the power of a belief system to block one's ability to act but the depth and tenacity of that power as well. We come a little closer to a compassionate understanding of the dynamics underlying a battered woman's failure to act in her own behalf. Ultimately we can come to a more compassionate understanding of ourselves and the Herculean effort involved in wrestling with our own tenacious belief systems.

QUIZ: DO YOU SUFFER FROM LEARNED HELPLESSNESS?

Presented below is a quiz that may help you identify the degree to which LH is operating in your life. The most important thing is to respond to the questions as you would be most likely to respond in everyday life. In other words, do not try to answer them according to what you think is the ideal behavior or even the one you aspire to, but rather choose the one that comes the closest to describing what your actual behavior would be.

1. Your patio screen door has come off the runner and is lying on its side on the patio. It's a hot summer day and you want to open your patio doors to get the air circulating, but if you do, the flies will come in. If you don't, you are going to swelter in the heat, since you have no air-conditioning. (If you have a husband or a landlord, assume he is out of town.) Are you likely to:

  A. Fix it yourself?
  B. Suffer with the door closed until you can get your husband, boyfriend, next-door neighbor, handyman, or landlord to come over and fix it?
  C. Go out and look at the door for a few minutes, sort of mess around with it a little, but when it turns out to be more difficult than you anticipated, suffer it out until you can get someone to fix it?
  D. Go out and look at the door for a few minutes, play around

with it a little, then, when it turns out to be more difficult than you anticipated, become even more determined to fix the door yourself?

E. Rig up some temporary situation (such as leaning the screen door up against the opening) that "will do" but is quite inefficient, until you can get someone to fix it?

2. You are at a party. The man with whom you have been exchanging glances all evening walks up and starts a conversation with the woman standing next to you. Are you most likely to:

A. Walk right up and start a friendly conversation with both of them?

B. Hate yourself, feel fat, ugly, or old, and try to fade into the nearest potted palm?

C. Come to the conclusion that the other woman is more appealing in some way (thinner, prettier, sexier, younger, etc.) than you?

D. Think the *guy* has a problem for not seeing *your* appeal?

E. Watch and wait until he is alone for a few minutes and then go up and talk to him?

3. The man with whom you live (either full- or part-time) becomes increasingly abusive—verbally, emotionally, perhaps even physically. Are you most likely to:

A. Pack your bags and leave (or alternatively pack his bags and change the locks) and refuse to cohabit until he sees a counselor?

B. Begin examining your own behavior to determine what you did that set him off?

C. Decide it's best not to provoke him because there are too many other things at stake?

D. Inform him that if he ever strikes you or indulges in *any* sort of violent behavior, you will wait until he is sound asleep and then attack him with a cast-iron frying pan?

E. Realize that he's the one with the problem but decide to work through it by suggesting the two of you go together to see a marriage counselor?

4. You are enrolled in your first computer class. You are having

much *less* difficulty with the material than you had anticipated. You will probably receive a good grade. Are you most likely to:

    A. Feel significantly more confident about your abilities?
    B. Decide that the course material was really quite easy and that you overestimated the difficulty of the material?
    C. Feel somewhat relieved?
    D. Feel a little bored, wanting more challenge?
    E. Feel bored but relieved?

5. You are enrolled in a new computer class, but this one is *not* going well. You are confused and lost in the material. Are you most likely to:

    A. Ask a lot of questions in class, do your homework regularly, seek extra help from the teacher, ask more questions in class, and even request private appointments if necessary?
    B. Do your homework but feel it is hopeless, begin hating yourself, and try to remain as invisible as possible in class by avoiding eye contact with the instructor?
    C. Get frustrated, gradually lose interest in doing your homework, get progressively more behind and eventually drop out?
    D. Allow for the possibility that perhaps the teacher is not a good instructor and get outside help?
    E. Plod along, doubting your intelligence and vowing never to take another computer class?

6. Make a brief list of some of your daily activities, both recreational and work related. Which of the following best describes these activities?

    A. Things you were once reluctant or afraid to do.
    B. Things in which you have always exhibited skill or natural ability.
    C. Things that will not provoke any negative criticism of you.
    D. Brand-new things you've never tried before.
    E. Things that give you a sense of accomplishment rather than challenge.

7. Due to a variety of circumstances, you have been eating poorly. Your clothes have become too tight for comfort. By the time you

get around to stepping on the scale, you have gained eight pounds. Are you most likely to:

A. Spend some time thinking about what caused you to gain the weight, decide upon a responsible course of action to correct the problem, and then plan a little daily treat for yourself that has nothing to do with food?
B. Have an anxiety attack, hate yourself, feel like a failure, and be immobilized by depression and fears of inadequacy?
C. Hysterically throw out everything in the refrigerator and cupboards, go on a starvation diet, which by four o'clock in the afternoon you have already broken, and begin the process of hating yourself and feeling like a failure all over again?
D. Cut out your midmorning and evening snacks?
E. Read diet books, talk to friends about dieting, plan your diet and exercise regimen, but never quite get started?

8. You're feeling very stuck in your present career. You are either at the top of your career ladder or very close; however, you no longer derive much satisfaction from your work. Are you most likely to:

A. Ask others who have made changes how they did it, take notes and ask questions, talk to them again and ask more questions?
B. Review the elements of your life that must be considered and get discouraged about the complexity of making a career change?
C. Feel that you don't have the energy or the know-how to make the drastic changes required?
D. Make lists, brainstorm with yourself and others, and strategize ways to overcome the inevitable obstacles?
E. Figure your investment up to now in time, energy, and money isn't worth giving up, continue in the same career, and just try to make the best of it by finding other areas of your life in which to make changes?

9. Again, you want to pursue a new career. It will require going back to school at the graduate level. Your investigations reveal that you must pass a math portion of the Graduate Record Exam. Are you most likely to:

A. Dig out old math books or invest in some new ones, starting on page one and working your way through?

B. Decide there's no way you could pass a math exam and get discouraged about pursuing your new career?

C. Go to a bookstore, buy a copy of the GRE math study guide, thumb through a few pages, and then decide there is no way you could pass a math exam and get discouraged about pursuing your new career?

D. Hire a tutor, review the material, do your homework, and stay with it no matter how frustrated you get?

E. Procrastinate taking any action for a number of years?

10. Your marriage (or long-term relationship) fails. Your husband (or long-time companion) tells you he still cares about you but has changed over the years and wants a new life, sans you. Once the initial shock and grief wear off, are you most likely to:

A. Accept that people and circumstances change and that although you will miss him terribly, wish him well and begin planning your new life and coping with being single?

B. Feel that if you had just been prettier, thinner, wittier, livelier, sexier, or just somehow *different*, he would still be with you today?

C. Go into your shell and feel lonely and bitter?

D. Realize that his leaving had more to say about him than about you and let him go?

E. Launch a plan to win him back?

11. Your family is taking you (and all your hard work) for granted. They simply expect you to do certain chores, never say thank you, or even acknowledge your effort. Are you most likely to:

A. Call a family meeting and tell them how you feel?

B. Suffer in silence, feel hurt and neglected, but continue to do the work without saying anything?

C. Figure it wouldn't do any good to say anything anyway, so why bother?

D. (If strategy A fails), stop doing the chores until someone notices and then discuss with them the failure of strategy A and indicate there will now be a massive change in household re-reponsibilities?

E. Get mad, yell a lot, keep right on doing the work, get mad again, yell some more, do some more work, and so on?

12. You go out with a new man, whose company you thoroughly enjoy. He says he will call. Three days go by. He doesn't call. You wait until it has been a week. Still no call. Are you most likely to:

  A. Realize that he may have gotten busy, lost your phone number, or any of a variety of things, and call him?
  B. Recall every moment of the evening (what he said, what you said, nuances of his behavior, etc.) attempting to ascertain what you might have said, done, or wore that turned him off?
  C. Decide that men are just a bunch of jerks?
  D. Figure, "Well, it's *his* loss," and proceed with your life?
  E. Decide he's not worth seeing if he doesn't want to see you too, but still feel somehow responsible for the failed evening?

13. Your mother comes to visit for two weeks. The first couple of days go well, but soon you start to bicker just as the two of you did when you were a child. Eventually the tensions erupt, you yell at your mom and get into a fight with her. Later, following the argument, are you most likely to:

  A. Sit down with your mother and have a heart-to-heart in which you explain your point of view and offer specific information concerning the behaviors that make you react negatively?
  B. Feel guilty all day, as if you've been a "bad girl," and try to make it up to her?
  C. Figure she'll never change her ways at this point in her life and say nothing?
  D. Chalk it up to the nature of intimate relationships and go about your business without further ado?
  E. Feel guilty as in B above, but then get angrier because she made you feel this way?

14. Imagine that you are going through a very stressful period in your life during which many unforeseen changes are occurring. You may wish to recall one of those actual times. (On the other hand, you may not!) Anyway, your general mood is anxious and worry filled. Are you most likely to:

  A. Accept that change always entails some degree of discomfort while seeking ways to turn the discomfort into a learning experience by talking with a therapist, enrolling in a self-help program, joining a support group, meditating, or all of the above?

B. Head for the refrigerator in an attempt to give yourself some pleasure and escape the anxiety?

C. Come home from work and pour yourself a drink (or light up a joint or take a tranq) to escape the anxiety?

D. Recall your last stressful time as a growth period and review how you coped before, what worked, what didn't, and develop better, more refined, strategies this time around?

E. See a therapist or join a support group while continuing to eat or drink your anxiety away?

15. You have just had a major success at work or on the personal front. A peer whose opinion you admire compliments you on your fine work. To their question What is the secret of your success? your most likely response is:

A. "Intelligence, experience, and effort."

B. "It wasn't that hard really. I was just lucky, I guess."

C. "I had a lot of help from others."

D. "Hard work, persistence, and determination."

E. "Well, I don't know. It was a lot of things really. Uh, it's kind of hard to pin it down to just one or two things. You know what I mean?"

16. In junior high school, when faced with your first big math decision (taking algebra versus general math), did you:

A. Take algebra, get confused, but work hard and master the course?

B. Take general math and feel utterly relieved not to have to take algebra?

C. Take algebra, get confused, stop doing your homework, cut class, and ultimately earn a low grade?

D. Take general math, prove to yourself and your instructors you could handle algebra class, and then take it the following year?

E. Take algebra, squeak by with a C, and never again take another math class?

17. Imagine that, for some reason, you *must* change your career or profession. Think about other options you would pursue. Did you:

    A. Consider all the wild possibilities?
    B. Tend to overlook or rule out anything in a completely new field?
    C. Look only within your current or related fields where you have already performed well and shown your ability?
    D. Reexamine all your different interests to see what new possibilities or old talents have been overlooked in the past?
    E. Long to pursue an old, neglected talent or interest but reject it once again due to the time or effort involved?

18. Think back to a particular risk (financial, physical, or intellectual—not relationship-oriented) that you chose *not* to take. What would be the most accurate description of why you chose not to take it:

    A. The timing was wrong.
    B. I conjured up everything that could go wrong and worked myself into a state of abject terror.
    C. Discovered that some degree of discomfort or "suffering" might be involved.
    D. Realized I needed more information or training.
    E. Didn't have the time or the money.

19. Once again, recall that risk you chose *not* to take. If faced with that same risk today, would you:

    A. Rehash the negative "what ifs. . . ," decide you have changed sufficiently to handle it, and take the risk this time?
    B. Rehash the negative "what ifs . . ." and avoid it once again?
    C. Reject it without really thinking too much about it based on having thought about it in the past and having rejected it then?
    D. Say, "Oh, what the hell," and go for it without thinking about it too much?
    E. Think about it, long for it, think about it some more, procrastinate some more, but definitely not give up on the idea?

20. Think back to the last risk you *did* take (once again, financial, physical, or intellectual, not relationship-oriented). In looking back, what was your most common feeling?

    A. Exhilaration
    B. Anxiety
    C. Dread
    D. Stimulation
    E. Excited but cautious

21. In the mail you receive a catalog from your local community college. An exciting new array of classes in a wide variety of fields and subjects is being offered. Would you be most likely to:

    A. Sign up for something that has always intrigued you but one about which you have no knowledge?
    B. Sign up for one most like what you are familiar with?
    C. Sign up for one in which you are likely to get a good grade?
    D. Sign up for something you have never even thought about before but that caught your eye this time?
    E. Be attracted to something new but figure you would enjoy it more if you had some experience with it?

22. You begin some kind of project (a class, a new job, acquiring a new skill, learning a new sport, living alone, whatever). It is difficult and requires you to exert a lot of effort. Is your tendency to:

    A. Understand that working hard is part of the natural process involved in reaching goals and that it is the same for everyone?
    B. Feel that if you must work so hard, you must not have what it takes and start to get discouraged?
    C. Have less and less interest in reaching the goal?
    D. Tell yourself that it takes time to learn new skills and give yourself credit for progress thus far?
    E. Feel discouraged but keep going without joy or satisfaction?

23. Suppose once again you have been wanting to make a change in your life. You start talking it over with friends. When they suggest ideas, your typical response is likely to be:

A. "How would one go about accomplishing that exactly? Can you help me with the steps?"
B. "Yeah, but, it would be too hard (take too long, be too expensive, etc.)."
C. "Yeah, but, I don't have the skills (money, talent, ability, time, etc.)."
D. "Let's brainstorm some more. I haven't found a viable idea yet, but this is helping me."
E. "I don't know, it's a neat idea, maybe I could, but it doesn't sound like me. I don't know, I'll have to think about it."

24. Pick a problem that seems to keep repeating itself in your life, like choosing the same kind of Mr. Wrong over and over or remaining chronically in debt or yo-yoing up and down with a weight problem. Think it over for a few minutes. Which of the following most accurately describes your feelings?

A. Maybe I didn't have enough information before, or didn't incorporate the right strategies, or didn't get any outside help.
B. It's unlikely ever to change. I've already tried everything I can think of. It's hopeless.
C. It's mainly my fault for being so stupid (undisciplined, screwed up, out of control, needy, etc.).
D. Maybe I'm going about this the wrong way.
E. I think maybe I could make some changes, but this problem affects everything else in my life, which is what makes it so hard.

25. Imagine that you have moved to a new city, or alternatively, that your closest friends have moved away. You are feeling lonely. Are you most likely to:

A. Join a new group in order to meet people?
B. Spend a fortune in long-distance calls talking to old friends?
C. Withdraw and feel more lonely?
D. Cultivate someone at work, at church, or at school and let them know you are open to a new friendship?
E. Read the paper looking for new groups, check out the church newsletters, talk to friends about meeting new people, mark your calendar with dates of events where people like yourself are likely to congregate, and then not go to any of them?

HOW DO YOU SCORE?

Tally up your answers by giving yourself a point for every *B, C*, or *E* answer. Generally speaking, the higher your score, the more that learned helplessness is influencing your life.

Before looking at your score in more detail, however, there are a couple of important things to say about the quiz and how to use it. First, if studied carefully, this quiz, although somewhat simplified, will show you three things: (1) how LH manifests itself in both your personal and your professional life; (2) the degree to which LH influences your willingness to take a risk; and (3) the degree of your emotional hardiness, which will be required to see you through the setbacks and frustrations that will inevitably occur.

Second, if you are willing to take time to review and study your answers periodically as you read through the text of the book, certain themes may emerge: areas of your life in which LH is more operative than others, areas in which you already exhibit mastery-oriented behavior, ways to apply current mastery behavior to new situations, and so on. As you read through the exercises and techniques that will be offered later in the text, you can apply them to your specific areas of need.

Also, be sure to read through all the paragraphs that explain the point scoring, not just the one that applies to you. Even though you may not fall into a particular range, you may glean important information from the other categories.

In sum, taking the test and then looking over your answers one time, or tallying your score and reading only the paragraph that seemingly applies to you, will probably not bring about change all by itself. On the other hand, studying, working with, and applying the information you glean in order to alter your belief system, inspire new behavior, and improve your specific situation—now, *there's* mastery-oriented behavior.

SCORES

20–25 Points
LH is operating in your life to a significant, even debilitating, degree and may be contributing to overall feelings of panic, depression, hopelessness, bitterness, lack of motivation, and the inability to initiate or deal effectively with change. You may also:

- Be reluctant to try new things
- Be relieved, rather than bored, by lack of challenge
- Decrease effort when frustrated
- Blame yourself for everything that goes wrong
- Deny any responsibility for those successes you do have
- Fail to develop alternative plans to reach a goal

13–19 Points

Although not as serious as the above, LH is still a critical factor in your life. Clearly it undermines your ability to reach a goal, persist through obstacles, and sustain your enthusiasm through the difficult times. Sometimes it can make even simple living seem like a formidable task. On a day-to-day basis you may function adequately but are likely to exhibit the traits listed above whenever unforeseen change or risk presents itself in your life.

7–12 Points

You probably function quite well as long as everything is running according to plan. No one would think of you as a helpless or dysfunctional person. However, if you are on the high side of this range, you still resist risk and change and probably do not initiate it. Furthermore, you face your greatest challenge in keeping your spirits up and believing in yourself when failures and setbacks occur in the midst of risk taking and change.

If you are on the low side of this score, you probably already take risks. Your greatest difficulty, however, will also be mid-risk, when you are likely to sabotage yourself by giving up too quickly. Be alert to this tendency and work on persistence.

1–6 Points

Congratulations! You are basically a mastery-oriented woman. You may close this book and be excused. Seriously, though, what will serve you is a close examination of which particular questions evoked the LH response (B, C, or E) in you. It will help target your vulnerabilities so that you can begin to apply your risk-taking skills to new areas.

Scores with 12 or more E answers

If most of your answers fell into the E category, you are something of an actress, hiding behind a persona or carefully constructed mask, which you don for public appearances. You probably talk a good line and seem quite mastery-oriented to others. On a more realistic level, however, you probably sabotage yourself with secret bouts of self-doubt, hesitation, or resignation to "the way things are."

This kind of subtle LH, like the subtle sexism of the new nineties, can be even more insidious because it is harder to spot. If you fall into this category, be alert to the clever ways in which you secretly undermine yourself. Attend to your behavior to see if you can determine when you are merely play-acting mastery behavior and when it is the real McCoy. As you read through the text of this book, be alert to the subtle ways in which you exhibit the behaviors while fooling others.

SUMMARY

When the majority of your answers fall into the LH category (B, C, and E), they reveal a general approach to life that lacks a belief in self-efficacy. Efficacy refers to the ability to produce desired outcomes. Lack of belief in self-efficacy, then, is the very foundation of LH. Clearly anyone suffering from this particular failure of confidence is going to be fiercely undermined in the pursuit of goals, in adaptability to change, and in the willingness to take risks and persist through obstacles. Just living with a lack of belief in self-efficacy can turn daily coping into a draining and dissatisfying kind of existence.

People who embody this belief range from those who are easy to identify, such as concentration-camp victims, POWs, and abused women, to those with more subtle manifestations, such as low self-esteem, a lack of initiative and persistence, decreased effort in the face of difficulty, or a generally fearful response to life. A lack of belief in self-efficacy can produce a variety of psychological conditions, ranging from panic to depression.

Furthermore, like Seligman's dogs, who were blind to the opportunity for escape because they no longer believed it possible, human beings exhibit similar kinds of blindness based on their belief system. The human version of this opportunity blindness manifests as a collapse of problem-solving skills—the ability to think strategically through a problem, to generate more than one means to an end, to persist through difficulties—and is a sad and difficult way to live.

If you scored in an LH range that you personally consider un-acceptable *and* you interpret that score as "the way things are with me," without at least the willingness to consider the possibility of change, then taking the quiz will have been a depressing experience indeed. If, on the other hand, you take the quiz in the spirit of transformation in which it is offered and interpret your score as a tool to assist you in the early stages of growth and development, its purpose has been fulfilled.

The aim of the quiz, then, is not to define your reality but to help you to begin to see the ways in which your reality can be changed. If you recognize yourself in the *B, C,* and *E* categories, you may be volunteering to be a victim, but remember, you can change this status, since all the components of LH—beliefs, re-sponses, and behaviors—are under the personal control of the in-dividual.

Perhaps the best way to get a handle on how LH works is to begin a general review (in Chapter 3), which will become even more detailed (in Chapter 4), of what has been uncovered by Seligman and his associates and other researchers over the last twenty-five years or so.

CHAPTER 3

Opting Out:
What the Research Says

If you cannot be happy here and now, you never will be.
—TAISEN DESHIMARU

EXPLANATORY STYLES

Everyone experiences bad things. Everyone encounters fear and failure, frustration and setbacks, anxiety, doubt, and dismay. Everyone must take risks in this life and cope with unexpected change. This is true whether we are helpless or mastery-oriented, male or female, rich or poor, young or old. So why do some people keep plowing through the obstacles to reach their goals eventually while others get derailed and give up?

Strangely enough, the answer turns out to be fairly simple. (It is the behaviors that become complex.) The difference between the mastery-oriented and those with LH lies in their explanation of bad events, aptly called "explanatory style." In other words, the way an individual explains a bad thing that happens to her seems to be more important than what actually happened.

Here is how it works. Human beings, with their infernal but endearing need to make sense out of life, persistently ask the question Why? of the events of their lives. Since reality is open to multiple interpretations, answer-seeking humans can attribute a vast array of explanations for the events that befall them. A negative explanatory style, one that basically says, "This is going to last forever; it affects everything else in my life; and it's my fault," is the explanatory style of helplessness.

Researchers have labeled this style as *stable* (this is going to last forever), *global* (it's going to affect everything else in my life), and *internal* (it's my fault). Contrast this to the mastery-oriented, who have an explanatory style that is *dynamic* (things can change), *specific* (this problem is limited to this one area only), and *external* (this is not necessarily my fault).

Let's look at a couple of examples. Two women find themselves suddenly single through divorce. One's explanatory style is helpless, that is, stable, global, and internal. She says:

"I'm never going to find another man that I will love as much as I loved Marvin." (Stable—*this is going to last forever.*)

"I'm going to be poor, socially isolated, and starved for affection and sex." (Global—*it's going to affect everything.*)

"If only I had been a better wife (or thinner or prettier or younger), he might still be with me now." (Internal—*it's my fault.*)

The second woman, undergoing the same unforeseen state of events but being a more mastery-oriented type, says:

"It will probably take some time, but eventually I will enjoy other men and get close to them." (Dynamic—*things can change.*)

"Well, the relationship area of my life has obviously got some problems, but my work is going well. I have my dog, my sense of humor, my friends, my love of swimming (or reading or hiking or art). I will use all of these to help get me through." (Specific—*this problem is limited to this one area only.*)

"I was a good partner all those years, but Marvin needed to make some changes that probably say more about him than they do about me." (External—*this is not necessarily my fault.*)

In another incident occurring across town, a major corporation is downsizing its operation, and two co-workers who sit right next to each other both lose their jobs in the restructuring. The one who has acquired LH will say to himself:

"I'll never find a job that pays as well as this one did." (Stable)

"During this time without a job, I can't be happy. My family will suffer, everyone will think I'm a failure, and my health will degenerate." (Global)

"I'm such a screwup. If I had just been more aggressive (or smarter or whatever), they would have kept me on." (Internal)

The fellow sitting next to him is the mastery-oriented type. Therefore, he thinks completely different thoughts:

"Things are constantly changing. New possibilities and opportunities, ones that may not have even existed yesterday, are unfolding every moment. Five minutes from now someone across town could make the decision to quit his job and provide an opening for me." (Dynamic)

"Well, at least the other areas of my life are functioning. I have a loving family and great friends and my health and my sense of humor and my experience." (Specific)

"It's not my responsibility that this organization got itself into trouble and must be restructured." (External)

Thus, the explanatory styles of bad events are as follows:

Learned Helplessness: Stable (no change)
                             Global (affects everything else)
                             Internal (my fault)

Mastery-Oriented: Dynamic (allows for change)
                             Specific (problem limited to specific area)
                             External (not necessarily my fault)

To make matters worse, in childhood we are taught a variety of phrases and ways of thinking about our problems that reinforce and perpetuate helplessness in challenging circumstances. They have all been uttered at my seminars:

Stable   "It's always been like this."
                             "It's in our family."
                             "Women are just not able to . . . "
                             "Men are just like that."
                             "It's not going to get any better."
                             "You can't fight city hall."
                             "The more things change, the more they
                             stay the same."

Global   "Nothing ever works out the way it's sup-
                             posed to."

Internal

"Everything is all screwed up."
"Everything else depends on this."
"Nothing works. I've tried everything."
"I can't think about anything else."
"It's all my fault."
"I always screw up."
"What's the matter with me?"
"I'll never get this right."
"If I wasn't so stupid, fat, ugly, undisciplined, etc., this never would happened."
"People who are successful never experience failure. Only failures experience failures."
"I just haven't got what it takes."
"I've lost my touch."
"How could I have been so stupid?"
"Where did you get a crazy idea like that?"

If you take a moment to look back over the quiz, you will see that the helplessness-oriented categories (*B*, *C*, and *E*) show a lack of belief in self-efficacy reflected in a negative explanatory style. The mastery-oriented responses (A and D), on the other hand, reflect a belief in self-efficacy based on a positive explanatory style. (These will be discussed in greater detail in later chapters.)

At a still deeper level, the LH style reflects an even more insidious and debilitating belief: that the nature of reality and personal identity are unchanging, that what happened in the past or how I behaved in the past will continue unaltered in the future, that past failures or foibles will determine future ones. The mastery-oriented style reflects the opposite belief, that what happened yesterday is no guarantee of what will happen tomorrow, that what I did yesterday is not an iron-clad predictor of how I will choose to behave tomorrow, and that past failures simply indicate a need to change my strategy in order to succeed in the future.

The irony is that neither belief necessarily reflects reality. Nor does either belief necessarily distort reality. In reality, reality is not even the issue!

How liberating this can be if taken into the heart and mind at the deepest levels. Frankly, "what happened" doesn't matter, only what you think happened and how you then behave based upon your explanation of the event. The realization that mastery-oriented individuals choose to explain their reality differently from LH individuals provides incentive to change one's own explanation of reality, so that the task of changing one's subsequent behavior becomes less daunting.

At one of my seminars a black woman in gold hoop earrings and a tiger-print scarf shared the following observation: "I remember something a therapist said to me once that really struck me at the time and now makes even more sense. I was talking to her about my father and telling her some story in the past. I stopped at one point and said, 'Well, actually, I'm not a hundred percent sure that is how it happened.' She blew me away with her response. She said, 'It doesn't matter how it happened, only how you think it happened.'

"That was the first time, really, that that idea was presented to me." She sort of chuckled and added, "It makes me laugh."

"Why laugh?" I asked.

"Because, girl, we all take reality so seriously, as if we could figure it out. Now I see that the truth is that we might just as well choose the explanation that does us the most good."

Sounds like good advice to me. In pursuit of the explanation that will do us the most good, the next chapter will delineate the specific behaviors of LH that follow from the LH belief system. Right now, however, examining the research on helpless versus mastery-oriented children would be useful, since it provides a virtual road map of the two different styles. Please do not dismiss this research because it was done on children. After all, it is in childhood that we learn the helpless- or mastery-oriented patterns that we carry forward into adulthood.

The children in these studies were chosen because their skills were basically equivalent in terms of speed, accuracy, and sophistication of thinking. They were presented with puzzles and/or problems that demanded the kind of skills required on a typical aptitude or achievement test. Since overall intelligence was not a differentiating factor, one would expect that the children would have similar responses when they encountered difficulty. This was not the case. In fact, difficulty caused some children to improve their performance, while it caused others to give up. Some children were so debilitated by simple mistakes that they were unable to solve the same problems they had solved previously!

In order to understand the dynamics of this phenomenon, the researchers designed another test in which the children would first experience success and then experience failure. In other words, confusion, obstacles, and failure were experimentally induced. The main differences among the children now were in their *thinking* about failure and success, or the way they *construed* their situation. Helpless children, for example, were quicker to label a mistake a failure than were mastery-oriented children, who, while recognizing a mistake, labeled it as accidental or temporary and something that would be corrected in due time. The helpless children tried to *explain* mistakes by attributing them to lack of ability or loss of ability ("I'm just not any good at this"), while the mastery-oriented children offered *no* explanations for their mistakes.

Helpless children became so distracted by attempting to account for their errors that they spent more time explaining *why* they failed than attempting to correct their errors, and their performances subsequently deteriorated. In contrast, the mastery-oriented children didn't even bother to offer explanations because mistakes were not defined as failures. Instead they spent their time figuring out where they went wrong and how to improve or change it. Subsequently they improved their performance levels. The bottom line was that helpless children saw a mistake as an indication of lack of ability, while mastery-oriented children saw the same mistake as a cue to change their strategy.

Same data, different conclusions.

The contrasts didn't stop there. The helpless children developed negative feelings about the task and themselves and wished to stop the activity. Mastery-oriented children became more positive and even expressed pleasure at the notion of being challenged, giving themselves encouragement in the form of little pep talks. Finally helpless children inflated their failures and predicted future failure as well, while the mastery-oriented children predicted future success *in spite of* their present difficulties. Since the learning situation (experimentally induced failure) was equivalent for everyone in the study, the differences had to be in the children themselves.

To make matters still worse from our point of view, study after study has shown that girls are more likely than boys to exhibit the helpless response to failure. First, they consistently express more anxiety about failing than do boys.[1] Second, they do not recover well from failure and lower their expectations of themselves in new situations.[2] One study measured the impact of confusion on girls and their subsequent learning and achievement levels. Mind-boggling as it may seem, the *brighter* the girl, the *less* likely she was to master new, confusing material.[3] Third, females who have a high fear of failure in childhood are more likely to have the same high fear of failure in adulthood than are boys, who may or may not carry the fear of failure into adult life.[4]

CAUSES OF LEARNED HELPLESSNESS

The reason that this helpless behavior exists among females, particularly in this day and age, is interesting to speculate about. After all, didn't the women's movement change attitudes? Aren't more and more females taking greater risks nowadays? Didn't our experience in Panama and the Persian Gulf show that women can hold their own, even in combat situations? Is it not a knee-jerk response to assume women are more helpless than men?

To some degree, the answers to all the above might be a resounding yes, were it not for two things: First, the above-mentioned changes are observed mostly among a minority of women, and second, research shows the opposite, that females tend to avoid conflict or danger and show lowered persistence and lack of initiative once failure is encountered.

The fact is that change is much slower than most of us think. Attitudes may change, but the behaviors that must follow take a good deal longer to evolve. For most of us humans (being the creatures of habit that we are) processing our attitudinal changes and transforming them into observable behaviors is a long, drawn-out affair. Consequently, a number of forces are still at work, culturally and personally, that continue to reinforce helplessness in females.

First is the issue of violence. Living in a society that is violent toward women, even regards them as prey to some extent, produces fear and LH in females. In this country every eighteen seconds a woman is physically brutalized by a man. Every year four thousand of them die at the hands of men who are supposed to love them.[5] Even in households where females are free of abuse, they are confronted with daily headlines of date rape, abductions, kidnapping, and murder; of slasher movies with young, usually female victims; of rap and rock videos and lyrics that often condone, even promote, male fantasies of violence and dominance. Thus, females feel unsafe in their own society. They become disinclined to take risks (who can blame them?) and instead seek out safe men to protect them.

Second is the devaluing of females in general. Though there have been some changes, society continues to send the message that the traits of femininity are not as valued as are those of masculinity. This is particularly revealed in differences in wages, with service-oriented (feminine) jobs earning much less than production-oriented (masculine) jobs, to use just one example.[6] Whenever a group is undervalued in this or some other way, the members of that group tend to internalize responsibility for their problems. In other words, when they encounter failure or experience setbacks, they mimic the cultural imperative and come to the conclusion that something must be wrong with them. This tendency within the female population is echoed in the black population as well and is consistent with the research on LH among minority groups.[7]

Third, parents become the torchbearers of cultural biases and beliefs, passing these on from generation to generation (often unconsciously) by socializing their children into the behaviors society deems appropriate. For the most part this is a harmless, even necessary practice that lubricates the social machinery and keeps things running smoothly. When cultural expectations are tainted with subtle aspects of sexism, however, the torches that are passed can burn some members of that society and leave lasting scars, such as those of fear and helplessness.

A study in which parents were observed helping their sons and daughters (separately) to solve a difficult jigsaw puzzle reveals the passing of just such a torch.[8] In this study both parents, but particularly fathers, emphasized the performance aspect of the task for boys. They stressed task mastery and the principles of problem solving. They answered more task-oriented questions for boys and set higher standards for them. Emphasis for girls, on the other hand, was on enjoyment of the game. Fathers focused more on interpersonal communication with their daughters, that is, joking, comforting, playing, in contrast to the task-oriented communication they used with sons. Finally, with daughters fathers showed more concern for their emotional well-being than for their performance of the task.

The most important facet of this study, however, involved a type of rescue. When, in the course of trying to solve the puzzle, girls became frustrated and emotional, fathers attempted to eliminate any discomfort for their daughters by putting the puzzle piece in place for her *before she asked for help*. This behavior, known as *premature rescuing*, clearly contrasted with the fathers' behavior with sons, whose emotional or frustrated outbursts they ignored. When their sons became emotional, fathers simply overlooked it and instead continued to stress task mastery and the principles of problem solving.

A father's premature rescue of his daughter is obviously motivated by love, but it teaches learned helplessness with deadly certainty. Think about it. The message behind premature rescuing is "You can't do this alone. You need my help." Though fathers certainly do not intend to make their daughters helpless, in their overly zealous desire to protect them from risk or the discomfort of anxiety-producing situations they wind up teaching LH instead.

It's only fair to say that we females are usually grateful for this rescuing. If our fathers are particularly zealous in protecting us from the consequences of our actions (paying off our credit cards, for instance, fixing our cars, catching us up on late rent, representing us in conflict situations with others), we may even come to expect it. But we pay a heavy price for this rescue—lack of confidence in our ability to do it ourselves.

Another study, this one conducted in 1974*, showed a similar way in which cultural biases can influence even our very perceptions of the sexes.[9] In the study male and female newborns were closely matched for height and weight. One group (consisting of both boys and girls) was dressed in blue; the other, also consisting of both sexes, in pink. Parents were asked to describe the babies. The blue group was described as healthy, robust, strong, and alert; the pink group as sweet, fragile, dainty, and pretty.

Obviously such beliefs will cause a parent to behave differently with the child, treating "strong, robust" babies differently from "fragile, dainty" babies. A number of studies show that fathers tend to play with their sons more than they do with their daughters.[10] Furthermore, with boys, fathers are more physically active and challenging. They lift and toss sons more than daughters, with whom

---

* Though 1974 may seem like an old study, bear in mind that girls born the year of this study are now approximately eighteen years old. What they learned as children, from a parental generation that was supposedly "enlightened" toward female potential, seems surprisingly old-fashioned.

they engage in quieter types of interaction, such as cooing, cuddling, and holding.

The great irony here is that girl babies are in fact more physically robust than boy babies. The mortality rate at birth is lower for females; they have a more mature skeleton at birth than do their male counterparts (although males tend to be slightly heavier); and they tend to fuss less and mature more rapidly.

As they mature, females continue to take the developmental lead. They talk earlier, read earlier, count earlier, and generally do better in school, even in math, until junior high school, when becoming "feminine" takes over their priorities, and grade-point averages decline.[11] (By the way, grade-point averages for boys improve at this period in their lives.)

The perceptions and descriptions of males and females are not based on fact, but on a set of culturally predetermined expectations. A perception of a female as weaker than a male reinforces the belief that she needs protection and rescuing, motivates parents to rescue their daughters prematurely from anxiety-producing situations, produces more LH in females, and endlessly perpetuates the cycle.

In yet another study, this one conducted in 1977 (children who are now about fifteen), two thousand parents were asked to list traits they wished for their sons and daughters.[12] Twice as many parents listed "hardworking" and "ambitious" for their sons as listed them for their daughters. Parents also felt it was important for their sons to be "self-reliant" and "responsible," while they wanted their daughters, to be "well mannered," "kind," and "attractive"—not exactly the traits of derring-do required for a mastery-oriented risk taker!

In many households Dad still makes the big decisions, such as managing money or choosing where the family will live. If not balanced with observable decision making by the mother, this practice sends some damaging messages to daughters—for example, "females make bad decisions," "females do not need to make decisions (others will do it for them)," "females do not have to take responsibility for their actions." None of these between-the-lines messages is conducive to building mastery-oriented behavior in a female.

Soon thereafter, society-at-large colludes with the nuclear family to reinforce the rescuing of females. Studies show that teachers give different feedback to underachieving boys than to underachieving girls.[13] Boys are chastised for their lack of effort and told they could succeed if they just tried harder. Girls are "helped" through difficult material. Teachers still ask boys to carry books and move furniture, while girls erase the blackboard and record grades in the gradebook. Boys are expected to learn how to take care of their cars and fix a tire. Girls ask their boyfriends and fathers to do it for them. Boys are expected to go out and get a job in high school, while many girls (not all) are just given money. Girls are not expected to learn to defend themselves physically, but boys are. Males and females alike are still taught that the male will have the primary responsibility as breadwinner of the family.

Thus LH is subtly passed to females, from generation to generation, through parenting styles, unconscious family interaction, and cultural habits. Although we *say* we want our girls to be strong and independent, our behaviors reveal a deeper, more hidden belief, that girls are frailer and should be spared hardship, risk, or discomfort. As a society, we believe that a male must learn to experience some discomfort in his formative years in order to prepare him for his future as a risk taker. We attempt to build his character by teaching him how to test his limits and expand his horizons. We avoid rescuing boys so that we don't make "sissies" out of them, but we show tolerance for the consequences of rescuing girls.

Most importantly, however, the culminating factor still at work in our society is this: We continue to define the traits of a mastery-oriented risk taker as "masculine." Indeed, research shows that many women still fear success because they view it as incompatible with their role expectations as females and anticipate negative consequences.[14] They suppress their capabilities, particularly in mixed-sex competition. This will be discussed in much greater detail in Chapter 5, but for now, suffice it to say that exhibiting mastery-oriented behavior is a dilemma for women who enjoy being thought of as feminine and attractive and are reluctant to have their behavior defined as masculine.

LEARNED HELPLESSNESS, COMPUTERS, AND MATH

> No matter how great your difficulties with mathematics, mine
> are still greater, I can assure you.
> —ALBERT EINSTEIN

Ultimately the maladaptive, helpless response that girls exhibit when challenged intellectually has its greatest impact in the area of mathematics. There may be no greater indicator of our lack of will to master risky or difficult circumstances than the overwhelmingly common feminine malady of math/computer/technology anxiety.*

Should aliens from another planet observe us, they would likely conclude that some sort of "computer virus" attacks the female of our species at around age thirteen. This "virus" would appear to weaken the math-competency center of the brain (which doesn't exist, by the way, in either the male or the female brain), then spread to anything remotely connected to math—computers, physical sciences, and technology—convincing the stricken female that she is either just plain stupid or, at the very least, terribly miswired somehow.

Over the years, research from a variety of fields has attempted to prove math incompetency in females on some biological basis but has failed to prove its case. In the Soviet Union, for example, the performance level of boys and girls is comparable in both math and physics.[16] Male and female Asian students also perform equally well in math and science, as do American boys and girls *prior to the age of thirteen*.

Here is how it works. In elementary school the material is usually not challenging enough to cause confusion, or, when it does, the opportunity to avoid it is not presented. In junior high, however, when math classes become more intellectually rigorous, students are presented with the opportunity to drop out of challenging courses that pose the threat of failure and/or confusion. Since girls tend to internalize their failure, a bad grade or state of confusion is proof to them that they lack ability (unlike boys, who take a more adaptive approach and just try harder). Unable to withstand the constant attack on their self-esteem, which males do not suffer, they give up.

---

* And things are slow to change. As late as 1988, when females had supposedly made terrific progress in these areas, only 12.2 percent of *all* doctorates in math, engineering, and physical science were awarded to females.[15] Because these fields have been so male-dominated in the past, *any* increase in numbers of women represents a *large* increase in their percentages. For example, if five years ago a calculus class consisted of three women and now, five years later, nine women are enrolled, statistics will show a 300 percent increase! Sounds terrific until you discover that the total class enrollment was fifty-two. (These numbers are from an actual class enrollment at a local junior college in Denver.)

Since mathematics is a discipline in which the individual is *likely* to experience confusion and failure, particularly at the beginning of each new level, learning math creates precisely the kind of conditions under which those with LH typically fold. For these reasons learning new explanatory styles and changing one's beliefs are paramount. Toward that end, meet Terri and Pat, two women with entirely different approaches to the challenges inherent in mathematics.

Terri, the Textbook Case

A thirty-five-year-old displaced homemaker* whom I'll call Terri showed up at one of my seminars because she was having a difficult time returning to school following a divorce. She provided me with practically a textbook case of LH, in this case that age-old female problem—math anxiety.

Following her divorce Terri had enrolled in a computer class at the local community college, both in the spirit of adventure and as a necessary career move. When the going got rough, however, she got discouraged and started missing a few classes. These piled up on her until she decided she wanted to drop out. Unfortunately she had missed the deadline to drop the class, and now her options were all unpleasant: try to pass the class (which she doubted she could do), take an incomplete (and be forced to take the course again), or fail (and put a permanent black mark on her grade-point average). As she talked about her situation, she revealed the beliefs and behaviors of LH, which were really at the root of her problem.

"If only I could be like my lab partner," Terri began. "Even when Steve's programs go wildly wrong, he doesn't fall apart like I do. He just calmly sits there and tries to figure out where he made the mistake.

"I'm just not like that. When I make a mistake or don't understand the material, I get so down on myself that it's a struggle not to cry. I think men are just naturally more able to understand math and stuff, don't you?"

---

* I've always hated this term. It makes me think of a suburban homemaker innocently loading her washing machine when, zap!, through some timespace warp, she finds herself in the frozen tundra of Antarctica boiling her clothes in a pot or on the banks of the Nile pounding them on a rock.

"Not necessarily," I responded.

"Well, my mother was lousy at math too, so that's probably where I got it," she continued, ignoring my comment. "I remember in the eighth grade I brought home my first and only D on a report card. It was in algebra. I thought my mother would kill me, but she only said, 'That's okay, honey, I wasn't any good at math either.' "

At this point I tried to steer Terri away from her justifications for succumbing to fear and doubt by getting her to describe some examples of Steve's mastery behavior.

"Well," Terri pondered, "he asks a lot of questions. I'm afraid the professor will think I'm stupid if I ask too many questions, but that doesn't seem to bother him." Then, once again seeking affirmation for her beliefs, she said, "I think some people just naturally have more confidence than others, don't you?"

"No, I don't," I replied. "What you are describing as natural I would call a learned behavior. It sounds to me as if somewhere along the line Steve has been taught how to ask for what he needs. In this case it's instruction. He has learned how to learn, that's all."

"Yeah, but it's easier when you're already good in a subject," she argued.

"Maybe you've got the cart before the horse," said someone from across the room. "Maybe he's good in the subject because he asks questions."

"Or maybe he's just not afraid to be wrong," suggested another.

"Yeah, but . . . I am," Terri added with the finality of someone determined to argue for her limitations.

At which point a frustrated woman across the room yelled out, "Then, what are you doing here? All you have done is yeah-but every suggestion we've given you."

This challenge brought forth an important issue. Terri had come to the workshop with her body but not her will. She could see what had to be done in order to succeed but didn't really want to make the effort. She was much more interested in arguing for her limitations than in attempting real change. In effect she was just going through the motions.

Her opening line of "If only I could be like my lab partner," for example, indicated empty wishing rather than strategic planning. Her statement "I'm just not like that" showed her belief in the stable nature of both the problem and herself. The next statement, "My mother was lousy at math too," provided historical evidence to solidify her belief further and fended off any suggestion that maybe she could try harder.

On the positive side she showed awareness of some of the differences between LH and mastery behavior. She said that Steve asked a lot of questions but then discounted that as a possible option for her because she was afraid the professor would think she was stupid. She could have taken a cue from Steve's nonchalance about making mistakes and learned an important mastery-oriented skill. Instead she discounted that, too, by describing his behavior, not as an acquired skill but as "natural" confidence—something she felt could not be learned or acquired.

Terri's responses are all somewhat predictable from an individual with LH. Once she realizes that her behavior is maladaptive, based on a negative explanatory style, and, most importantly, *correctable*, she will be on her way to acquiring the skills to master her fear of math (or anything else). Once she decides to tell herself a new story, like Pat, the woman you will meet next—a story in which smart, successful people also make mistakes, a story in which risk takers also experience fear and doubt but push through it, a story in which acquiring mastery behavior is more important than arguing for the limitations imposed by helplessness—then and only then can she avail herself of the techniques presented later.

Pat, the Math Whiz

A female computer whiz and math major in college whom I interviewed for my first book presented a point of view helpful to those of us with mathematical LH.

"When I was an undergraduate math major, I never really had a good grasp on what I was doing until I got to the next-level math course," said the dark, gaminelike woman sitting across from me in the student section of the university lounge. She looked at me through long bangs and stuffed a French fry in her mouth. "When I got to the next level, it would all become miraculously clear. Of course, by that time I would be confused all over again at the new-level math course. I finally learned that confusion was just part of the process, and I accepted it."

"Why do you think males seem to understand this better than females?" I asked her, since we had been discussing it earlier.

"I think it has something to do with self-esteem. Guys seem to forgive themselves for making mistakes or not understanding, but females beat themselves up for every little thing. It really undermines them in a field like mathematics."

"What advice would you give women thinking about tackling a math, computer, or science class they are fearful of?"

"They need to be more patient with themselves and avoid jumping to premature conclusions that they can't understand the material just because they are temporarily confused. What they forget is that *anyone* who does higher-level math gets confused."

"Actually I don't think that they forget it. I don't think they believe it in the first place," I countered.

"True, but the ones who make it, like me, are not necessarily more intelligent. We just have a higher tolerance for confusion. We don't blame ourselves or think we are stupid when we don't get it. We understand that it is temporary and that it goes with the territory."

We owe it to ourselves to cut through the miasma of self-doubt associated with math, computers, and technology, not because we all have to be rocket scientists but because our LH in math prevents us from fully participating in a mechanized world and severely weakens our earning potential. Failing to take the risks necessary to overcome our mathematical LH can leave us to languish in dead-end jobs with inadequate pay and benefits.[17] We will be cut off from many professional goals that require math, such as:

- Business, accounting, or engineering
- The physical sciences and medicine
- Graduate degrees in *any* field (that requires achieving a certain score on a math portion of the Graduate Record Exam and often passing a statistics class later on)
- Computer programming rather than word processing and data retrieval (which are clerical skills)

Even managing our money profitably or learning to invest it rather than just save it, requires us to exhibit mastery over numbers.

Real change is hard. Overcoming LH is hard. No use pretending it isn't. One must be willing, intellectually and emotionally, to be confused, to be wrong, to exert effort, to take oneself lightly, to take a risk, exert more effort, fall down, skin one's knee, get up, exert more effort, be wrong again, laugh about it, and be wrong once again! Sounds rather like an exercise in masochism *if* one associates confusion and mistakes with stupidity, like Terri. If, on the other hand, one accepts confusion, blundering through, and making mistakes as an inevitable part of the process—as Pat does—then the fear loses its emotional charge and its power to make us feel sad and inadequate.

When you hear yourself yeah-butting like Terri, stop for a moment and consider what this may indicate. It may indicate an unwillingness to do what must be done, to tolerate confusion, to resist explaining to yourself or anyone else why you are confused. No need to explain. You're learning something new, that's all. Whether it's math or skiing or a whole new behavioral style, you are entitled to fall down and make mistakes. Anyway it's inevitable. Everyone does, including the mastery-oriented.

ONE LAST CAVEAT

Learned helplessness is a complicated and intricate weave of beliefs and behaviors, of internal mechanisms and external manifestations. The jury is out concerning the exact model of LH versus mastery orientation. In other words, it is an evolving theory and, as such, contains overlap and paradox. In the study of human behavior, however, there are no models free of anomalies.

For the purposes of this book, the term *learned helplessness* will be broadened somewhat from the narrow clinical definition, because in the last five years of conducting workshops I have observed that people often fail to recognize their own helplessness when held strictly to the clinical definition. In other words, when asked if they think there is a connection between their actions and the final outcome of events (the clinical definition), they will nearly always reply glibly, "Of course." They must, really, in order to retain any perception of themselves as responsible adults. But as their understanding of the subtleties of LH increases, they begin to perceive the ways in which they do, in fact, exhibit the beliefs and behaviors of this debilitating syndrome.

A second reason for broadening the definition of LH has to do with my contention that individuals with an overall fearful response to life should also be included in the LH population. This group has learned to *generalize* fear from one moment to the next, unlike animals, who rely on what is known as a *startle response* to protect them and do not appear to continue to function in a fearful state once a danger has passed. Humans, on the other hand (who also possess a startle response, by the way), use their minds to generalize fear from one moment to the next or from one situation to another, even if they are only remotely connected. This causes all kinds of problems, as I'm sure you are aware, from phobias to panic disorders, from mild suspiciousness of others to outright paranoia, from a general malaise that pollutes the river of life to an immobilizing depression that effectively dams the flow altogether.

For these reasons, the definition of LH, for the purposes of this book, while founded upon Seligman's clinical definition, will be broadened to include those with a less well-defined diagnosis but whose behaviors remain congruent with the behaviors Seligman has noted.

HOPE

The symptoms of LH do not convey the pain and emotional devastation that can accompany it, nor does a clinical recitation of mastery-oriented behavior even begin to touch the joy and power that are available to any individual who learns mastery and practices it.

The rest of the book will reveal how the drama is played out in the lives of women who have been there, from one end to the other, from lives of victimization and helplessness to lives of personal power and joy. They invite you to join them in the pleasure of their metamorphoses. I invite you to embrace the hope that lies within their transformations.

CHAPTER 4

The Set of the Sail

One ship sails east; the other ship sails west
While the very same breezes blow.
But it's the set of the sail and not the gale
That gets you where you want to go.
— AMERICAN FOLKSONG

"I was preparing to be alone for a long time, waiting for the right time, meaning when the kids were out of diapers, out of the stage when it was too hard for me to cope alone and still be a mom for them."

The woman speaking, petite, blond, and wide-eyed, dressed in a khaki jumpsuit, chewed on her pencil. Janet's voice shook with emotion. Her childlike expression belied the story of courage that only a full-grown woman could tell.

"I worked part-time. I earned two hundred and fifty dollars every two weeks. My paycheck went for groceries and a baby-sitter. Groceries were two hundred dollars and the sitter was forty dollars.

"The entire year before we split up, when I would make out the grocery list, I would think, 'Should I rent a U-Haul and get out of here, or should I go to the grocery store?' I could either get out or feed us, but I couldn't do both. A very limited set of options. Or, at least, that was how it seemed to me.

"Even though I was preparing for this internally," she continued shakily, "when we finally split, I was god-awful scared.

"The first month was probably the worst. We lived in the mountains, and it was the dead of winter. I thought, 'How am I going to get us up and down this mountain? How am I going to light a fire in the wood-burning stove to keep us warm?' I didn't know how to chop wood, and of course he left when there was no wood left in the woodpile. It was a basic survival situation for us.

"I was so scared, it was like being physically ill. Looking back, I don't think that was just the challenge of surviving in the mountains, because ultimately I was able to take care of us. I think it was feeling I was trashing my whole life, everything I had been working for, that made me so sick.

"Anyway, I didn't eat for two months. Every once in a while I'd thaw out a piece of meat, thinking, 'I'll get some protein. I can't let myself die. I have to stay alive for my kids.' "

The audience, hushed into respectful silence, waited compassionately as she fumbled in her purse for a tissue to wipe away the tears threatening to spill over and spoil her mascara.

"Anyway," she continued, "every day, just a little bit at a time, I started proving to myself that I was capable of taking care of us, me and my two kids, through this winter. It was unbelievably hard, and even though no one else knew what was happening, I could feel my strength building.

"Chopping the wood was the big milestone for me. At first I thought, 'I cannot chop this wood,' Then I thought, 'I shouldn't have to chop this wood,' although this was irrelevant because if I didn't chop it, it wouldn't get chopped and we would freeze to death.

"I went outside. I was weak because I hadn't eaten in days, but I was so determined. I picked up the ax. I swung it, praying I wouldn't chop my foot off. With every swing of the ax, I thought, 'Look at me not need him.' With every trip up and down the mountain in snowstorms, I thought, 'Look at me not need him.' By the time spring came, I felt like Nanook, Woman of the Wilderness. I got out the chain saw and cleared the overgrowth blocking the driveway and thought to myself, 'Look at me still not need him.' "

At which point a woman across the room chimed in with, "Yeah, and then she got out her vibrator and thought, 'Look at me still not need him!' "

As the room rocked with laughter and the release of emotion it brought, I was once again touched by the humor, clarity, and poetry with which women describe what is more clinically discussed in the literature on LH. Real-life women, speaking from their experience, liberally sprinkled with the warmth, candor, and wit of their personal styles, are able to re-create vividly their experiences with LH and offer the critical aspects of recovery into mastery-oriented behavior.

Often, as with my episode aboard the jetliner to Germany, this transition happens because a woman has no other choice.

"I had gone to Europe with my boss to cover a trade show in the fashion industry," added another woman. "I was just a little small-town girl with writing skills who had landed a job at a fashion magazine. I didn't know the first thing about foreign travel.

"Midway through the show, which lasted two weeks, he starts coming on to me. I tried to put him off, politely at first, but when that didn't work, I had to get tough.

"Well, one thing led to another and I finally had to leave the trade show, even the country, to make my point. I was scared, but, after all, I figured, here I am in Europe, I might as well make the best of things, so I decided to go to Italy to see the sights."

She pauses to take a breath.

"After some misadventures trying to get to Italy (one involving me in a designer suit and a matching felt hat with a stylish veil, boarding the wrong train and ending up in a freight car amid a bunch of squawking chickens and pigs in cages being transported to market), I found myself sitting alone on my bed in a hotel room, somewhere in Rome, lonely and terrified. I felt so forlorn and isolated without so much as a common language to comfort me. Of course, I imagined all the dangers in my head: getting mugged, accosted, lost, kidnapped into white slavery. . . .

"I would definitely have preferred to be rescued. I mean, I thought, okay, who usually gets me through bad times? My husband or my mother, but they're a bit far away. My boss, who was supposed to get me safely through Europe, turned out to be someone I needed to be rescued *from*! The American embassy probably doesn't care that I'm here.

"Sitting on my hotel bed, going through the possible means for rescue and eliminating them one by one because they weren't feasible, I finally got to the obvious, 'Well, then, it's gotta be me.' The last resource I have is me. Hell, the *only* resource I have is me, so, okay, now what can I do?"

Summarizing, the woman added, "The process you described to us earlier of changing one's explanatory style I went through on a very abbreviated basis. It was a combination of forced risk taking and a desire for change that motivated me to change my explanatory style."

"Could you explain this for us?" I asked.

"The stable part was that I saw myself as a small-town girl. That definition of myself was, up to that point, set in stone. I thought that was all I was or, more importantly now that I think about it, all that I could be. But I knew something had to change. I didn't want to be a small-town girl sitting alone crying in her hotel room in Rome, so I was forced to go out and act as mastery-oriented as I could.

"Well, I was pickpocketed, just as I feared. The second after it happened, I understood the scam. I hung around and watched these two guys continue to work the crowd. I thought, 'Well, if I move fast, I can go to the police and haul them back here, and maybe I'll get my money back.'

"I went to the Vatican police, and they wound up interrogating *me*. They wanted to know what I was doing, a woman alone in Rome. To them I was the one who was suspicious. I was told later this was due to an influx of hookers. Being blond and alone just reinforced their suspicions.

"So it turned out that I had assessed the situation accurately. The dangers were out there, just as I thought. But my alternative was to hole up in my hotel room and pass up this once-in-a-lifetime opportunity to experience one of the truly great cities of the world, which I was determined not to do.

"Every morning I would have to give myself another pep talk to get out the door. I would think, 'I did it yesterday, and if I did it yesterday, I can do it today.' The challenges continued. I *did* get accosted, I *did* get lost. But through this daily process my skills of negotiating the city were noticeably improving, my confidence was building, and my self-image was changing. It wasn't long before I stopped seeing myself as a naïve small-town girl and began to think of myself as an international woman of sophistication and savoir faire.

"The global part was that, at first, I kept thinking, 'Now everything's ruined. This whole trip is a disaster. Nothing ever works out as it's supposed to. It's all just a waste of time and money.'"

"How did this change?" I asked.

"Well, as I said before, a lot of it had to do with forced risk taking. I had to act mastery-oriented, even though I didn't really feel it at first. I had to fake it. As I started going out and negotiating the city, I realized that it wasn't true that my whole trip was ruined. Only a couple of days, really, and even that was just my description of it at the time.

"And the internal part?" I asked, knowing what she would say.

"That was the part where I blamed myself for my predicament. I kept telling myself that I never should have come in the first place, that I should have known, somehow, that my boss would be a problem, that I never should have left him and set out on my own. But then I got mad and thought, 'Wait a minute. This is *not* my fault! It's not my fault that my boss is a jerk and I had to leave.' That anger gave me the energy and motivation to go out and enjoy myself in spite of him. I thought, 'I'm not going to let that ass spoil what will probably be my only opportunity to see Europe.' "

"I can relate to her story," added Nanook, Woman of the Wilderness, who with chain saw vanquished her helplessness. "Mine was forced risk taking too. Once I was forced to do certain things, I had to change my self-concept. It's quite simple really."

JUST DO IT

Simple but paradoxical. You see, most of us think that internal changes must come before we are ready to make changes in the external circumstances of our lives. Sometimes that works. More often, however, what works is the opposite. By taking a risk (or being forced to) we become mastery-oriented, not the other way around.

The truth of the matter is we cannot avoid risks. We only pretend that we can. Risks are woven into the fabric of being. As living creatures we are always only one breath away from nonbeing. Although we take the next breath for granted in a most cavalier fashion, the truth is that every heart, as long as it is beating, is vulnerable. Like it or not, life is one big gamble, one whopper of a risk from the get-go. Just getting out of bed is a colossal risk. Most of us pretend this isn't so. We pretend we are safe so that we aren't immobilized imagining the possibilities of everything that could conceivably go wrong.

As I see it, we have two choices. We can either wait around, living in an illusory cocoon of safety, hoping that life won't catapult us into forced risk taking, ready or not, *or* we can begin calculated risk taking now, developing our mastery-oriented skills and preparing ourselves for the challenges, risks, and payoffs that life will inevitably present.

If we choose the latter, we become increasingly comfortable with risk and change. We learn to tolerate, then evoke, and finally welcome varying degrees of ambiguity in our lives and to overcome the interpretation of risk and change as frightening and unpleasant.

This matter of interpretation is critical. Security seekers (those with LH) interpret the feelings that accompany risk and change as "terror." Consequently risks are to be resisted because they are frightening and unpleasant. Risk takers (those who are mastery-oriented) experience the same feelings when they take a risk, but they name the feeling exhilaration. Therefore risks are desirable for their ability to stimulate and excite. Most of us are some combination of the two, labeling the feelings differently depending on the situation.

A pervasive mistake that we women make is to believe that somehow the emotional risks we are taking are not as hazardous as the other types of risk. We delude ourselves that at least we are not endangering our jobs or our lives as men do. This is patently false. Many a woman has awakened, mid-risk, to discover that the emotional gamble she thought was relatively safe did, in fact, endanger her financial security or indeed her very life. Let's face it, there is no such thing as a safe risk. There are only calculated risks. To paraphrase Gertrude Stein, a risk is a risk is a risk.

Those of us stuck solely in the emotional realm of risk taking will never allow ourselves to experience the joys of those who are willing to take big chances—like the woman you will meet later, a "lowly little secretary" with a high school education and no wilderness experience who took the leap of faith in herself and helped to make history in a landmark study of the snow leopard in its native habitat of Nepal. We will never know what it is like to watch the sun slip behind a snowy, windswept peak high in the Himalayas. We will never know how it feels to synchronize our body with the tranquil rhythm of nature's timepiece as it measures out the days and nights without the benefit of clocks. We will never know the trembling eloquence of an encounter with a wild animal in its natural environment. Sadly, we will not allow ourselves to be touched and changed in the ways that only experiences like these can touch and change us.

Finally, this is as good a place as any to offer the reminder that the reluctance to take a risk may show up in one area of life and not another. A woman may gleefully dive out of a plane without a second thought, but go weak in the knees at the prospect of investing the family fortune. In whatever aspect of our lives we exhibit LH, or a lack of belief in self-efficacy, that is the aspect of our life where we take little risk. It is there that we can observe a lack of development and consequently a lack of discernible growth.

It is safe to say that risk taking is a reasonably reliable yardstick of one's belief system. If you want to know what you believe, just look at what you have produced and what you had to risk in order to do so. Then you will appreciate where you have had faith in yourself to produce desired outcomes (self-efficacy) and where you haven't.

Try the following exercise to help you take stock. Start with two columns. The first column should show what you have produced in your life thus far, and the second should show what you had to risk in order to do so. Then, follow these columns with statements about self-efficacy, about what kind of faith you had to have in yourself in order to take the risk. For example:

WHAT HAS BEEN PRODUCED   **WHAT WAS AT RISK**

1. *Purchasing a home.*   *Money and (to some degree) freedom.*

Self-efficacy statements:
"I had to have faith that I was a responsible individual, that I was ready to settle in one place and take on the responsibilities of a homeowner."

"I had to have faith that I could hold down a full-time job and make house payments."

"I had to have faith that I could maintain my salary at a particular level and perhaps even earn salary increases and/or promotions."

"I had to have faith that I could take care of a house, that I could either do the work myself or hire someone to get it done."

2. *Having children.*   *My life, my body, my freedom.*

Self-efficacy statements:
"I had to have faith that I was strong enough and healthy enough to live through childbirth, both figuratively and literally (the physical risks)."

"I had to have faith that, once again, I was a responsible adult capable of handling the incredible responsibilities of parenthood."

"I had to have faith that my husband would be a good parent, help raise and nurture the children, and be a support to me, both emotionally and financially."

"I had to have faith in my ability to create and maintain a certain lifestyle and level of security to provide a stable environment for my children."

3. A *move to a new city.*   *Money, friends, security, loneliness.*

Self-efficacy statements:
"I had to have faith in my ability to find a job."

"I had to have faith in my ability to make new friends."

By the same token, you could do the exercise from the opposite point of view—risks you have refused to take and what that *may* have indicated about faith in yourself (the belief that you could produce desired outcomes). For example:

1. Not *purchasing your own home.*
Uncertainty about your earning capacity, your desire to maintain a stable location, or your ability to take care of a house.

2. Not *having children.*
Uncertainty about your ability to go through childbirth, to be a good parent, to support a child financially, or your desire to settle down to the responsibilities of parenthood.

Obviously the above situations could involve other things besides a lack of belief in self-efficacy. Perhaps you work in an unstable work environment (layoffs, etc.). Perhaps you do not have the down payment required for a house. Perhaps you do not have a spouse to help you raise a child or you genuinely don't want children. The value of this exercise, however, is in determining whether your choices are based on circumstantial realities or simply a lack of faith in yourself.

When we incorporate the behaviors of the mastery-oriented, even if it's only an act in the beginning, something inevitably happens

—change, growth, development, transformation, alchemy, meta-morphosis, self-actualization.

"The payoff for the day's risk taking came at night," said the woman who rode to Rome with the chickens. "Back in my hotel room I would be so exhilarated, I could hardly stand it. I felt so aware, so alive, so confident, you know?

"So, here's where it gets good. One night I go down to have dinner in the hotel dining room. Across the room is this gorgeous Italian with these smoldering eyes, scrutinizing me over his menu. I knew he was upper-class because he had good teeth. I learned in Europe that smile determines class.

"Anyway, we began discreetly peeking at one another over our menus, exchanging eye contact, the whole bit. Tentatively, shyly, but with terrific charm he comes over to the table and says, 'Are you an American? I would like so much to practice my English. May I join you for dinner?'

"His name was Everisto—Ito for short. Through dinner we sat with our heads together poring over an English-Italian dictionary, drinking wine, laughing, having a marvelous time. I remember he told me he was married to Avagardner—And that's just how he said it every time he mentioned her—my wife, Avagardner. One word. It cracked me up.

"Anyway, he asked me if I wanted to go to a very trendy nightclub in Rome, saying the floor show was being billed as the most so-phisticated entertainment in all of Europe. I protested that we were both married, but he reassured me that Italian men were different from American men, that they could appreciate romance without infidelity. I ask you, What woman in her right mind would turn down an offer like that?

"In the taxi I tried to imagine what the floor show would be like. After all, this was jaded and decadent Rome. There was nothing here they hadn't seen before, I reasoned. I wanted to be prepared for whatever I might experience, so I imagined nudity, of course, and maybe even some live sex. Are you ready for this? It turned out to be dancing bears! This sent both of us into fits of uncon-trollable laughter, and we were asked by the maître d' to leave the establishment.

"Hanging our heads in mock shame, like kids being sent out to the hallway for disturbing the class, we barely made it out onto the street before completely collapsing with laughter. We were hanging all over each other, shrieking uproariously, trying to stand up, and hailing a taxi, all at the same time.

"To make a long story longer," she quipped, "we spent three very romantic days together in Rome. True to his word, he maintained the romance without the infidelity.

"When it came time for him to leave Rome, it was a scene right out of the movies. Standing on the terrace of my little room, looking down at a quaint, narrow street, I saw an artist's easel on the sidewalk, street musicians casually strolling by, and Ito, actually dressed in a full, black cape. He turned from the curb, tipped his hat to me, and called, 'Ciao, Deborah.' 'Ciao, Ito,' I called back. All I kept thinking as I watched him disappear into the crowd was, 'Danielle Steele, eat your heart out.' "

The audience burst into spontaneous applause.

She finished her story, "The thing is, I can still be a fearful and helpless person, but whenever I encounter an opportunity that is both scary and appealing, I remember Rome—the risk and the payoff—and I can talk myself out the door and into life."

The essence of mastery-oriented behavior—taking action and taking risks—is that it creates change, the very thing helplessness (with its stable explanatory style) does not believe possible. Deborah not only created the kind of memory to die for, she transformed her self-image as well. Sometimes the change we create just results in a wonderful memory; sometimes it transforms our lives. As you will see, women have changed careers, gone into business, traveled the world, hiked through Nepal, left abusive partners, altered their self-images, and changed their whole lives—all because they decided to stop volunteering to be victims of circumstance and relinquished the cherished belief that they could avoid risk and change.

My invitation to you, then, is to weigh the payoff of risk against the price of helplessness. Then, when you encounter an opportunity that is both scary and appealing, or a necessity that is frightening but inescapable, you will be able, as Deborah said, "to talk yourself out the door and into life."

The best way to talk yourself out the door and into life is to understand the behavioral differences that result from the two different explanatory styles. The following is a brief summary of these behavioral differences.

BEHAVIOR DIFFERENCE 1—GOALS:
GROWTH-ENHANCING OR STATUS QUO?

Studies of motivation and persistence show that people generally fall into two categories: those who choose what the experts call *performance goals* (usually chosen by those with LH) and those who choose what the experts call *learning goals.* [1] Performance goals show the desire to obtain favorable judgments of one's performance (or avoid negative ones). Learning goals indicate the desire to master a new task or increase one's competence.

Here is how it works. Those with LH believe that intelligence and ability are fixed commodities, traits that are basically impervious to change and unresponsive to strategies for development. When they encounter the perfectly natural situation of confusion/frustration that is an inevitable part of learning something new or adapting to change, they therefore interpret it as a signal that something is wrong with *them.*

What they do is personalize an impersonal process. They conclude that the cause of their confusion is a lack of intelligence or ability. By doubting their intelligence or ability every time they face uncertainty, confusion, or frustration, they wind up feeling ever more insecure. They therefore choose performance goals (areas in which they have already proven themselves) over learning goals (areas containing the potential for confusion) in order to avoid this painful state of self-doubt. The irony is that this painful state is a result of their own negative explanatory style.

Happily, the research does not support the "fixed-entity theory" of intelligence or ability. Studies have shown that IQ scores can and *do* increase over time. Some research suggests that there can even be improvement in IQ scores, by as much as twenty points, after age thirty-four. [2]

Furthermore, when learning a new task, people with high IQs or an impressive list of accomplishments *also* become confused and make mistakes, just like the rest of us. This is a basic truth that people with LH either do not believe or simply forget.

To summarize, then, a strong inclination toward performance goals is a symptom of LH. This inclination to keep doing only what you are already good at perpetuates the status quo and impairs functioning in the face of adversity. Ironically, a woman's fixation with winning approval may lead her to shun the very challenges she needs in order to develop the skills that will win approval. It is tantamount to saying, "In order to achieve a high level of ability in this new endeavor, I must already have a high level of ability." Such thinking has about as much usefulness as dehydrated water.

"A Helpless Phi Beta Kappa?"

"I made the mistake of choosing a performance goal over a learning goal right out of high school and headed down the wrong path for three years as a consequence," offered Betty, an engaging, articulate, middle-aged woman deeply involved in a mentorship program for young girls.

"Like a lot of girls, I had always done well in humanities classes but poorly in math. Although my ambition was to earn a business degree, my counselor took one look at my math scores on my College Boards and announced, 'You are not college material and will never make it through a business program.' Well, I went through the process you describe of thinking that I was just too stupid to do well in math and that all the effort in the world wouldn't change that. I thought the only option was to be a humanities major.

"In my third year as a communications major I was forced to take a statistics class. I was terrified of being seen as stupid, so I worked hard, kept up with the homework assignments, and sought extra help from the teacher. None of which I did in high school, when my style was to give up when I got confused. Well, I passed the class, not with an A but with a B, and I was proud of what I had accomplished. My thinking began to change: If I was wrong about my ability to get through statistics, maybe I was also wrong to avoid the challenge of business school.

"The upshot was that I changed my major my third year, much to my parents' dismay, I might add. Anyway, after graduation, I sent a copy of my business degree and my Phi Beta Kappa key to my counselor so that he wouldn't teach helplessness to someone else."

In other words, when we act on the belief that intelligence or ability can improve—which the research indicates it can—we choose the type of goal (learning) that does in fact lead to our intellectual growth. Conversely, when we believe intelligence is fixed, we choose a different type of goal (performance), which can lead to intellectual stagnation or even decline later in life.

When we believe we can improve, we do. When we believe we

can't, we don't. As Henry Ford once said, "Whether you believe you can or whether you believe you can't, you're right!"

This is both ironic and profound. It means that we've got it backward. It means that our belief systems (which produce our explanatory styles) are fully capable of producing the very reality that our explanatory styles are designed to explain. We've got the cart before the horse. In other words, belief systems do double duty. They can be used, modified, transformed, rearranged, altered, tempered, and adjusted not only to explain past and present but to *create* the future as well.

BEHAVIOR DIFFERENCE 2—ATTRIBUTIONS: WHO GETS THE CREDIT? WHO GETS THE BLAME?

When successful men and women were asked to what they attributed their successes and failures, their answers were very revealing. Men, on the whole, tended to attribute their successes to internal traits, such as ability, intelligence, and effort. They attributed their failures, on the other hand, to external events, such as difficulty of task, bad timing, or lack of help. Guess what? Women, on the whole, were exactly the opposite.[3] They tended to blame their failures on internal deficits, making statements like, "I just wasn't smart enough," or "I wasn't good enough," or "I didn't try hard enough." Their successes, on the other hand, were attributed to external things, such as luck, assistance, or ease of task, and were accompanied by statements such as "It was nothing," or "I had a lot of help," or "It's just that it was easy."[4]

This research on what psychologists call *attributional style* dramatically underscores the contrasts between those who have learned a mastery-oriented style (usually men) and those who have learned the helpless style (typically women) in their reactions to success and failure. It is distressingly simple: On the whole, *men internalize and accept responsibility for success, and women internalize and accept responsibility for failure.*

These attributions for failure and success have a profound impact, both on our self-esteem and on the likelihood that we will persist in a difficult or risky situation. Listen to the following two stories. The first is my own. The second was told to me by a woman in a workshop.

My story began when the sliding screen door to my patio refused to work. It would neither open nor close properly. (Actually, walking into it the day before might have had something to do with the problem.) Anyway, my tenant, a male, said he would fix it for me when he came home from work. I happily agreed. However, as the day wore on, I began to think, "Well, if he can fix it, why can't I? I'm not stupid. It's not a moving-parts engine, for God's sake. If he can figure it out, I can figure it out."

Bravely I ventured forth, a woman warrior, poised to meet the challenges of force and torque, armed with only my manual dexterity, a Phillips screwdriver, and my positive explanatory style!

Two hours later, my screen door lying broken and bleeding on its side, tools strewn everywhere, beside myself with frustration and awash in angry tears, I called Brian to tell him I had tried to fix the damn door myself and had made an even bigger mess of things. I felt so stupid and helpless. He tried to make me feel better by reassuring me he would take care of it when he got home.

"That's not the point!" I shrieked at the poor man. "I'm so discouraged. I'm not even as smart as the door. I just feel so stupid."

"In my opinion," he replied calmly, "you're not the stupid one. Whoever the guy was who designed that door was the stupid one. I looked at it last night and thought how poorly constructed and designed it was. No wonder you had trouble."

Get it? I, behaving in a typically female fashion when faced with failure, instantly attributed the problem to my stupidity and lack of ability. Brian, behaving in a typically male fashion, attributed the stupidity elsewhere. In the long run the "truth" was irrelevant. His explanation was far more encouraging of self-esteem, far more supportive of a belief in self-efficacy, far more likely to produce persistence in the face of difficulty.

What is so amazing to me was how easily and quickly it came to him. How naturally even. *I'm* supposed to be the authority. I'm the one writing a book on the subject! But the tendency is so habitual, so pervasive, that even in the midst of writing about the feminine tendency to internalize failure, I internalized failure! It taught me (and I hope you too) how deeply ingrained are these beliefs and behaviors and how consciously, vigilantly, and energetically we must strive to defeat them.

I thought I was being mastery-oriented by rallying myself to go outside to fix the door. I was. However, when faced with a failure, I slipped back into the old LH (and feminine) response.

The other story was given to me in a workshop by a woman who worked as a corner flagger at a racetrack on the weekends. Apparently an accident had taken place in her corner one weekend, and she was required to fill out an accident report detailing the events she had witnessed. At that point it had to be approved by a supervisor.

She dutifully wrote out her account of the accident. When she took it to the supervisor to be signed, he insisted that it be written by the other flagger (a male) who had been standing in the same corner at the time of the accident. In other words, the supervisor completely discounted her account of the accident.

"Driving home that night after the race, I felt so bad. I kept telling my husband, Peter, that I must be incompetent because the supervisor had not accepted my witness report.

"Peter gave me this incredulous look and said, 'What? You think he didn't accept it because you are incompetent? I can't believe you. You have just been the victim of sex discrimination, pure and simple, and here you are blaming yourself!'

"Other than being embarrassed that it took a man to point this out to me, I was so relieved. It hadn't even occurred to me that I had been discriminated against. I just automatically internalized the failure. Peter, on the other hand, automatically attributed the problem elsewhere, and more accurately, I think."

That Peter and Brian were probably accurate in their explanations doesn't necessarily mean they will always be right and that we will always be wrong (there's that tendency to internalize failure again). It's just that a man's choice of attributions gives him better access to what he needs to meet challenges and—this is vital—the motivation to develop multiple strategies should he encounter failure. In other words, by refusing to internalize the failure he does encounter, he is motivated to consider the changes in strategy that can ultimately produce changes in outcomes.

Let us take our cues from these mastery-oriented males and learn to see other possible reasons for our failures. Let us see that we may be as responsible for the *successes* in our lives as we are for the failures. Let us know that perhaps all the failures are not our fault. If that seems like a tall order at this point, never fear. Specific strategies for learning how to change your thinking will be presented in Part 3 (Chapters 7 through 13).

BEHAVIOR DIFFERENCE 3—INAPPROPRIATE REFERENCES: DON'T COMPARE

Another behavioral difference between those with LH and the mastery-oriented involves making inappropriate comparisons between oneself and others. A woman at a workshop related this story.

"My daughter is a gifted musician. When she was about ten, she was taking private lessons from a well-known teacher and studying quite seriously to be a concert cellist. Then, a couple of years ago we took her to see Yo-Yo Ma, thinking that this would be an inspirational experience for her. It turned out to be the worst thing we could have done.

"Following his performance she concluded that no matter how hard or long she practiced, she would never be as good a musician as he and promptly gave up all further efforts to play the violin. We were just sick. We tried everything to change her mind, but I guess she already had the helplessness syndrome and just wouldn't listen."

To measure herself against one of the greatest virtuosos ever to grace the concert stage, performing at a time when he was a seasoned and mature musician, was not only inappropriate but was downright unrealistic and counterproductive. This behavior is common among those with a helpless style, who develop the habit of measuring their self-worth based on someone else's performance (or, as adults, on someone else's display of wealth). When we measure ourselves against an inappropriate reference, *as if we were supposed to be a peer of the greatest artist or scientist in the world*, we create the conditions that lower self-esteem and decrease our efforts in the pursuit of goals. *

Another participant from the same workshop revealed a different example of inappropriate referencing. She came up at the end to talk, and after listening briefly to her story, I invited her to my home for an interview.

---

* You may have also noticed that the young woman had burdened herself with a performance goal over a learning goal. We have already discussed the effects of performance goals when employed prematurely in the learning process. Here, the choice of a performance goal in combination with an inappropriate reference completely debilitated a talented individual and short-circuited a promising career. Once again, "reality" had nothing to do with the failure, only the explanatory style.

Linda and Barbara

As Linda sat facing me on my sofa, talking into my tape recorder, her charisma was almost unnerving. She was wearing jeans, an ethnic print blouse, and dangling silver earrings, which caught the late-afternoon light, providing a striking contrast with her dark hair and olive skin. She gazed at me through intensely expressive almond-shaped eyes nestled above high cheekbones. Curled on my sofa, sipping tea, she was not conventionally pretty but was endowed with the kind of regal beauty and aloof mystery usually reserved for Native American princesses. She began her story.

"This woman named Barbara and I used to belong to the same women's support group a couple of years ago," she began. "I always felt like such a failure around her because she seemed to have it all—a high-status job with security and a good salary, a contented married life with a caring husband, above-average children, a lovely home in the right suburb, nice face, nice figure, you name it. On top of all that she was six years younger than me. To make matters worse, I felt petty for being envious of her. I just couldn't win on any front," she said, warming her hands on the teacup.

"We all got very intimate over the course of the year, and the truth of the matter was that she really *did* have it all! She was only in the support group to make some new women friends. All the rest of us had big problems, but there she was, happy, but just a little lonely for female friendship."

Linda laughed self-consciously, "God, I still sound so envious, it's embarrassing. I want to say, though, that it's not just envy. When I was around her, I always felt inadequate, kind of worthless, you know?"

According to Linda, Barbara was born pretty. People used to tell her she looked like a blond Mary Tyler Moore. Her family was stable and happy, white and Republican. Her father was an engineer, her mother a homemaker. The three of them lived in a five-bedroom home in an affluent neighborhood. Barbara went to private schools. During the summer her parents would take her on exotic trips to places like Europe and the Orient. When she was sixteen, they bought her a car.

"As far as I could tell," said Linda, "her parents paid for college, she breezed through, married a nice guy who could afford to support her. When I knew her, she had just received her MBA, without even having to work part-time, I might add, and was just about to start a lucrative new job.

"At the workshop the other day, I realized that Barbara was one of those people called an inappropriate reference. I had been measuring myself against her. Then, as you talked, I realized it really wasn't fair to compare myself with her. Our lives are too different. My life, my background, the events that made me who I am are so totally different from Barbara's, it's as if we're from different planets."

"Go on," I urged.

"Well, my family was about as unlike Barbara's as you could get. Mine was a mess from the beginning. My poor mom gave birth to me when she was little more than a kid herself—sixteen to be exact. She was pregnant when she married my father. She realized her mistake and divorced him when she was eighteen, but not before having another baby.

"My mother struggled to make ends meet for the three of us as a single parent and waitress for the next seven years. She took her time remarrying because she wanted a good man. At twenty-five she met someone she thought was a nice, responsible guy, but two more kids and three years later he abandoned us. We were plunged back into poverty. Since I was the oldest, I had to take care of the kids while she worked two, sometimes three jobs, just to keep us going."

Linda shifted around on the sofa, transferring her weight, wincing noticeably and rubbing her left leg.

"The thing was, I had something going for me. I was smart. I had attended parochial school on scholarship, and all the nuns encouraged me to go to college. We didn't have the funds, so I worked for a year and saved my money. I got started late, but with a little scholarship money from the nuns, a grant from the university, and the money I had saved, I felt like I was on my way."

Midway through her junior year tragedy struck. Linda sustained a severe leg injury when a car hit her while she was bicycling to class and sent her hurtling through the air with such force, she took out a fencepost with her leg. When the ambulance took her away, the only thing connecting her foot to her knee was a long tendon.

Doctors who were faculty members of the university medical school where she was a student agreed to treat her leg without charge if she would permit them to experiment with new techniques to save her leg. They reconstructed the bone and grafted pigskin to her leg because the graft would have been too large to use pieces of her own tissue, and pigskin is the most like human skin. They were able to save the leg, but two years later she remained in almost constant pain.

"During my rehabilitation I almost gave up. Not only was I coping with the trauma of my injury and learning to walk again, but all my money was gone, I had been out of school for two years and had become addicted to the morphine-based painkillers the doctors had prescribed during my treatment.

"At the urging of friends, I entered a drug-rehab program and kicked my doctor-prescribed morphine habit. I took out a loan and finished my last year at the university."

Linda stared out the window for a few moments at the softly falling snow, lost in a private place, unconsciously massaging her left leg. I sat quietly and waited for her. She came to suddenly, took a philosophical sip of her tea, and continued.

"I date occasionally, but most guys seem unable to cope with my disfigurement. Not only is my leg pretty ugly, but I limp too. I live alone, my life is okay, but mainly it's all I can do to cope with the pain and dysfunction, both physical and emotional, that this injury has caused."

Now, if Linda, or anyone else for that matter, measures her worth by the outward trappings of Barbara's life—advanced degrees, loving and successful husband, high-paying job, lovely face and figure— she will indeed feel like a "failure." She is measuring herself against an inappropriate reference and, predictably, will feel inadequate.

Barbara is an inappropriate reference because her life, in stark contrast to Linda's, contains all the elements that spell privilege in America. Linda's courage, tenacity, strength of will, and persistence in the face of adversity are all characteristics of performance at an extremely high level of functioning, a level at which perhaps Barbara herself would be unable to perform. As outsiders this is easy for us to see, but for Linda the inappropriate reference against which she measured herself created a blindness to her own achievements. Although to us Linda is obviously a mastery-oriented individual, she did display one trait of the LH style.

"Anyway, as I listened to you talk about inappropriate references in the workshop, I came to understand why I felt so terrible around

Barbara. I was just being unrealistically hard on myself by making an unfair, inappropriate comparison."

The mastery-oriented tend *not* to compare themselves with others, particularly at the beginning of a new endeavor. They stay focused on their own growth and development. They look at where *they* started and how far *they* have come rather than at the distances traveled by others. They understand that comparisons with others serve little purpose, except to create conflicts and dramas that undermine their persistence and enthusiasm through the difficult times that accompany the journey toward any goal.

BEHAVIOR DIFFERENCE 4—FAILURE OF STRATEGIC THINKING

Martin Seligman himself said that one of the disruptions caused by LH is the organism's impaired motivation to respond. One aspect of this impaired motivation is the failure to think strategically, something the mastery-oriented do regularly and repeatedly. In other words, they don't mind going back to the ol' drawing board as many times as is necessary.

Strategic planning is the willingness to think creatively by generating new options, considering the wild possibilities, and changing outmoded ways of doing things. Unfortunately, when LH is operating, creativity is diminished by the opportunity blindness that accompanies LH, so that even the ability to see existing options, much less generate new ones, is severely curtailed. An LH individual's failure to think strategically ultimately derives from the same things that compel her to avoid learning goals—that is, fear of negative criticism, distress, confusion, and lack of tolerance for frustration.

On the other hand, the mastery-oriented are able to generate multiple strategies and be creative because they remain unconcerned with the potential for negative criticism from others. In other words, they don't fret about the inevitable wet blanket who will say, "Where did you get a crazy idea like that?" The belief system of the mastery-oriented does not compel them to seek certainty (performance goals) in order to avoid that criticism, so their creativity is not reciprocally diminished.

Developing strategies takes time, so if you want to make changes in your life, stop wishing and start planning. Wishing is passive, planning is active. Wishing is helpless, planning is mastery-oriented. Since change is really a process, not a product, when you accept that it will take time, you will be motivated to begin your planning as soon as possible. Furthermore, strategic planning transforms what may seem like waiting time into planning time, a much more mastery-oriented and productive approach.

If you feel stuck in a hopeless situation, unable to see a way out, perhaps the story of one woman's planning will help you feel less alone.

Sue Ann's Flight for Life

"My husband didn't hit me for the first two years, but he was emotionally and verbally abusive. He would call me 'fat cow,' stuff like that. I put up with it, thinking it could be a lot worse. As a kid I saw my mom get knocked around, so I used to think, 'Well, at least he doesn't hit me.' The first time he slapped me, though, I realized things *were* getting worse. When he hit me again, a couple of months later, that time with his fist, I started working on a plan to get out. [5]

"I knew what I needed most was money, but Carl wouldn't let me work. The only cash he gave me every week was for groceries and gas. If I was going to get any money, I would have to eke it out of that little bit.

"I started cooking a lot of soups and noodle dishes and casseroles with rice and beans so that I could use cheap cuts of meat and save some money out of the grocery budget. I also cut out lunch. It was great for my figure." (Chuckles from the audience.) "I began to save a few bucks out of the gas money, too, by bumming rides with friends to the grocery store and shopping center and stuff. After they heard my plan, my girlfriends were happy to help.

"I started asking my family and friends for cash presents for my birthday and Christmas. I would tell them to buy me some cheap little thing that I could show to Carl but to give me the rest in secret cash that I could put away.

"One night when Carl came home and passed out on the couch after getting drunk with his buddies, something he did every Friday night, I realized I had another source of cash. I'd steal some of his money, usually five bucks or less, out of his pocket. Because he was drunk, he would never remember how much he had come home with."

At this point a woman in the group made a thumbs-up gesture and yelled, "Right on! Steal from the bastard!" The others cheered and whistled their approval.

Sue Ann smiled and continued, "I gave the money to my sister, who put it with her money in a money market account, which was earning better interest than a regular savings account. She kept the books so that we would know whose money was whose, but that way I earned a better interest rate.

"I know five to eight dollars a week doesn't sound like much, but in two years, during which time Carl just got weirder, more violent, and more unpredictable, I had scraped together a little over seven hundred dollars. It was enough to put down a deposit and pay the first month's rent on a little studio apartment.

"I planned it very carefully. I alerted my family when I would be leaving so that they could get their stories together."

At this point Sue Ann, who had been talking at warp speed, paused to take a deep gulp of the cold coffee in the little Styrofoam cup she was holding in her lap.

"This is the part where I get shaky just thinking about it," she said.

"Take your time," I replied. "You are inspiring all of us."

She blushed, then continued. "Like I said, Carl always went drinking on Friday nights with the guys. Knowing he would come home drunk, that's when I planned to leave. After he passed out, I let the air out of his tires so that he couldn't follow me. And I did it fast. I stuck a knife in them." (More cheers.)

"I had packed the trunk of the car earlier that day with the barest necessities: a few clothes, including one outfit nice enough to go job hunting in, one plate, one saucepan, a skillet, a fork and spoon and my favorite coffee mug, a sleeping bag, and my Swiss army knife.

"I knew I had to get out of town, because he used to tell me he would kill me if I ever tried to leave him. He used to say, 'If I can't have you, nobody can.'

"I drove to a town across the state line, rented a cheap apartment, and got two jobs: one as a waitress, a job I highly recommend, by the way, because of the constant cash flow from tips—a real necessity when you are starting all over again—and the other doing telephone solicitation, which I hated.

"My mother called to tell me Carl had reported me as a missing person, which was stupid. He knew I'd left him. Who did he think slashed his tires? Anyway, I called the police in my hometown and told them not to bother to look for me, I was not missing and had left of my own free will."

Sue Ann stopped here, rather abruptly, apparently finished with her story. Sensing the audience wanted more, I pursued, "How long ago was that?"

"A little under two years."

"And now?"

"Now? Well, it's okay. Not great, just okay. For a long time it was really hard. I mean *really* hard. It seemed like all I did was work. But that's better than living in fear. I think Carl has simmered down and accepted my being gone. But, to tell you the truth, I'm afraid to file for divorce. I'm afraid to stir it all up again. I'm not sure what I'll do at this point. Since there's no one in my life right now, I can't see a reason to pursue a divorce."

"Are you dating?" another woman asked.

"No," Sue Ann answered, sighing, "I get real lonely sometimes and I want someone to hold me, but I'm afraid I'll pick another bad one. I'm not going to push it. If someone comes along, maybe I'll get brave and go for it, but for now I just want rest."

Sue Ann's story is full of the mastery of strategic planning. She took time and strategized a course of action. She budgeted money, elicited money from others, stole money from her abuser, and then shrewdly saved it in the most lucrative way possible. She was persistent, taking two years to develop her plan. She planned the right time. She slit his tires to prevent his following her. She went to a place he wouldn't suspect she would go. She left the state. She took the risk, called upon the warrioress within her, and saved her own life. No wonder she feels like resting.

Later you will hear other stories of strategic planning, particularly in Chapter 12 where I discuss ways to develop multiple strategies. But for now, remember, creative problem solvers, true mastery-oriented individuals, see strategy development as a continuous process, not one that ends once we think our plans are securely in place. Since life is full of surprises, we must be willing to keep altering the plans we have made in order to meet the constantly changing demands of the ever-changing moment.

BEHAVIOR DIFFERENCE 5—NEGATIVE VERSUS POSITIVE SELF-TALK

Self-talk refers to the internal tapes we play in our heads and, make no mistake, they pack an emotional wallop. Research indicates that those with a helpless style engage in more negative self-talk than do the mastery-oriented, who talk to themselves in positive and energizing ways. Those with a helpless style have acquired a self-talk pattern that demoralizes them. Those with a mastery style have developed a self-talk pattern that energizes them.

Two particularly subtle, and therefore insidious, examples of negative self-talk are the "If only . . ." and the "Yeah, but . . ."

The if-only weaves a tale based on a circumstance *in the past* that the individual is now powerless (helpless) to change. Now, there is nothing wrong with fantasizing; in fact, fantasies are an important aspect of creative thinking and problem solving. But mastery-oriented individuals put that same precious mental energy to better use by fantasizing events *in the future* and strategizing the means to bring them about—a shift in focus that is more likely to generate motivation and action. Instead of self-talk full of if-onlys, their self-talk involves a lot of "I could try this. . . . I could change that. . . ."

The second phrase, the yeah-but, was first recognized by Dr. Eric Berne, who coined the term to name a psychological game played to gratify one's inner Child.[6] Within the LH framework, yeah-but is also used by the inner Child, this time to avoid taking responsibility. Yeah-but thinking runs along these lines: "Yeah, I could still go to college, but I don't have the money. Yeah, I could apply for a grant, but scholarships are only given to minorities. Yeah, I could take night classes, but it would mean giving up a social life. A person needs a social life."

The yeah-but enables the individual with LH to procrastinate taking any action whatsoever for an indefinite period of time. As a form of negative self-talk it is quite effective in its subtle ability to short-circuit risk taking by eliminating all options.

The mastery-oriented, in contrast, ignore the past, identify the goals of the present, and strategize the most effective means to achievements of the future. Their self-talk runs like this: "To improve my life, I need a college degree, and to get a degree, I need money. I'll investigate requirements for grants and apply to even the most obscure financial-aid organizations. I'll investigate and apply for government loans. I'll see if there is a tuition program where I work, at my church, within my community, at my stamp collectors' club. I'll check into work-study programs through the university."

Finally, while you probably do not think of yourself as an abuser, if your internal self-talk is fault-finding and censorial, you *are* being abusive. It is just as morally unacceptable, indeed, just as obscene, to abuse yourself as it is to abuse any other living thing. Now don't go off blaming and hating yourself for this too! Simply love yourself as much as you can. Maybe all you can muster is a little love. That's okay, love yourself a little. Do what you can. (My mother, bless her wise old heart, used to say, "Do what you can and can the rest!") Your ability to love yourself will grow as you learn how to do it. As Teddy Roosevelt said, "Do what you can, with what you've got, from wherever you are."

The main problem with practicing years of negative self-talk is that it becomes a habit. When we are in crisis or are in need of nurturing, we find that we have either forgotten how to speak kindly to ourselves or automatically revert to the negative stuff. Later chapters will provide exercises and techniques to help you change this negative and debilitating habit.

INTERPRETING AND CREATING REALITY

What should be obvious by now is that mastery-oriented behavior is a matter of defining events in a way that serves, motivates, comforts, and sustains. "Reality," by which we usually mean a list of so-called facts, such as what happened, who's to blame, what will be affected, how long it will last, and so on, is really kind of irrelevant. Ultimately it is not reality but how we construe it that either keeps us going, moving, changing, and persisting or gets us stuck in self-doubt, procrastination, hesitation, and fear. The pair of glasses through which you choose to see the world then becomes the determinant of your future reality.

Two charts are offered on pages 80 and 81. The first one delineates and summarizes the behavioral differences between the LH response and the mastery-oriented response. The second one illustrates the "flow," if you will, from belief system and explanatory style to behavior and outcome of events; it shows the reciprocal nature and reinforcement pattern between beliefs, behaviors, and outcomes. These charts are provided as a quick overview and reference, once you understand the components. Put them on your refrigerator as reminders.

THE LAST OF THE RED-HOT MOMMAS

The red-hot momma in this anecdote also happens to be my momma.

It was 1938. Momma (Maxine) was a clerk in a department store. My father, Nick, was a butcher. Both were also professional musicians (Mother: piano; Father: sax) who played occasional gigs and shared a hankering for a different kind of life together. After seven years of marriage and living the kind of conventional domesticity everyone expected, they took the leap, bought what my mother always called a little beer joint, renamed it the Shangri-la, and entered that rarefied atmosphere in the Realm of Wild Possibilities.

"Basically we starved to death for the first three years," my mother recalls.

"Was it hard to keep going?" I prompt her.

"Oh, yeah," she continues. "We definitely felt like failures at first. I had to borrow money from my mother just to get my dress cleaned. But we hung in there long enough to learn what we were doing.

"See, in the beginning we didn't know a damned thing about running a joint. Up to that point we were just a couple of typical musicians, who would show up, set up the instruments, and play. At the end of the night the owner would give us our checks, and we'd pack up and go home. That taught us next to nothing about running a club."

My mother's memory is jogged by pictures in an old scrapbook. I hold up a dingy, yellowing, cracked photograph of a large building, with a stone fireplace, huge parking lot, and great big, glitzy neon sign written in script that says, "World-Famous Shangri-la."

When I was little girl, I would ask her if it was really world famous. She would say, "Advertising requires a certain amount of

SUMMARY OF BEHAVIORAL DIFFERENCES
BETWEEN THE HELPLESS AND THE MASTERY-ORIENTED

Helpless	*Mastery-Oriented*
Ruminate on failure, internalize blame, and offer explanations	Offer no explanations for failure *or* give external attributions
Attribute failure to internal factors, such as lack of intelligence or ability	Attribute failure to external factors, such as bad timing or bad luck
Setbacks experienced, defined, and internalized as failure. "That didn't work, therefore I am a failure."	Setbacks not experienced or defined as failure. "That didn't work. I'll try this!"
Failure is globalized.	Failure is kept to specific area.
Focus on past failure and seek escape in the present	Focus on future and seek solutions in the present
Attribute success to external factors, such as good luck or help from others	Attribute success to internal factors, such as effort and ability
Tend to avoid failure by setting performance goals	Tend to strive for success by setting learning goals
Overestimate the performance of peers	Are unconcerned with the performance of peers
Use inappropriate reference groups to measure their own performance	Do not compare themselves with others
Indulge in negative self-talk	Indulge in positive self-talk

THE SYNDROME OF LEARNED HELPLESSNESS

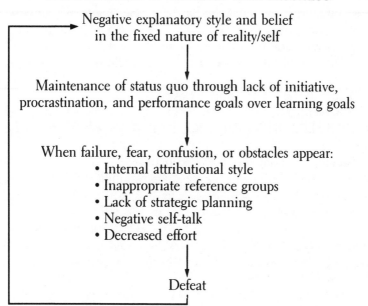

Negative explanatory style and belief
in the fixed nature of reality/self

Maintenance of status quo through lack of initiative,
procrastination, and performance goals over learning goals

When failure, fear, confusion, or obstacles appear:
- Internal attributional style
- Inappropriate reference groups
- Lack of strategic planning
- Negative self-talk
- Decreased effort

Defeat

THE MASTERY STYLE

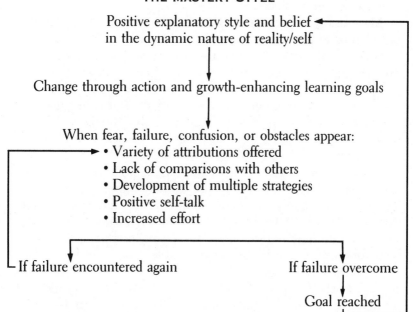

Positive explanatory style and belief
in the dynamic nature of reality/self

Change through action and growth-enhancing learning goals

When fear, failure, confusion, or obstacles appear:
- Variety of attributions offered
- Lack of comparisons with others
- Development of multiple strategies
- Positive self-talk
- Increased effort

If failure encountered again   If failure overcome

Goal reached

poetic license, honey." I never knew what she was talking about. Now I do. Anyway, what she has been referring to as a little beer joint all these years turns out to have been very posh digs, art deco design, swank and trendy in its time. She and Nick transformed a sleazy little joint into *the* see-and-be-seen nightspot in prewar Denver.

"You call this a beer joint?" I query.

"Force of habit," she replies. "That's how we started out, so even after we added the big dance floor, we continued to call it a beer joint."

"So tell me about why it was so hard."

"When we first bought the business, we didn't even know how to mix a drink! I'm not kidding. The first day all we knew how to do was draw a beer. Neither one of us was even a social drinker, so Nick went out and bought a bartender's mixology book, which we kept stashed behind the bar. When someone would ask for anything more complicated than a beer, we would sneak a peek at the book in order to make it.

"But we didn't let that stop us. We figured, hell, we can tough it out until we learn. Maybe we were just too damn dumb to realize what we were getting into, but we took it one day at a time. Gradually our confidence increased."

My musical but nondrinking parents consistently chose learning goals (how to run a bar business, how to pour a drink) over performance goals (setting up their instruments for another gig just like the last gig). To do so, they had to be willing to "tough it out," as my mother said, to tolerate a temporarily low level of performance (in front of their customers, no less) in order to learn their business. As their confidence increased, they were able to take still bigger risks and tackle even greater learning goals, such as deciding to expand the "beer joint."

"The minute we got a little money ahead, we hocked everything we owned and went into debt to build the dance floor and bandstand. Of course everyone disapproved, but that's when the business really took off. And that's when we had to work even harder. Still, I had so much fun, it never seemed like I was going to work, even though I worked harder than I ever had in my life."

"Tell me about that."

"Well, when you lay yourself on the line like that, your life kind of lights up. It's hard to put into words. You feel exhilarated, even though you are scared. It can be kind of unnerving, but one thing is for sure, it's not boring! You really feel alive. You *know* you are living. You're not just going through the drudgery of work anymore. It's exciting, and eventually, for us, it became a lot of fun."

"That's easy to say once you know you've succeeded," I counter, acting as voluntary spokesperson for my more skeptical readers.

"But what if we had never tried? Then for sure we couldn't have succeeded."

"Good point."

"You know, we didn't go off quite as half-cocked as I have made it sound. For example, when we were first thinking of buying the bar, Nick said we shouldn't take the owner's word on how much business he was doing, regardless of what his books said. So we parked our car across the street, hidden in a wheat field, honest to God, and for a solid month we counted the number of cars that came and went and how long they stayed. We started every night at five when we got off work and sat out there till about one. We had a little book that we kept all the information in.

"Then for a couple of nights we went to a different bar and counted how many drinks people averaged in an hour. Then we took all our numbers and averaged them out and tried to estimate his real nightly earnings." She grins and smooths her hair. "For a couple of dummies we were really pretty shrewd."

Shrewd indeed and progressively more mastery-oriented. All the ingredients were there. Nick and Maxine developed a strategy, a carefully constructed plan to minimize, as much as possible, their risk factors. Then they had to be willing to endure a low level of performance and to tolerate the insecurity of learning goals in order to gain mastery gradually. Finally they built upon each new success by replacing the performance goal with a new learning goal and a new strategy for getting there.

"We finally got rich," my mother says matter-of-factly. "I once had sixty-five thousand dollars in my regular checking account. Can you imagine that?"

"I'd like to do more than just imagine it, I'd like to spend it."

"Apparently so did we!" she says, as we both laugh.

"You know what?" she volunteers, "now that I think about it, owning Shang turned me into a completely different person. Before, I was kind of a quiet little thing, afraid to speak up or go against the grain. Now I'm the last of the red-hot mommas. Running the business, especially that kind of a business, required me to get strong. Throwing out drunks and dealing with creditors and hiring and firing musicians makes you . . . what did you call it?"

"Mastery-oriented."

"Yeah, mastery-oriented, real quick."

It is true that Nick and Maxine might have failed, although the likelihood of failure for two people who had had the gumption and strategic foresight to hide in a wheat field and count cars seems slim. Nevertheless a statement like that can be made only in hindsight. At the time their actions constituted bona-fide risk taking, and their mastery-oriented behavior serves as a great example.

PART II

Change and the Self: The Irresistible Force Meets the Immovable Object

CHAPTER 5

The Irresistible Force: Change

The only person who behaves sensibly is my tailor.
He measures me anew each time he sees me.
—GEORGE BERNARD SHAW

No book on overcoming LH would be complete without a discussion of change, that mighty and sovereign force that acts without human permission to metamorphose faces, transform bodies, modify careers, move residences, tease perceptions, alter choices, tamper with philosophics, shuffle the cards, rearrange the deck chairs, and bend the road. Why? Because change puts a double whammy on those with a negative, LH explanatory style.

First, as you may recall, those with LH do not believe change is possible (the stable aspect of their explanatory style). Furthermore, they don't even want to believe it is possible because then they must face the unpredictable processes and outcomes of change. This activates their darkest fears concerning their ability to influence outcomes (belief in self-efficacy), making change a very risky business indeed.

So the double whammy for those with LH is this: They do not believe change is possible nor do they want to. This is why, even when they understand that a negative explanation of life events undermines their ability to respond positively, individuals persist in reconstructing a negative explanation again and again. They are trying to maintain a feeling of safety.

Paradoxically, then, explanatory styles, which humans use to shed light on what is supposedly "really happening," instead shed light only on their belief systems. The more helpless and negative an individual's belief system and explanatory style, the more easily daunted that person is by changing and risky circumstances. Such people are the ones most likely to avoid risk and change with thoughts of "I don't dare . . ." or "What if . . . ?" or "Women are just not able to . . ." or "*I* am just not able to . . ." or "You can't fight city hall."

On the deepest levels, the explanatory style of LH becomes yet another way of resisting change and avoiding risks, another way of arguing for limitations. Fortunately, though, LH need not be a life sentence, an iron-clad prison cell, or a final resting-place. Overcoming LH isn't easy, but then, neither are fear, anxiety, depression, pessimism, and inertia. The bottom line is this. You are born. You will die. How do you want to spend the time in between? If you believe that you can escape change by believing it is impossible, you are mistaken. Just ask the woman trapped in an unheated cabin in winter with hungry mouths to feed, or the one recovering from traumatic physical injuries, or the one crying alone in a hotel room in the Eternal City. The question is, Does it have to come to this? Is it not possible to begin training in mastery behavior *before things get desperate?*

If you are serious about overcoming LH before reaching a crisis situation, or if you are simply tired of being stuck in old patterns, you must be willing, like an alchemist, to transmute the base metal of helplessness into the gold of mastery behavior. Like the alchemist, you can concoct an elixir from which to draw motivation and sustain energy, but you must be willing to tolerate some uncomfortable feelings that accompany changing one's self. Is that too scary? How about this: Are you willing to be willing?

If you can get that far—to just simple willingness—the following ideas will help get you started. (Chapters 7 through 12 will show you how.)

First, are you willing to entertain the possibility that your explanatory style, the one that has kept you stuck and fearful, may not necessarily be an accurate representation of the world or your place in it? Are you willing to entertain the possibility that you have been, well, not wrong exactly but, like all human beings, at least very subjective; that your description of reality is just that, *your* description, not an airtight, hands-down final word on the nature of things?

Second, are you willing to consider the possibility that, whether you consciously realize it or not, you are always a woman-in-transition, and it is only that some transitions are more obvious and compelling than others? If you want to emerge from these endless transitions and changes (whether superficial or deep and profound) each and every time as a more mastery-oriented person, you must be willing to alter your thinking, which is the most effective way to alter your behavior.

And finally are you willing to radically alter your concept of who you are; that is, to change, not so much your self-concept as your concept of Self, and to tolerate, perhaps even learn to appreciate, the wild feelings this will engender?

LIFE BETWEEN THE TRAPEZES

In the midst of change, particularly deep or radical change, one often feels like a trapeze artist who has just released her hold on one of the trapezes, is turning in midair to reach for the other trapeze but has not yet grabbed hold of it. In one sense, this midair moment can be terrifying and awesome, even intolerable, if it goes on longer than is anticipated. In another sense, life between trapezes is most certainly an exhilarating period that heightens one's presence in the moment as well as one's appreciation for life itself. We never feel more alive than when our lives are hanging in midair, when the outcome is unpredictable and the future unforeseeable (which, of course, it always is anyway).

The difficulty in living between trapezes for any period of time arises from the human desire to categorize experience almost immediately. By freeze-framing a moment in order to define and categorize it, we stop the flow of change. In this way we attempt to make an unruly, unpredictable, potentially chaotic world safe and secure. The sooner we can control our experience by labeling it, the safer we imagine ourselves to be.

Another way we stop change and the flow of experience results from our belief that we know how things should be. If we go to a social gathering, for example, we go with expectations. We constantly monitor all activities to see if they match our expectations. "I need to have a lot of fun tonight," or "I'm not sure whom I can trust here," or "I need more attention than I'm getting," or "I should be trying to make others feel welcome," or "I have to appear friendly and sociable," or "People should have noticed that I lost twelve

pounds," or "I don't care for these people, I wish I'd stayed home."
This involves constant judgment. We are so busy calculating to
what degree our experience is matching the one we decided ahead
of time we wanted that we miss the one going on right under our
noses. We end up having an experience totally shaped by our prior
expectations, rather than participating in what actually takes place.

Such expectations imply that we already know what is best for
us. We know that we should have fun or that people should pay
attention to us or that we should be friendly or what-have-you. We
believe we know what's best.

But how can this be? Our present way of looking at things (our
explanatory style) is the limited framework that causes the distress
in the first place. It creates the very story lines that perpetuate LH.
If this limited framework has not made you happy in the past, it is
not going to make you happy in the future. Your current LH beliefs
will simply compel you to force things to be the way you think they
already are. In other words, your present explanatory style is the
one that decides what kind of experiences you will have in the
future. Your experience will not be determined by a natural flow
of events in which you fully participate, learn, and grow, but rather
by the narrow and limiting beliefs you bring with you.

All our present perspectives act as filters through which we understand experience. *Therefore, in order to change our experiences,
we have to change the filter.* If your current filter is LH in nature
and has not brought the changes you desire, it's time to change the
filter. Perhaps a radical change in thinking is what is needed. Perhaps
it is time to take a risk.

The truth, of course, is that you are always taking risks and are
always between trapezes. Letting go of the moment just past, looking
toward an uncertain moment in the immediate future, you are
always hanging in the midair of present time.

Take a moment actually to visualize this situation. I'm serious.
Read the following paragraphs, then put down the book and do the
visualization described. Remember to let your imagination go, allow
it to create vivid pictures, and use your awareness to pay close
attention to your experience.

Exercise: "Under the Big Top"

Upon closing your eyes, spend a few moments settling down and
quieting your mind.

Once settled, begin to visualize the setting of a large and colorful circus tent crowded with the expectant and happy faces of children and adults enjoying the antics of crazy clowns or admiring the grace of the wild cats. Watch the circus yourself for a little while from the wings, where you are waiting to go on.

Now see yourself enter the center ring to stand in the spotlight. You are the featured performer of the evening—a high-flying trapeze artist! Have fun imagining your costume, complete with sparkling sequins and fringe in your favorite color, an intricate hand-beaded bodice, fishnet stockings (with a sexy seam up the back), and a graceful ostrich feather in your hair. (While you're at it, you might as well visualize a perfect body too!) Take a few preliminary bows.

Then turn and walk over to the side of the ring, where there is a ladder leading to a tiny platform high above the circus floor. See yourself as you begin climbing that ladder. Climb slowly, gradually experiencing the height as you climb, listening to the music and the hush that descends upon the crowd as they realize you will be working without a net.

Keep climbing, up and up, until you reach the platform high in the rafters of the dome of the tent. Jump onto it. Turn to face the cheering crowd below. Smile. Take another quick bow.

Now, gradually, begin to gather your concentration and your energy for what you must do. At any moment you will be jumping off the platform to swing powerfully through the air on the trapeze. Your partner, who is already on the platform, will set the other trapeze in motion at precisely the right moment so that when you turn in midair, it will be there for you to grab ahold of. Of course, since this will be taking place behind your back, you will have to have faith that the other trapeze will indeed be there when you reach for it.

Now, holding on to the bar of the trapeze, jump off the platform and begin to swing gracefully back and forth high above the circus floor. Point your toes and use your legs to push through the air, propelling yourself forward while gravity inexorably pulls you back. Swing rhythmically for a few moments, back and forth, back and forth, the breeze created from your motion through space ruffling your hair and cooling your skin.

When you feel ready, signal your partner. Allow your visualization to go into slow motion at this point. Now, on the upswing, release hold of the trapeze on which you are swinging. See yourself begin to turn slowly high above the circus floor, not holding on to anything, suspended in midair like a hummingbird, not knowing if, in fact, the other trapeze will be there for you when you turn around.

Give yourself plenty of time to fully experience this midair moment. Don't rush it. This is important. Explore the physical sensations occurring in your body as you execute your slow turn. Pay attention. How does your stomach feel? Your throat? Your arms and legs? Your head?

Once you have fully and deeply experienced the physical sensations of uncertainty (of life between the trapezes), continue your visualization but allow the slow motion to return to regular time. You discover, with great relief, that the trapeze is indeed there for you. Grab ahold of it, feel your arms take the weight of your body as you grasp the bar, swing powerfully through the air a few more times, experiencing the satisfaction of your perfectly executed trick. Then jump back onto the platform, turn to face the wildly cheering crowd, and take your bows.

Stop now. Close your eyes and do this exercise. Take a full five minutes.

Well, how did it feel? Did you feel light and free? Energized and expanded? Exhilarated and ready for anything?

Perhaps you feel frightened and anxious, light-headed and dizzy, thoroughly shaken and out of control.

Exhilarated or frightened, light and free or out of control, energized or anxious—these are different labels for the same physical sensation, the same bodily response to uncertainty. One thing is sure, whatever your response, you are undoubtedly at a more heightened state of awareness than you were the few minutes prior to doing the visualization.

This exercise can help you develop an appreciation for how the language you use (self-talk) affects your ability to take a risk and cope with change. The words you choose to describe your experience (in other words, your explanatory style), determine how you *feel* about the experience and the likelihood of wanting to repeat it. Everyone experiences similar bodily sensations in this exercise, but while one individual labels these sensations exhilarating, another may label them terrifying.

One example that comes immediately to mind is my own self-talk as I wait in the wings right before giving a presentation to a large audience. I used to call the agitated feeling in my stomach stage fright and thought it was something to overcome (which really meant that I didn't want to feel it). Then one day a wise man gave me a different way to explain the feeling.

"When you present to a large audience in a large room," he said, "you must generate the amount of energy required to project both into the space of the room and into the hearts of your listeners. What you are calling stage fright is not necessarily fear at all but simply the generation of energy and personal power to do what must be done—reach your audience."

How does one measure the value of a gift like this? The only way I can repay him is to pass it along to you. When you begin to practice reframing your experience of fear, you will discover the inherently profound wisdom already existing within your mind and body. In other words, everything you need is already there, the energy to execute any undertaking, once you stop resisting it by giving it a negative label.

Since this man reframed the experience for me, my attitude toward the feeling in my stomach is completely different. I no longer resist it. I embrace it. I embody it. I use it. I welcome it. I love it. Perhaps you, too, can learn to embody the energy that seeming fear can generate when you give it a new name, a different label. Perhaps you, too, can learn to use it, welcome it, love it.

Like life between trapezes, the risks we take in life (or are forced to take) can be wildly exhilarating or wildly terrifying. Usually both. We choose the label. We choose the experience.

A MATTER OF TIME

"Helplessness is a state, not a trait."[1] This quote from two prominent researchers in the field of LH is perhaps the best news of all for those suffering from LH, because it affirms that helplessness, like everything else, is subject to change.

In other words, a state refers to a state of being. A state of being is temporary, subject to change, and likely to shift. My state of being last night—lonely and fatigued—was entirely different from my state of being this morning—energetic and cheerful. A trait, on the other hand, is immutable, something set in stone, intrinsically part of one's identity, such as being female.

If helplessness is a state, not a trait, then for once, time is on our side. Even the most immovable, rigid, and unbending situations can be made more fluid, friendly, and forgiving by the changes that time will bring, and by time's power to alter perceptions and change who we are and who we can become—a lesson I was to learn as I trembled on a rock face, one hundred fifty feet in the air.

ON THE ROCKS

Remember back in Chapter 1 when I told of my friend's one-syllable response to my fear of skiing: "So?" This one little syllable continued to have an effect on me for years to come, curing me of the opportunity blindness caused by my helplessness-oriented belief system and negative explanatory style.

The story begins over twenty years ago when I first read about Outward Bound, a wilderness survival school that advertised "Self-Discovery Through the Medium of Adventure." From the moment I heard those thrilling words, I was hooked.

Further investigation, however, revealed that technical rock climbing would be required as well as a three-day solo experience in the wilderness, with no food, no fire, no shelter, and no books, just my sleeping bag, my journal, and me. Suddenly, discovering myself through the medium of adventure took on a whole new meaning. To say my passion for self-discovery was significantly cooled is a bit of an understatement.

My lack of belief in self-efficacy, namely to produce the desired outcome of survival, along with my negative explanatory style, set the stage for failure, which in this case meant not trying in the first place. It meant gathering up the slick, colorful brochures sent to me by Outward Bound and, as if they were a cherished friend to whom I was saying good-bye, tenderly tucking them away in the back of a drawer, so that I would not have to be reminded of my failed ambitions.

For years I told myself that the reason I hadn't enrolled in Outward Bound was because I hadn't had enough time or money: If I had one, it always seemed I didn't have the other. The truth was I was just plain scared.

Sometime later, while writing my first book, I was at the word processor, waxing poetic about females and risk taking. Suddenly I realized the hypocrisy of my words. Remembering the loss of my cherished Outward Bound aspirations, it seemed to me that my cowardice (which was really LH) tainted my ability to write honestly about females and risk taking.

On the other hand, the passage of time and experience had changed me. Learning to ski in spite of my fear, for example, had taught me a new way of perceiving myself. This new perception helped cure the opportunity blindness of LH, and I was able to see another possibility. Suddenly I thought, I wonder if Outward Bound has a scholarship program?

I dialed the phone. A cheerful voice on the other end assured me that scholarships were available. A letter stating my need would be required, but there would likely be no problem.

I sat down immediately and wrote the scholarship application letter. I advised them of my intentions to interview my fellow trailmates (all women), which would provide free advertising and another forum for Outward Bound in my book. The whole time I was writing the letter, I was praying I wouldn't get the scholarship but knowing that I would.

I was setting myself up, you see, developing a strategy. I now had the time, so if they provided the money, what excuse could I possible have?

Eight weeks later I found myself quivering on a rock ledge. One hundred and fifty feet below me was one instructor, a hundred feet above was the other. I was stuck between them. The rock above me jutted out in such a way that the only living creature that could have conceivably passed this point was a fly.

"There's nowhere to go," I yelled down to my instructor.

"Look around," she yelled back.

I looked around.

"No, there's still nowhere to go. Can I come down now?"

At this point I fully expected her to allow me to descend, or to at least give the signal to those above to pull me up by my belay rope (the umbilical cord used by some climbers to tether them to life). She waited until it was very quiet and all my trailmates below were paying attention and then she said, very loudly, "Whether it takes you two minutes or two days to figure out that no one is going to get you off that rock but *you*, we've got the time."

I was stunned. She couldn't be serious. Not rescue me? But I was in trouble! Always before in my life, if I was in serious trouble, *someone* would help me. Who did she think she was anyway? Didn't she have any feelings? Her superiors would certainly hear a thing or two about this! I proceeded along this productive line of reasoning all the way from blaming my instructor to blaming myself to blaming even the rock, all to no avail. I was still stuck in the same place, it was forty minutes later, and night was about to fall.

By this time my legs were trembling with fatigue and the toe bearing all my weight had gone profoundly to sleep. When it finally dawned on me that the instructor really meant what she said, I was filled with hatred for what I thought was her callousness, but I did begin to climb again—resentfully, angrily, bitterly, to be sure, but climb I did. (Later that night, as I lay in my sleeping bag, I tried to figure out how I got up that rock. The truth is I don't know. All I do know is that once my belief system changed, I made a path up the rock that hadn't existed five minutes before.)

A little farther up I got stuck again. This time I looked at the instructor above me and said, "What do I do?"

"Just place your foot and trust yourself," she said calmly.

Oh, great, I thought, just what I need, another little homily. But this time I didn't waste precious energy hating her for not rescuing me. I took her advice, placed my foot, trusted myself, and to my great delight, scrambled up over the top.

Now, during my little ordeal, had a group of hikers passed by on the trail below, they might have thought, "Well, she is obviously a failure at rock climbing. She has been stuck on that ledge now for forty minutes."

Had they passed by again forty minutes later, they would have realized that that judgment had been too hasty: Not only had *time* altered circumstances again, but it had altered *me* again too. My "failure" was really just a temporary state of being, not a trait of my character, an impermanent way of thinking that kept me stuck in one place.

The point is, never underestimate the power of time to bring about changes in who you think you are or what you can become. In my case, time had altered my self-image, which then enabled me to see opportunities, which then enabled me to develop a strategy that propelled me beyond my next fear zone.

Specifically here's how it happened. I took a risk (learning to ski), which changed my belief system (fear doesn't have to stop me), which wiped out my opportunity blindness (idea to request a scholarship), which enabled me to develop a strategy (writing a letter and interviewing trailmates for book). Just as the flowchart in Chapter 4 shows, the dominoes fell, and where previously I had seen myself as a writer, teacher, speaker, and skier (among other things), after Outward Bound I discovered, to my complete astonishment, that I had to add rock climber to the list. Maybe not a skilled one, maybe not a brave one, but a rock climber just the same!

Time is the most powerful dynamic of all in bringing about change—change in events, circumstances, relationships, and even the idea of self. We are all subject to it, regardless of our station in life. When time brings about the imperative for a change in one's view of self, we must place our foot and trust ourselves or stay stranded on a rock ledge throughout a very long and terrifying night.

Moreover, the acceptance of the temporal quality of all things (including the self and one's state of being) marks the critical difference between the active, mastery-oriented response to adversity, which, you will recall, is dynamic and allows for change, versus the passive, LH response to adversity, which argues that things are static. Passive and helpless individuals freeze-frame a moment of failure and proceed to make all their decisions based on one frozen moment in time, like the hikers passing by as I quivered and quaked on my rock ledge. The mastery-oriented regard the moment of failure as just one more moment in an interminable flow, a moment no more significant than any other moment, with the next moment bringing about totally different and unforeseen possibilities.

So what appears to be a failure at one point in time may turn out to be just a pause on a rock ledge, a temporary bug in the program, or simply an unforeseen circumstance that must be handled before moving on. Just because you have not yet overcome helplessness or fear or succeeded at a cherished project doesn't mean you never will. See yourself as still in process.

There is a Japanese proverb about a farmer who was so anxious for his little sprouts to grow into mature plants that every night he went out and tugged on them ever so gently. Of course they all died. His interference with the natural but time-consuming process of growth killed his fragile plants clinging tenuously to their new life and ruined what might have become a lush and bountiful garden.

Attempting to rush time or the slow, imperceptible process of growth, judging the passage of time as failure (seeing it as a trait, not a state), extinguishes the budding and tender little sprouts of your new mastery-oriented identity. Trust that the lush and bountiful garden of your growth and development is as inevitable as change itself, that it may have its own timetable, but that the new you will be unfolded *to* you.

CHAPTER 6

The Immovable Object: The Self

> The true value of a human being is determined primarily by
> the measure and sense in which he has attained liberation from
> the self.
>
> —ALBERT EINSTEIN

Those involved in the study of LH know that one of the most potent kinds of resistance to change is something known as *self-consistency motive*, or the wish to protect one's self-picture from change, to create and maintain stable, coherent identities.[1] After all, one's self-concept is the central axiom around which one's whole life philosophy revolves. Without this guiding attitude, the individual can become immobilized, confused, and baffled as to how to proceed in life. Whether for good or ill, our self-concept guides our behavior and makes us feel secure in an unpredictable world, which explains why we strive to maintain consistency, even when it doesn't really serve us.

This motive (self-consistency) when combined with the negative explanatory style of LH, is what prevents an individual from developing mastery behavior. It is this motive that leads those with LH to conclude that any failure in the past is an indication of failure in the future. It is this motive that leads them to choose performance goals over learning goals. It is this motive that results in a lack of growth, responsiveness to change, and willingness to take risks.

With a radical change in perspective, such as the possibility of *many* selves, for example, a space is created for a more fluid, dynamic, and responsive approach to multifarious and manifold reality. Consider, for a moment, the many selves that are you. There is the Good Mom/Bad Mom, the Professional Woman, the Slob, the Temptress, the Little Girl, the Competent Adult, the Wicked Witch, the Blessed Saint, the Adventuress. The list can go on and on, depending upon the individual. These are not just roles I am talking about, for a role implies an illusion of some kind, like when an actress creates a role. But these selves that exist within you are not false. They are not illusions. They are different facets of the diamond that is you, and they emerge at different times to meet different situations, just as facets of a diamond flash when the light strikes them.

Stretching this kind of thinking to its limits can be fun. For example, even all the selves listed above do not encompass all the possibilities of who I am. When I look at my "self" from the perspectives of other beings on the earth who experience me, my definition of self becomes even more blurred. A dolphin, using sonar, would know me as an object that transmitted and reflected acoustical waves. Viperous snakes, who use infrared, would know me as a larger physical entity than the boundaries indicated by my body because my body heat radiates beyond my actual physical boundaries. The bacteria in my body know me as an environment!

Though these experiences of me are definitely of the nonordinary variety, they are not any the less real. That may strike some as ridiculous, but that is because they are unaccustomed to viewing their existence in any way other than the conventional way. Unfortunately the greater our resistance to unconventional thinking about our "selves," the more we can be trapped in the self-consistency motive, which will only perpetuate the negative explanatory style of LH.

When we cling to the idea of only one self, a consistent self, then our other selves (those not being expressed at a particular moment) are forced to become "unreal," yet we know they are real because we have experienced them. Why not acknowledge their existence? Refusing to acknowledge their existence as bona-fide selves thrusts us into the vexation of trying to figure out which one is the "real" one. It isn't necessary to go through such mental contortions. Like the woman at my seminar who said she gave up trying to figure out the "real" story, it is far easier simply to accept the empirical reality of many selves changing and flashing within the field of experience than to try to fit oneself into a prefabricated form.

Some of the work done by the National Institute of Mental Health on real-life multiple personalities is not only fascinating but pertinent to our discussion.[2] On record are cases in which serious allergies exhibited by one of the personalities do not manifest under a different personality—that is, the physical body of an individual with multiple personalities reacts differently when under the influence of different host personalities. This defies all conventional medical wisdom, which says that the immune system is lifelong, that although the body may build up a certain degree of tolerance to various substances, in the main once a body is allergic, it remains allergic. The same findings have occurred with multiples diagnosed as having diabetes, a supposedly incurable disease.

Even more intriguing, I think, are cases of female multiples who, as one personality, may just finish a menstrual cycle when a different personality (one with a different menstrual cycle) will then begin her period. In other words, the same body has more than one menstrual cycle, within one or two days of each other. Furthermore one personality may experience cramps and serious discomfort while the other may show no symptoms at all. (And you thought you had it bad once a month!)

Granted, these unusual phenomena are found in true personality disorders, but don't miss my point. I offer these extreme examples as evidence of the wild possibilities that manifest under a changing sense of self. This research shows that the personality, or self, with its accompanying belief systems (all of which are products of the mind), is capable of creating changes within the human body that medical science deems impossible. If this sort of thing is possible at the physical level, the one we think of as immutable, what may be possible at the level of behavior, at the level of the ability to cope with ordinary daily living or to respond to crises? What may be possible in the development of mastery-oriented behavior to cope with life more effectively?

Believing that you are either bright or stupid, helpless or mastery-oriented, depressed or happy, fearful or courageous, good in math or bad in math, sets up the following traps: (a) the trap of dualistic thinking, which asserts that you must be either this or that; and (b) the trap of identity preservation or self-consistency, which asserts the existence of only one, unchanging self and denies the existence of all the rest.* If you believe you are a loving person, how do you explain it when you act angrily? If you believe you are helpless, where is there room to behave in a mastery-oriented fashion?

Similarly a behavioral problem can be viewed in much the same manner. Learned helplessness (or rage or fear or shyness) is only a problem an individual has—is only a part of that person—at the moment it is manifesting. Dr. David K. Reynolds, author of *Playing Ball on Running Water* and practitioner of the Japanese Morita psychotherapy based on Zen Buddhist principles, mentions that occasionally shyness is a problem for him when speaking to groups. But, he goes on to say,

> When I am deeply involved in a discussion . . . and no self-conscious shyness intrudes at that moment, then there is no need to assume that the shyness is lurking around somewhere waiting to emerge. I am never entirely assertive nor entirely shy, neither clever nor stupid, neither neurotic nor healthy. I am sometimes this, sometimes that. I am a constantly changing flow of awareness. I am only me-now.
>
> Simply discard the notion that you have a single personality. Notice the variety that is you. You will find a lot of experiential validation when you drop the outmoded theory of one person–one personality.[3]

Coping with change, then, becomes applicable to the self as well. If we insist on seeing ourselves as only one self, then that rigid, fixed self must be forced into every situation. If that self happens to be a helpless self, then we are forced to behave in a helpless manner in each and every situation in order to preserve our self-concept and remain consistent. If, on the other hand, we allow for a changing self or manifold self, then there is room for mastery-oriented behavior to manifest at any point in time or with increasing frequency.

---

* Before I have every psychotherapist in the United States on my case, allow me to say that this kind of thinking is not meant for the individuals with the serious personality disorders described above—the borderlines, schizophrenics, and true multiples. These individuals have a tenuous grasp on a personal self in the first place and need to develop one, integrated self before they can cope with many. The suggestions made here are rather for ordinary individuals who generally cope with life but who, for one reason or another, have particular areas where they have exhibited helplessness and wish to change this pattern and belief system.

In the marvelous and enlightening interviews between Bill Moyers and Joseph Campbell, Moyers asks Campbell about reincarnation as a metaphor and what it may suggest. Campbell replies, "It suggests that you are more than you think you are. There are dimensions of your being and a potential for realization and consciousness that are not included in your limited concept of yourself. Your life is much deeper and broader than you conceive it to be here. What you are living is but a fractional inkling of what is really within you, what gives you life, breadth and depth."[4]

When fully absorbed into the heart and mind, this view allows for transformation at the deepest levels and of the most profound kind. It suggests that change, or a type of perennial reincarnation, is the great vehicle of life (not death). It suggests that *change*, the only reliable aspect of reality, the one we resist with such gusto, is the very aspect we should embrace with gratitude, for it is *the* dynamic powerful enough to move us into new, more expansive realms of being, identity, and self.

Certainly the narrow, limited, rigid view of self that we protect so hawkishly is not powerful or expansive enough to initiate or accommodate this transformation. One must surrender to the constant flow of experience, the metaphoric reincarnation potential within each circumstance, event or moment, in order to breathe new life into old situations, by enabling the rigid definition of self to open and expand.

This approach to change and self, then, invites you to see the-many-in-the-one and to experience the renewal that this viewpoint can bring. Not only is it more experientially valid, but it will allow the refreshing breezes of mastery to blow more freely through your daily existence.

A SECRETARY IN SHANGRI-LA

Consider the change in self-view of a self-described "lowly little secretary," Darla Hillard, the Snow Leopard Lady I mentioned earlier, who participated in a five-year, landmark study of the elusive cats in one of the deepest, most treacherous gorges in all the Himalayas—the Langu Gorge. The gorge, a trailless wilderness much too rugged for human habitation, was described by Hugh Swift, author of *The Trekker's Guide to the Himalayas and Karakoram*, as the most precipitous and forbidding valley he had ever seen.

I met Darla in the green room of a California talk show as we both waited to take our turn to be interviewed on our just-released books. At the time, this book you are reading now was just a glimmer of hope, but when I heard about Darla's adventure, her expansion of self from lowly little secretary to Snow Leopard Lady, I knew I had to interview her.

Apart from a brief stint hitchhiking around Europe one summer, there was nothing in Darla's background to indicate she had the inclination or the gumption to embark on such a colossal under-taking. Only a nagging dissatisfaction with what she considered the boredom and claustrophobia of her life as a secretary prompted her to seek new horizons. The closest she came to any wilderness experience was camping as a kid with her family in the Sierra Nevada of northern California. Not exactly the kind of qualifications one would expect for a trip guaranteed to produce life-or-death struggles!

Never dreaming she would one day find herself in the snow-swept kingdom of Nepal, Darla innocently arrived on the doorstep of the office of the California Institute of Environmental Studies (where she had participated in a backpacking trip), to apply for a position, any position really, that would bring her a little closer to a different lifestyle. She was accepted as a volunteer.

One of the institute's codirectors, Rodney Jackson, who had been to Nepal in the winter of 1976 to study the snow leopard, was eager to continue his research in the field but was running into all kinds of bureaucratic and financial difficulties. Working side by side on institute projects, Darla and Rodney drew closer together and began to date.

One day, while reading a magazine, Rodney spotted an announcement sponsored by the Five Rolex Awards for Enterprise offering the princely sum of 50,000 francs ($25,000) to be awarded to five projects that promised to break ground in their particular fields. Rodney asked Darla if she would help him type and edit his proposal, entitled "A Radio-Tracking Study of Snow Leopards in Nepal," which he was readying for submission. Eight months were to pass. Eight months of working on projects together, spending time together, planning together. Eight months before they would hear that Rodney's proposal had been accepted.

A week-long celebration was to be held in Geneva, Switzerland, culminating in the presentation ceremony to the five Rolex laureates. That Darla would be accompanying Rodney to Geneva was understood. But beyond that? It was then that Darla had to face hard, cold reality. (Be careful about what you want, you just might get it.) The expedition to Nepal would require living under the harshest conditions imaginable, in winter, in a two-person, unheated tent sixty miles from civilization.

"Did you have any self-doubts?" I began.

She burst out laughing at what I now realize must have seemed like an absurd question.

"Yeah, you could say that. You think to yourself, 'What if I get sick? What if I break a leg?' I suppose the way I thought was, 'Well, if something happens, I'll deal with it when it happens.' There was always the question 'Can I take it?' Even Rodney, who had been there before, was unsure if *he* could take it. The answer was, in every case, 'I don't know.' You have to just get out there and find out. That's the only way."

In the initial fifteen months (which turned into four years), Darla and Rodney endured the relentless physical and emotional challenges of the Himalayas, hardships that would drive most of us over the edge. (Pardon the pun.) No contact with other human beings for weeks at a time; raw exposure to the natural fury of weather in the high Himalayas; hiking on exposed trails suspended over bottomless chasms and dizzying cliffs; the elusiveness and (when cornered) ferocity of the rare cats they were tracking; the endless bureaucratic hassles and dealing with governmental agencies; an incredibly monotonous and unappetizing diet; no doctors, no hospitals, no showers, no emergency vehicles; not to mention the constant threat of rockfalls and avalanches. As if that wasn't enough, Rodney was bitten by one of the wild cats and they spent eight days stumbling and falling through blowing snow, blinded by the sun as the two of them hiked out to get him to a doctor. All this bravery and competence, not from the kind of person most of us expect, such as a wizened old field researcher or a seasoned, eccentric anthropologist, but from a middle-class, San Francisco Bay Area secretary!

"What did you do with your fears?" I asked.

"Ignored them. That's the only way to deal with it. You can let them build up, you know, think about them all the time and worry about them all the time, turn them into even bigger monsters, but think how destructive that is. There's really no point in that. There is nothing to be served by dwelling on your fears. That doesn't mean you don't feel them. It means you don't let them stop you.

"My worst physical challenge was conquering the fear of climbing Tyson's Cliff. There was me and this Nepalese biologist and we were both chicken to go over this cliff. But to do anything, to get closer to the cats where they were beyond human interference, required going over it. Rodney would do it. He'd just get up and go. I'd wave and watch him through the binoculars, which made it look much worse than it really was.

"By doing this, I dwelt on my fear and built up my feelings of inadequacy until it was really a death-defying act. But I didn't want to sit there by myself for the whole summer. As time passed, I was getting more and more disgusted with myself, so I just did it."

"Like they say in the Nike ad? Just do it?" I responded.

"Yeah, sort of like that. Like standing on a diving board and sucking in your breath and jumping."

"What if your worst fears had been realized and you had been hurt?" I probed.

"But I wasn't. Look, you can always say, 'What if, what if?' That's the greatest block of all."

She shows me some pictures of the gorge they inhabited, a topography so steep and severe that even the native Nepalese tried to dissuade them.

"So how did the trip change you? Obviously you couldn't be the same person today that you were before you left."

"I don't procrastinate anymore," she said, surprising me with her answer. "It's so easy to put things off if there is some task that you don't want to do for whatever reason, whether it's making a phone call or leaving an abusive husband. Just do it and get it over with, because the longer you put it off, the worse it gets.

"Also, I learned that you don't necessarily have to know how to do something in order to do it. There are a lot of things you can do with just the willingness to learn. The whole trip was like that for me. Everybody said that what we were trying couldn't be done, but we did it. There was certainly an element of satisfaction in that, particularly regarding those well-known biologists who were so snotty about it," she laughed.

"What kept you going when all those snotty, well-known biologists said it couldn't be done?"

"For everything they said we couldn't do, we found that if we kept trying, we could find a way around the obstacles, and there were plenty, believe me. It took a lot of patience and planning and more patience and planning. And tenacity.

"Plus, for me, there was the desire to be more than I was before. And you have to learn to enjoy the changes on certain internal levels, I think, or else you're not going to make it successful."

"God, you're brave," I gushed unabashedly.

"You know, I find it so weird to be in this position. I mean, who am I to tell anybody else what to do?"

"You are somebody who overcame great obstacles, endured great hardships, mastered great fear to have a life-altering experience, completely change your self-concept, and make a lasting contribution, that's who," I responded.

"Well, the only thing I can say is, if there's something that you want to do, tour the world, create dolls, whatever it might be, don't underestimate your own capabilities. I'm a prime example. I'm not educated. I have a high school education. I had no wilderness experience, and yet look what I did.

"You have it within you, even though you may not know it. For some it may rise to the surface on its own, as mine did. Dissatisfaction with my life stirred it up."

"Stirred what up?" I probed.

"Whatever it takes. I'm sorry to be so vague, but 'it' is whatever it needs to be, given the circumstance. Courage. Fortitude. Determination. Curiosity. Call it what you like. You will find it within yourself when you need it. But underestimating your capabilities is such a waste. Go out there and find out what you can do and who you really are."

Darla didn't really know if she could handle it or not. She didn't know if the "self" needed to meet the challenges would be available to her. All she knew for sure was that her desire for change was greater than her desire for sameness, her need for a heightened sense of living was stronger than her need for safety, her urge to expand into a new self more urgent than maintaining the old one. She opted for a learning goal over a performance goal, took the risk first, and in so doing became a new person, one vastly more mastery-oriented, vital, and alive.

She also refused to indulge in negative self-talk, what-if-ing herself out of trying. As Darla points out, you can always say "what if?" What if I get in an accident on my way to work? What if someone breaks into the house while I'm gone? What if I marry Tom and he finds a younger woman when we're fifty? What if I take a trip and don't have a good time? What if I get pregnant and have a difficult time with the birth? What if I buy this house and the real-estate market declines?

The what-ifs are endless. If we engaged in this kind of thinking all the time, we would be totally immobilized, unable even to get out of bed each morning. But we don't. We *selectively* what-if when we are looking for an excuse to avoid the risk of changing our concept of self, of who we think we are.

Throughout the entire ordeal Darla and Rodney engaged in endless strategic planning. From writing the proposal for Rolex to tracking the leopards in the gorge, everyone said it couldn't be done. But it was done. In Darla's words, "It took a lot of patience, planning, and tenacity. If we just kept trying, there was always *something* that could be done." It took the willingness to generate options should one or more plans fail; to plan, and plan again, and change those plans and plan once again. It took the willingness to learn new skills and shrug off mistakes as part of the process rather than as failures. Most importantly it took the willingness to see failure as the failure of strategy, not the failure of self.

HER HAT IN THE RING

Another woman whom I interviewed had to fight for her life, not in the wilds of the Himalayas, but rather in the wilds of Milwaukee, or Cleveland, or wherever.

"When I decided to run for office, I had to quit my job in order to devote myself full-time to the campaign. I had thought about doing this the previous election but was so terrified, I was unable to pull it off. Even though it was just small-town politics, I wasn't ready to see myself as a winner."

The woman telling me her story reminds me of Maureen O'Hara—flaming hair, brilliant-green eyes, freckles everywhere, and cheekbones to die for. She is involved in the local politics of her city, and although you would probably not recognize her name, she prefers to remain anonymous. Should she win the election, she does not relish the idea that her bout with LH may come back to haunt her.

"I remember just sitting in my car, staring at my white knuckles as I gripped the steering wheel. It was as if I was trying to hold on

to the security of my past. You see, I was on my way to resign from
a career that was seventeen years in the making. Here I was about
to dismantle a nice, safe, secure life I had painstakingly constructed
as a buffer against the very kind of insecurity I was about to create!
It was too weird.

"Something like vertigo came over me, and I had to pull the car
over. What if I lost the election? God, then, I wouldn't even have
a decent job. Now I know what naked terror feels like, terror at the
possibility of becoming one of the throwaways: a bag lady. Of course
I knew, on a rational level, that this was probably extreme thinking,
but it seemed very real at the time.

"When the vertigo passed, I pulled back out into traffic. Great
as my fear was, I was simultaneously exhilarated with the prospect
of a new life. It was intoxicating. I was lurching down the street
like a car that needs a tune-up, first accelerating rapidly, then slowing down in doubt. I was doing an approach-avoidance number."

The clashing emotions described by Lorraine are common to
anyone who has been forced to take drastic steps in order to begin
a new life or re-create one's self. (The bag-lady visions of self don't
do much to help us either.) What she calls her approach-avoidance
number was evidence of a new being within her seeking to emerge
and drafted into battle with the forces of her old self, the motive to
change and the motive for self-consistency engaged in a deadly
struggle. Fetal and unformed though it was, this new self was still
strong enough to assert itself against the dominant old self and to
propel Lorraine forward in this ambivalent fashion.

"I made it to the parking lot of the office where I was going to
hand in my resignation but could not manage to get out of the car.
Gagging back my tears, all I could think of was what I was
sacrificing—a comfortable routine, a job so secure I would practically have to commit an ax murder to be fired, a professional
reputation that had taken years of dedicated labor. Most important,
though, were the practical necessities of a guaranteed income and
things such as health insurance.

"These were real fears, things I needed to consider and weigh.
The problem was, I had already weighed and considered them and
thought I had come to a conclusion. But as each insecurity reasserted
itself there in the parking lot, I felt myself growing younger and
younger until the adult required to meet the challenge was swal-
lowed up by a scared little kid. Finally I just burst into tears.

"I felt like a little girl again," said this elegant and beautifully matured woman, "sitting behind the steering wheel of my mom's car with mascara running down my cheeks. I remember thinking, 'What if my supporters could see the candidate of their choice slobbering into a dirty old Burger King napkin she found stashed in the glovebox?' "

"I didn't want to do this alone, dammit, with no job prospects, no security, no guarantees, very little savings, and no man to protect and rescue me should all my best efforts fail.

"I started the car and backed out of the parking lot with my resignation letter, written with such hope, and, I might add, lying impotently on the seat beside me. I was just imploding with failure. I was numb. I steered the car back to my unacceptable little life. When I got home, I threw the letter into the trash, got undressed, and went to bed. All my friends were calling to see if the deed was done. I was so ashamed and embarrassed, I didn't answer the phone or talk to anyone the whole weekend."

It is difficult to be philosophical about failure, particularly when we are in the midst of it. Lorraine's inability to act had confirmed her darkest fears, that she was *not* the high-flying risk taker she had fancied, *not* the seasoned politician who could handle life's vicissitudes without so much as smudging her mascara. She was an easily daunted little girl, destined by her own helplessness to subsist at a level of experience far less thrilling than what she had envisioned. Because her thoughts created a mind space that was too narrow for her new self-concept to expand into, she would not feel the refreshing breeze of a new life for several more years.

Lorraine's story is a truthful account of the type of ordeal one often undergoes upon attempting the birth of a new self. Like the other stories, it has been included so that you will know that even risk takers struggle with sheer, naked terror, just as you do. Sometimes they succeed and vanquish the terror. Sometimes, the fear wins and they must patiently endure a few more bouts before trying again. Usually it is just a matter of time.

It is no use underestimating the impact of our fears and their power to make us feel helpless. Every day they prevent most of us from becoming who we could become. They are fiendishly, even diabolically, clever at keeping us stuck in old roles, old belief systems, old ways of doing and being. It takes a concentrated and conscious effort, *and maybe several of them*, to give birth finally to a new self.

"What finally changed for you? How did you manage to pull it off four years later?" I asked her.

"I stopped telling myself things like 'You're going to be a bag lady' for one," she laughs. "You really do have to be quite careful about what you are saying to yourself. Now, even if I don't win, I tell myself that I have the brains and the chutzpah, thank you very much, to do something else."

She pauses to take a sip of her coffee. "Plus, remember what Darla said about just doing it?"

"Yeah, about just sucking in your breath and diving in?"

"Right. Well, something in my gut knew that this was the only way. Just do it, whether I felt ready or not. I realized that if I waited until I felt completely ready, I'd never do it. I would just continue to think up more reasons why I wasn't quite ready.

"Once I took the risk, then I felt mastery-oriented. I couldn't wait until I felt mastery-oriented first. It took me several years and a couple of tries, but that's okay, I made it."

You may also recall that my mother, who opened the nightclub back in 1938, also mentioned that change-in-self that occurs once a risk is taken and time is allowed to do its work. What she said was, "The experience of owning Shangri-la turned me into a completely different person. Before, I was kind of a quiet little thing, afraid to speak up or go against the grain. Now I'm the last of the red-hot mommas. Running the business, especially that kind of a business, required me to get strong . . . and mastery-oriented, real quick."

Here's the paradox once again: Take the risk first and then you get mastery-oriented, not the other way around. Take the risk first and that will change your idea of who you are.

Finally, my mother adds, "The trouble with a lot of people who go into business for themselves these days is that they expect to get rich overnight. I always tell them, these things take time, don't expect to get rich overnight. Don't expect even to get out of the red for a couple of years, much less get rich!"

Point well taken. Whether you are trying to get rich or just expand your idea of self into a broader, more courageous, mastery-oriented type, remember, these things take time.

THE FEMININE SELF AND HELPLESSNESS

Before I alienate some readers, let me clarify what I am about to say in the next section. Upon first reading, it may appear that I am demeaning femininity. I do not mean it to be so. I heartily agree with those who believe that the feminine traits are to be admired and emulated and may represent our last glimmer of hope for engineering a society capable of actually becoming a softer, gentler nation. I believe that the traits of the feminine self (whether they reside in a woman or a man) are to be prized, particularly so whenever a situation calls for sensitivity, compassion, flexibility, and intuition.

Unfortunately, despite seventy years of feminism in the United States (including the years of struggle for suffrage), the concept of femininity has been tainted with an aspect of helplessness. Since we are conditioned to our gender identity as children, before we are capable of discrimination, we pick up the negative connotations of femininity and incorporate them into our self-concept and self-presentation as well as the positive ones. To the extent that one has incorporated the concept of helplessness into one's idea of femininity (and granted, this is a very subjective thing, some doing it much more than others), one's enthusiasm for risk taking is diminished. I was first made aware of this in the seminars upon which I based my first book.

I would ask the participants to list adjectives describing individuals whom they thought of as feminine. I also asked them to do the same for individuals whom they thought of as masculine. Here is the list I have compiled over the last seven years.

MASCULINE	FEMININE
Adventurous	Nurturing
Assertive	Emotional
Aggressive	Sensitive
Independent	Soft
Confident	Sweet
Vigorous	Domestic
Strong	Unpredictable
Powerful	Intelligent
Firm	Understanding

MASCULINE	FEMININE
Decisive	Flexible
Rugged	Intuitive
Sturdy	Compassionate
Brave	Playful
Daring	Gentle
Courageous	Sensual
Intelligent	Sexy
Logical	Pretty
Rational	Attractive
Reasonable	Conniving
Athletic	Slim
Active	Dainty
Forceful	Fragile
Virile	Frail
Sexual	Refined
Stoic	Submissive
Tough	Childlike
Muscular	Weak
Robust	Helpless
Straightforward	Powerless
Protective	Talkative
Violent	Self-sacrificing
Rigid	Passive
Coarse	Defenseless

As is evident from this list, the descriptions of femininity and masculinity are vexing from the viewpoint of LH and mastery behavior. The feminine traits of self are highly congruent with helplessness and dependence, while the masculine traits are highly congruent with mastery and risk-taking behavior. In other words, the traits exemplified by mastery-oriented individuals are the very traits described as masculine by most people. Although there are a few so-called feminine traits mentioned that are congruent with mastery behavior, for the most part they are the ones that must be *overcome* in order to achieve this. For example:

Belief in self-efficacy
Requires confidence, decisiveness, assertiveness, courage

Is undermined by emotionality, sensitivity, frailty, and submissiveness

Willingness to take risks
Requires daring, adventurousness, robustness, decisiveness, independence

Is undermined by passivity, fragility, frailty, helplessness, vacillation, and softness

Autonomy
Requires assertiveness, vigor, courage, straightforward behavior, and power

Is undermined by passivity, softness, sweetness, childlikeness, excessive connectedness to others, and a need to be protected

Even after twenty-five years of supposed consciousness-raising, during which time society allegedly made a huge leap of consciousness and came to understand these stereotypes as limited and limiting, we are still functioning with expectations of helpless behavior from females. Apparently that leap qualified for the high jump, not the broad jump, if you'll forgive the pun. In other words, after a leap of great height, the attitudes of society landed very close to where they began in the first place.

Therefore, even when a woman's behavior is colored by helplessness, the woman herself and others in her life are unlikely to notice it, because she is functioning within the parameters defined by most people in our culture as "feminine" or "normal for women." If a man behaved in the same way, people would think there was something wrong with him.

What does this have to do with change and the self and the invitation to see the-many-in-the-one? If we perceive only a single self and it happens to be a very feminine self, which it likely *is* due to gender identification, we may be thus limited in our ability to respond to life's challenges. This limitation may preclude mastery or risk-taking behavior altogether. If, on the other hand, we perceive many selves, then we are not limited to the feminine traits alone. We can choose to exhibit the set of traits that is most appropriate to the situation in which we find ourselves—a highly adaptive and quite mastery-oriented thing to do.

When it is appropriate to be soft, sweet, emotional, sensitive, domestic, nurturing, self-sacrificing, and intuitive, we can confidently exhibit that behavior. By the same token, when it is appropriate to be strong, independent, decisive, logical, rugged, adventurous, powerful, and brave, we can confidently exhibit that behavior as well. One does not have to preclude the other, unless we are too strongly identified with only a single, highly "feminine" self.

One key ingredient, then, to risk-taking mastery behavior and successful change, is the ability to vary behavior according to *circumstance* rather than according to gender or any set of rigid and predetermined traits we call the self. On an individual level, the more selves we recognize within, the more able we are to develop other ways of being and to adapt successfully to circumstances, which ultimately develops mastery behavior.

Capitulating to the narrow, unchanging cultural definition of a strictly feminine self and identifying with it too strongly (or singularly) can strike a serious blow to the potential for mastery behavior. In other words, the feminine traits alone do not do us much good in situations requiring derring-do and risk taking. Since the possible variations of circumstances life will present is unlimited, why limit ourselves?

Several studies have examined femininity and masculinity as independent dimensions of LH and have concluded that gender issues are indeed involved in learning helplessness. Research usually begins by ranking participants according to their sex type. This means that an individual (male *or* female) can rank high in masculine sex typing (called *high masculinity*) or high in feminine sex typing (called *high femininity*). A third alternative exhibited by some individuals is known as balanced sex typing.*

Studies show that women who rank high in femininity (low in masculinity) are more prone to exhibit a helpless response after having experienced failure or loss of control.[5] In one experiment women were tested to determine their desire for future control after having experienced failure. Interestingly, 71 percent of women with some of the traits on the masculine list made choices to regain control while *none* of the feminine-sex-typed women did so![6] These results suggest that women with high femininity are less likely to

---

* A word of caution here. It is important to stay open to the idea that members of each sex can display traits typically thought of as belonging to the opposite sex, without overtones of homosexuality. It simply means that the adjectives on the lists shown on pages 111–12 can be applied to any individual, regardless of sex. These adjectives are not truly masculine or feminine traits anyway, just human traits, but most of society doesn't really accept this on any deep level yet.

make the kind of choices that result in control of their environment and are more likely to respond with LH when an obstacle is encountered.

Still another study examined the degree to which peers would be willing to grant control to women with differing sex-role identities if working with them individually on a two-person task. Women with high femininity were granted control on tasks deemed methodical and unenjoyable, while women higher in some of the masculine traits or those who were more balanced were given control on tasks deemed creative and enjoyable.[7] Studies also show that there is a correlation between sex-role identity and depression, with high femininity being a factor contributing to depression.[8]

"I MAY BE A PH.D., BUT I'M CUTE"

A piece of mail the other day served as a reminder of how much we, as women, undermine our own desire to be taken seriously as mastery-oriented types when we incorporate the more frivolous aspects of femininity in the wrong setting. I received a newsletter written entirely by a Ph.D. with over twenty-five years' experience as a researcher, educator, author, lecturer, and consultant. She knew her stuff. The newsletter itself was on the cutting edge—informative, well documented, articulate, and thought-provoking. She signed this newsletter in the following manner:

Sincerely,

Constance Goldbloom, Ph.D.
Editor

My question is: How seriously should we be expected to take someone who signs her professional correspondence with a "happy face" next to her credentials? It is as if she is saying, "Sure, I'm an expert in my field, researcher, lecturer, author, and consultant, but don't worry, I'm not an authority figure. I may be a Ph.D., but I'm still cute!" If this doesn't strike you as bothersome, I ask you to imagine a man signing his professional correspondence the same way.

Once again, the foregoing examples and studies are not cited in order to demean femininity or to glorify masculinity. I am not here to ask, in the words of Professor Henry Higgins, "Why can't a woman be more like a man?" Our society does enough of that. However, to the extent that we incorporate the negative or ridiculous connotations of femininity into our self-concept, especially those that result in an LH response to risks and challenges, we will block our ability to overcome old patterns, create new, mastery-oriented selves, and be taken seriously by the external world.

WHAT YOU DO AND WHO YOU ARE

A study published in 1986 by Dr. Kristen Yount of the University of Kentucky demonstrates the expression of multi-selves. Dr. Yount asked male and female coal miners to describe themselves. In doing so, they employed the same adjectives whether they were male or female, and the adjectives tended to fall primarily in the "masculine" or mastery-oriented set of traits listed above.[9] Similarly, when male caregivers, such as nurses and teachers, are asked to describe themselves, they use the same adjectives as females in the same professions.

In other words, adult self-perceptions tend to be dependent upon, and congruent with, the type of work they do. When women are engaged in daily work that is risky and dangerous, they come to see themselves as brave, courageous, and mastery-oriented. When men are engaged in daily work that is caregiving and service-oriented, they come to see themselves as nurturing, caring, and understanding.

This reveals that old concepts of work, gender, and self may literally be reversed. Typically it was assumed that women have chosen caregiving occupations because they are naturally more nurturant. Likewise, males choose more dangerous occupations because they are natural risk takers. This research shows that, instead, it is possible that women have come to see themselves as warm and nurturant *because* they work in the service professions. Since their reproductive destiny has historically placed them in the caregiving role, they have developed this self-concept and therefore choose to work in service occupations.

Something truly provocative lies in this idea. If what we do influences who we think we are, then changing who we are depends upon changing what we do. Stop and think about this for a minute. It is a profound shift from the usual, accepted sequence of events. It reverses the common notion concerning how to effect change in one's life. Typically, conventional wisdom demands that we change ourselves internally first, then change what we do, when in fact the exact opposite may be necessary. We may need to change what we do in order to change who we think we are!

This provides the best argument of all for risk taking as a vehicle for change, as the inducting mechanism through which a completely new self-concept can be born. In other words, if we want to become mastery-oriented, we have to take the risk *before we actually feel ready for it*. One doesn't become mastery-oriented *first* and then take the risk; one takes the risk first and then becomes mastery-oriented.

I am fully aware that this advice is not only paradoxical but irritating as well. When you can't "just do it," you wonder how it will get done!

Here is one way. Start with some small, calculated risk you have been resisting, one with only minor negative consequences. Instead of thinking about this risk as one you must succeed at in order to be granted membership in the Masters of the Universe Club, go into the risk with a much simpler (and easier) goal: to cultivate your curiosity. In other words, use your curiosity to help you disengage from your fear of failure. Success or failure will not even be an issue at this point. Instead, you will be using this minor risk *in conjunction* with your curiosity in order to observe your personal reactions to risk taking. (See pages 193 and 194 for some ideas.)

Allow your curiosity full, permissive play. Question everything. Ask yourself the following questions and write your answers in your journal:

1. How does it feel to take this risk? How am I interpreting the physical sensations of risk taking?

   - Make a list of adjectives describing your feelings and body sensations.
   - Return to the list. For every negative connotation of a sensation, see if you can find a positive synonym for the same feeling, such as "exhilaration" instead of "terror."

2. In what ways am I reacting with old belief systems? (List them.)
3. What patterns of thinking are more stubborn than others?
4. What is my internal talk? (Identify statements as stable vs. dynamic, global vs. specific, and internal vs. external.) This is just the first step. For help, see page 36–39, where this is discussed in greater detail.
5. Am I developing strategies or quitting in frustration?

Curiosity about and attention to your own process will help keep
you detached from the fear of failure. Anyway, so what if you fail?
Everybody does, including the mastery-oriented. They just don't
personalize it. Instead they see it as part of the process of learning
something new or developing a new behavior. They use it as a cue
to change strategies.

If we take Dr. Yount's study of the female coal miners and male
nurses seriously, as a cue to becoming mastery-oriented, we must
engage in activities that require us to demonstrate assertiveness,
strength, strategic planning, and courage. If we try to wait until we
possess these qualities before taking the risk, we will never acquire
them.

This wisdom is operant in Outward Bound, the wilderness survival school I attended that stressed the no-rescuing philosophy. By
forcing participants into situations they do not believe themselves
capable of and then refusing to rescue them, they change the participants' views of themselves. In so doing they give the greatest gift
of all—they teach you that you can do what you didn't think you
could do. They teach that you have capabilities, talents, *selves* that
you never even knew existed.

Life does the same thing. It reveals to us internal selves we never
knew existed. I would not have believed myself capable of living
through the mental breakdown of someone I loved. Janet never
would have believed she could survive a winter alone with her
children in a cabin in the wilderness. Linda never would have
believed she would recover from such traumatic injuries. Deborah
never would have believed the little small-town girl could become
a woman of the world. Darla would never have learned that she
could be an adventurer, naturalist, and scientist. The fearful and
helpless selves that existed in each of us prior to unforeseen life
events were far narrower, more limited, and more circumscribed
than the expansive, mature, and confident selves that emerged following these experiences.

This means, ultimately, that the quest for self-consistency has a
kind of anti-life quality to it, compelling us to resist the notion that
self-concept rests on the shifting sands of change, sands whose con-
figurations and surfaces are transformed as the winds of time swirl
new contours into being. Even the Sphinx, whose resolute gaze
stares into eternity with the knowledge "I am . . . ," does not define
herself further. We must be satisfied only that she is.

PART III

A Six-Step Plan for Mastery

Despite all my exhortations to "just do it," I realize that this advice is easier to give than to take. While for some of you a little push will be all you require to get going, others will be blocked by helplessness-oriented belief systems and explanatory styles and will need more than a little push. (I am resisting the temptation to say that you will need a great big shove because that implies the use of someone else's energy to get you going, and that is another form of rescue.) Ultimately *you* must be the one to take action.

Therefore, the next six chapters will provide a plan for helping you to do just that:

Chapter 7—Step 1: Dealing with procrastination and resistance
Chapter 8—Step 2: Changing one's explanatory style
Chapter 9—Step 3: Opening up a rigid self-concept
Chapter 10—Step 4: Persisting through the stress of change
Chapter 11—Step 5: Tapping creativity
Chapter 12—Step 6: Developing multiple strategies

Finally, while the nature of written communication forces me to present this plan in a linear fashion (starting at Step 1 and ending at Step 6), the process of moving from LH to mastery is not a linear one. You may start at Step 3, go to Step 5, then to Step 1, then start all over again at Step 3. Do what works for you.

CHAPTER 7

Developing the Will to Persist

If you don't get it from yourself, where will you go for it?
—ZENRIN
The Gospel According to Zen

PROCRASTINATION OR LH?

We typically think of procrastination as a trait of laziness. At deeper levels procrastination may be a trait of LH. In other words, you are not necessarily a lazy and undisciplined person if you procrastinate. It is quite possible that your belief system has debilitated you and depleted your reserves of energy. So, the first recommendation for dealing with procrastination is:

I. Be alert to excuses and avoidance behaviors as a reflection of your belief system and explanatory style.

Women with LH can be extremely ingenious at concocting reasons for not taking risks and then believing them. Upon more careful examination, however, these excuses (and the avoidance behaviors that follow) reflect an LH belief system and explanatory style. If a woman says that she can't go to graduate school because she didn't do well in math in high school, for instance, she is revealing a belief in the unchanging nature of her "self." This is the stable aspect of her explanatory style. She argues that her cognitive apparatus and problem-solving skills are no more evolved than they were when she was a kid.

This is not necessarily realistic or accurate. Maturity can bring with it a commitment to study, a willingness to suffer through confusion, an ability to ask for help when confused—all aspects of learning and success that she may not have exhibited as a high school student, when she was not only less mature but did not have the motivation to learn the subject matter that she has now that she wants to go to graduate school.

Begin by writing down all the reasons you have given in the past for not taking a risk or making a change you desire. Put these in a column headed "Excuse" or "Reason." Then identify the specific beliefs that are served by that excuse and write them in the second column, headed "Belief."

EXCUSE	BELIEF
1. "I'm too busy to learn how to ski."	1. I'm too uncoordinated to learn how to ski. I'll hurt myself. People will laugh at me.
2. "It will take too long to get another degree."	2. I'm not smart enough. It's too hard. It's too late. People will think I'm crazy or selfish.
3. "I am staying in a bad relationship because it's better than being alone."	3. I'm afraid of loneliness. I don't deserve a good relationship. I'm too fat (ugly, boring, old) to attract another man.
4. "I'm scared to go white-water river rafting."	4. I'm afraid I'll die. I'm afraid to be afraid.
5. "I don't know enough to start my own business."	5. I'm afraid to suffer through learning something new. I'm afraid to fail. My husband won't like it.
6. "I can't write a screenplay."	6. It sounds too glamorous for little ol' me. My friends will think I've gone Hollywood.

EXCUSE	BELIEF
7. "I can't get a face-lift."	7. Only rich women get face-lifts. It's wrong to change what God created. It's wrong to spend that much money on myself. I'll die in surgery. One should age gracefully.

Now take the beliefs in the right-hand column (those that have been served by the excuses), put them in the left-hand column, and counter them with more positive, mastery-oriented explanations and beliefs. Remember, these explanations do not necessarily reflect reality, nor do they distort it. Reality is not the issue. Reality is not even that relevant. Your explanation of reality is what is relevant.

LH BELIEF	MASTERY-ORIENTED EXPLANATION
1. I'm too uncoordinated to learn how to ski.	1. Everybody is uncoordinated when they are learning how to ski.
I'll hurt myself.	I could hurt myself walking out the front door this morning.
People will laugh at me.	Even the best skiers were beginners once. They understand how it feels.
2. I'm not smart enough (to get a degree).	2. Intelligent people get confused and make mistakes too.
It's too hard.	It just takes effort.
It's too late.	According to whom?
People will think I'm crazy or selfish.	Who cares what they think? Look at their lives. Do they make such great decisions?

LH BELIEF	MASTERY-ORIENTED EXPLANATION
3. I'm afraid of loneliness.	3. It won't last forever. Besides, solitude can be delicious.
I don't deserve a good relationship.	There are some really lousy individuals who have good relationships. Why shouldn't I?
I'm too fat (ugly, boring, old) to attract another man.	I could lose weight, get a face-lift, and take classes. (Or, alternatively, when I look around, I see many women who are not thin, young, or beautiful with good men.)
4. I'm afraid I'll die (if I go whitewater rafting).	I could get hit by the garbage truck in the alley and die too.
I'm afraid to be afraid.	So? Fear doesn't have to stop me.
5. I'm afraid to suffer through learning something new.	So? Fear doesn't have to stop me.
I'm afraid to fail.	Smart people fail too. I can try again and again until I succeed.
My husband won't like it.	So? His disapproval doesn't have to stop me.
6. (Writing a screenplay) sounds too glamorous for little ol' me.	So, I won't be glamorous. I'll wear sweat clothes when I write and refuse to comb my hair.
My friends will think I've gone Hollywood.	I won't tell them until after I've sold the screenplay. Then they'll be green.

LH BELIEF	**MASTERY-ORIENTED EXPLANATION**
7. Only rich women get face-lifts.	I could get a loan.
It's wrong to change what God created.	I wouldn't say that to a handicapped person.
It's wrong to spend that much money on myself.	Don't I deserve to be happy and at peace with my looks?
I'll die in surgery.	Remember the garbage truck. . . .
One should age gracefully.	That would be fine in a society that allowed that. It's more difficult in youth-worshiping America.

AVOIDANCE BEHAVIORS

Avoidance behaviors, like excuses, are also symptoms of a lack of belief in yourself (self-efficacy), and, like excuses, seem to be perfectly plausible reasons for not getting started.

You know how it works. You sit down to plan a strategy or crack open a book to study and suddenly your brain has the actual, physical sensation of turning to mush. You become so sleepy that it is virtually impossible to stay awake. At this point you decide to "rest your eyes for a few minutes," promptly fall sound asleep, and, upon awakening, feel guilty, remorseful, and defeated.

When this happens, rather than resting your eyes, take a walk, make a cup of coffee, put on an old Jerry Lee Lewis song, and rock out in your living room (I prefer "Whole Lotta Shakin' Goin' On" to "Great Balls of Fire," but whatever you choose, Jerry Lee is guaranteed to wake you right up), do some deep breathing to oxygenate your system, call a friend to brainstorm ideas, stretch, meditate, but *don't go to sleep!*

Another favorite avoidance behavior has to do with what most of us call getting organized. It works like this. Suddenly you remember a basement room or attic closet you have been meaning to clean out for the last five years and it becomes imperative that that closet be cleaned out *this minute.* Somehow you convince yourself that it is impossible to begin this project until that closet is organized!

This particular avoidance behavior happens to be my personal forte. Every time I start to write another book, I wind up with closets, bookshelves, and desk drawers that rival the military for organization and efficiency. Even the infamous junk drawer gets organized. When I'm not working on a book, however, the dust balls under the bed and piles on the desk are free to be fruitful and multiply without my interference.

What both of these avoidance behaviors show is that, when LH rears its ugly head, making us fearful of taking a risk, nearly any excuse or behavior will do, even closet cleaning. A woman in one of my seminars cracked up the audience with this concise description: "I have even been known to stay home and alphabetize my lipsticks to avoid going scuba diving with my husband."

These avoidance behaviors happen to everyone and will not seriously sabotage you, *unless you fail to recognize them as such.* In other words, if you actually come to believe that that closet must be cleaned or those lipsticks alphabetized or that nap taken (to be refreshed, of course!) before you can get started, you could be in trouble because there will always be yet another couch beckoning or closet to be cleaned. Becoming aware of your own avoidance behaviors, however, and *calling them by name* makes the behavior that much harder to indulge in. So, when you suddenly find yourself on your hands and knees digging out junk from a closet you haven't even looked in in several years or arranging your eye shadows according to the colors of the rainbow, don't say, "I simply must get this done before I can start the project." Say, "Here I am avoiding my project again by sorting eyeshadows!"

Typical Avoidance Behaviors:

- Eating
- Cleaning
- Organizing
- Sharpening pencils
- Overplanning
- Extraneous reading
- Talking on the phone
- Exercising
- Napping

- Trying to "get everything else done" before starting the project
- *Anything* that is not related to the project

The second recommendation for dealing with resistance and procrastination is to recognize, once again, that your self-talk (explanatory style) is probably creating a vortex through which all your energy is being drained. Therefore:

II. Begin asserting your rights as a woman-in-transition.

Write, read, and recite the following affirmations daily, over and over again, until you know them well and actually believe them:

1. Feeling confused, lost, or frustrated is natural in the process of growth and change. Everyone experiences these things, including the mastery-oriented.
2. It is okay to go slowly.
3. It is okay to ask others how they have done it.
4. I have the right to ask for as much help as I need, to ask for explanation and clarification until I understand.
5. It is all right to make mistakes.
6. It is okay to see a therapist.
7. I want to change my self-concept.
8. I will be the one to determine when I feel good about my achievements, even if they seem minor to someone else.

For those returning to school, add:

9. It is okay to learn slowly and to make mistakes.
10. It is okay to discuss my fears with my tutor or therapist or instructor so that he/she understands the obstacles I am dealing with.
11. I will interview prospective tutors or therapists thoroughly in order to determine if he/she is right for me and understands my needs and/or fears.
12. I will not hesitate to dismiss a tutor or therapist who makes me feel inadequate in any way.
13. I can exert effort without attributing the need to do so to a lack of intelligence, just as the mastery-oriented do.
14. I have the right to allot time in my day and space in my environment to study or do my homework or do whatever is necessary so that I may succeed.

If you read over the foregoing statements carefully, you will see that none of them is unreasonable, selfish, or untrue. They are mastery-oriented ways of explaining things to yourself so that you are less likely to procrastinate about getting started and more likely to persist through the difficulties once you have.

The final recommendation for coping with resistance and procrastination depends upon your figuring out what messages you received in childhood that contribute to your lack of self-confidence.

III. Write your academic autobiography (or scenes remembered from childhood during a period when you were trying to learn something new).

Many times we function on beliefs that were instilled in us as children but that are not necessarily supportive or even accurate. In order to ferret out these beliefs, write a brief autobiography of your academic experiences. While doing so, be alert to the messages that were given to you by influential adults, such as teachers, parents, siblings, peers, friends, and don't forget society at large. Make a list of all the statements you can remember having heard as a child when you were learning something new. To get you started, I have compiled the responses given by workshop participants when asked to do this exercise:

"What's the matter with you? Why can't you get this?"

"Everybody knows that girls are not good in math."

"Our family was never any good at that."

"College degrees are not important for girls."

"I'm only going to explain this to you once. If you don't get it, it's your problem."

"Mary will have to get by on her looks and charm."

"It's not healthy to expect too much from a child. It creates stress."

"Would you please learn to keep your mouth shut? Boys won't like you if you talk too much and seem smarter than they are."

"Sue got the beauty, Karen got the brains."

As you write and recall your childhood experiences in learning situations, you will realize that many of the things that were said to you were internalized as the truth, since as a child you had little else to go on other than what adults told you. Now, however, if left unexamined, these inaccurate explanations (which have become beliefs) will cause you to function as if they were true. Those with the severest cases of LH may learn that they received the most damaging messages.

Having just listed some of the most damaging messages, allow me, now, to illustrate by contrast. In my own case I was lucky to receive a very positive set of messages from my parents. One story in particular comes to mind.

When I was a teenager, it was my job to mow the lawn—a chore, I might add, that I loathed. One day, in the midst of this dreadful activity, the lawn mower broke down. I couldn't have been happier. I now had the perfect excuse to stop what I was doing and go hang out at the drive-in with my friends. I combed my hair, grabbed my purse, and called my father's office to tell him the news. Instead of saying, "Okay, I'll fix it when I get home," as I expected, he said, "You can fix it. I'll tell you what to do."

I could have killed him. I was all ready to go. I even had my car keys in my hand. My teenage priorities did not include an interest in fixing that stupid old lawn mower, even if it did result in mastery behavior, but my father believed I could fix the lawn mower, so I was expected to do just that. Phone call by phone call, he talked me through it. By the end of the day, when the beast roared to life beneath my hands, my self-esteem soared. At four o'clock I called him back for the last time.

"It worked!" I shouted happily in his ear. "It's running!"

"I told you you could fix it," he said, matter-of-factly, but I could hear the smile in his voice.

Now, fixing machines is still not my favorite activity, nor do I always succeed at it, but I am much less helpless than most women dealing with machines and more willing to try because my dad gave me a message that I internalized as truth. "You can fix it," was all he had said.

By way of contrast, imagine if his response had been what I expected: "I'll fix it when I get home." This would have reflected an unspoken belief on *his* part, which I would have internalized, that I was not capable of fixing a machine. Then, as an adult, when faced with broken appliances, I would be less likely to tackle the situation. If there was no one to help me, I would continue procrastinating because ultimately I would not believe in my ability to fix it, to influence the final outcome of events, to be self-efficacious.

CHAPTER 8

Get Real: Changing Your Explanatory Style

There is no way you can use the word "reality" without quotation marks around it.
— JOSEPH CAMPBELL

Sandra: Well, Murray, to sort of return to reality for a minute . . .
Murray: I will only go as a tourist.
— HERB GARDNER, A *Thousand Clowns*

THOUGHT MONITORING

By now it should be apparent that your explanations of reality do not necessarily reflect reality, nor do they necessarily distort it. As I have mentioned before, reality is only what you construe it to be, and the issue is how you then act upon this construction. When taken into the heart and mind at the deepest levels, this view of reality is utterly liberating, for it frees you to pursue the explanatory style that does you the most good.

By now you should also have a feel for how your thoughts (belief system and explanatory style) are critical to whether your behavior is helpless or masterful, since thoughts are what produce the emotional responses that can catch you, like a helpless fish. If your internal response to a thought is negative or painful, you wriggle and fight, squirm and struggle, to get free. (Actually, a pleasant internal response can hook you just as effectively, but because you label the experience as enjoyable, you do not struggle to be free of it.)

What bears repeating is that *although you cannot always control your emotions, you can control the thoughts that trigger those emotions*. Once you have truly grasped the link between your thoughts (your explanatory style) and your feelings, you will know how to avoid the hooks that snag you. You will be motivated to monitor your self-talk so that your thoughts remain positive and supportive, so that you will be less likely take the bait of a negative LH belief system and explanatory style.

"I guess what has made me so crazy about food is the way I think about it," said Sheila, a slim, eating-disordered woman whom I met at an Overeaters Anonymous meeting I had been invited to observe. "I didn't realize before what was causing my panic. Now I see how my thoughts produced this incredible fear."

The group had invited a counselor specializing in eating disorders to lead a therapy session in the hopes that it might help them begin to sort out their problems with food and eating. Sheila, setting a great example as a risk taker, had volunteered to be his guinea pig. Here is what happened.

"Okay, Sheila, please fill in the blank to this sentence: If I am fat, I am _____.

"You mean just list some words?" she asked.

"Right."

She paused for a bit, considering her answer.

"If I am fat, I am . . . um . . . I am . . . I hate to say this."

"Just say whatever you're thinking," he replied.

"Okay . . . you asked for it. If I am fat, I am stupid. I am lazy. I am undisciplined. I'm a dirty, low-class slob."

"Mmmhmm," said the therapist, in contrast to everyone else, who was registering shock at her uncompromisingly cruel judgment.

Then he said, "Okay, now let's take these one at a time. Are you in fact stupid?"

She actually paused, unable to answer the question. At that point he got exasperated and said, "Come on, Sheila, you've got a master's degree in economics."

Kind of sheepishly she admitted she wasn't stupid.

"Well, then, are you lazy?"

"Not really."

"Are you dirty?"

"No."

"What size dress do you wear?"

"Do I have to answer that?"

"Of course not."

"A ten."

"Are you fat?"

"I think I'm fat."

"I know, I understand that, but according to the insurance charts let's say, are you fat?"

"No."

"Okay, now let's look at what you have said about getting fat. Do you think that if you gained ten pounds, you would stop taking showers?"

"Of course not."

"How about if you gained twenty-five pounds, would you stop taking showers then?"

"No," she glared at him.

"Would you stop going to work, taking care of your kids, going to graduate school?"

"No."

"Would your IQ drop? Would you lose your wit, your insight, your problem-solving skills, your verbal skills that make you a fascinating conversationalist?"

"No," she said, blushing.

"Would you change, in any way, except to be a larger person?"

"I guess not."

"So, in other words, your thoughts about being fat and even about what you would be like if you gained weight are not founded on anything real, right? They are just beliefs."

She just sat there. Finally she reluctantly admitted that that seemed to be true. At that point the group broke into a discussion, each woman voicing her individual response to the fill-in-the-blank exercise. I was interested in talking to Sheila. During the break I cornered her to see how she felt about the exercise she had done.

"You know, I didn't even realize I thought that way until he made me look at it," she said. "I think my response shocked me even more than it shocked everybody else. Those are beliefs I have acquired from my father, who had very harsh stereotypes of overweight people, and somewhere along the line I must have adopted his beliefs as the truth. No wonder the thought of gaining any weight was so terrifying.

"Now I see why food and eating send me into such a panic."

The meeting was about to resume, so I asked Sheila if I could call her in a week and ask some follow-up questions. She agreed. When I finally contacted her, she was extremely enthusiastic about the results of the session.

"I can't believe all the insights that have flowed from that one little exercise," she said. "There is this whole sequence of events. First I think those thoughts, then I go into a panic that leads me to starve myself because I don't want to be thought of by others as a stupid, lazy, dirty slob. When I get so hungry that I am desperate, I go into the inevitable eating binge. Then I have to throw it up because I don't want to be a stupid, lazy, dirty slob. The whole horrible ordeal just keeps repeating itself.

"I'm not saying my eating disorders (both anorexia and bulimia) have been miraculously cured or anything, but at least now I see how the 'one thing leads to another' game sent me down a self-destructive path. Now I have a strong desire to get control of the first step in the process—my thinking. I've been paying closer attention to my thoughts to avoid triggering negative emotions. I take my thoughts seriously."

Exercise 1: "Filling in the Blank"

Taking a tip from Sheila's experience, you might want to consider doing the exercise yourself, varying the fill-in-the-blank statement to suit your needs. For example,

If I fail my math exam, I am _____.
If I ask Mike out and he refuses, I am _____.
If I invest some money and lose it, _____.
If I go skiing and fall down, I am _____.

If you discover that your responses are of the LH variety, that is, stable, global, and internal, you can begin changing them to more mastery-oriented responses. For example:

1. Internal and   "If I fail my math exam, I am stupid. I will
   Stable   never succeed at math."

                     Can be changed to:

| External and Dynamic | "If I fail my math exam, I am like anyone else learning something new, I make mistakes. I will get a tutor and study harder next time." |

OR

| 2. Internal | "If I ask Mike out and he refuses, I am ugly, fat, old, boring, stupid, and so on." |

Can be changed to:

| External | "If I ask Mike out and he refuses, maybe I'm just not his type. Anyway it's his loss." |

OR

| 3. Global and Internal | "If I invest some money and lose it, I will be homeless and destitute. How could I have been so stupid?" |

Can be changed to:

| Dynamic and Specific | "If I invest some money and lose it, well, you win some, you lose some. I would prefer not to have lost it, but it's not the end of the world. Lucky I didn't invest *all* of it. Next time I have a little to play with, I'll try again. Maybe next time I'll be luckier." |

OR

| 4. Specific | "If I go skiing and fall down, I am a clumsy, uncoordinated clod." |

Can be changed to:

| External | "If I go skiing and fall down, I am just like everybody else. Even the best skiers fall down." |

Such an exercise can be the first step in learning how to monitor your thoughts. Not only does it give you practice in coming up with positive connections, it is also very useful for seeing the connection between what you are thinking and how you are feeling.

Exercise 2: "Depersonalizing Failure"

As discussed earlier, helpless individuals are likely to explain a setback or failure by saying, "That failed, therefore *I* am a failure," in contrast to mastery-oriented individuals, who say, "That failed. I'll try this." In other words, mastery-oriented individuals are willing to attribute failure to a number of different causes long before coming to the conclusion that they are inadequate to the task. Thus an elemental step in becoming mastery-oriented is the ability to use your explanatory style to depersonalize failure. In this way so-called failures lose their emotional charge, enabling a variety of other possible causes to present themselves. Remember, the explanation you have been using all these years (and believing) may not necessarily be accurate!

To begin depersonalizing failure, choose an undertaking of the past that brought pain, difficulty, a feeling of failure or insecurity. Now on paper write the heading "Possible Other Reasons Why This Event Occurred." Then, in the detached manner you would use to explain this event if it happened to someone else, list all the other reasons you can think of that might have contributed to this event in your life. When you think you are done, think of three more—seriously. If you want to, engage a friend in this exercise in order to help you gain perspective.

Let's use the example of a young woman in one of my seminars who had just interviewed for her first teaching position but had not landed the job. She was certain she didn't get it because of personal inadequacies. "I guess I just wasn't smart enough," she said. If she were to do the exercise above, it would show a myriad of other factors at work, none of which had anything to do with personal inadequacy. Her list might look something like this:

OTHER REASONS WHY I DIDN'T GET THE JOB:

1. Due to prior events at the school, the principal had predetermined exactly the kind of individual he wanted. He did not want a young teacher because he needed a strong authority figure, and it is much harder for a young teacher to pull this off.
2. The principal even hinted he wanted a male (for the same reason as above).

3. Besides age, the principal needed someone with teaching and disciplinary experience, not a first-year teacher who is still learning the ropes.
4. Prior events at the school had led to the principal's decision. The previous year a particular class had gotten so out of control (due to an incompetent teacher) that a student had actually thrown a desk out the window.

Now for those last three I would've asked her to come up with:

1. The principal was a sexist.
2. The principal was trying to cover his backside because both the county administrators and a parent group were on him to correct the disciplinary problems at the school. (This happened to be true.)
3. To some extent the principal was also trying to protect the new teacher, knowing that hiring a young, inexperienced teacher in this case would be like throwing her to the wolves.*

As you do these exercises, remember the discussion back in Chapter 6 on the power and inclination of your old self to keep you stuck in a familiar self-image, explaining events in negative LH ways, thus preventing the very thing that self fears the most—change. Allowing for the possibility that what seemed "wrong" with you was just another negative explanation of a bad event, but not necessarily the truth, is the kind of thought monitoring that will help you change your explanatory style from a helpless one to a mastery-oriented one.

Exercise 3: "Cultivating Curiosity"

We higher primates have a built-in, standard feature we can utilize to help us avoid the hooks of negative thoughts and LH explanatory styles. It is called curiosity.

---

* It was necessary to acquire more information in order to provide these alternative reasons, and the teacher in question did call the principal back to find out why he didn't hire her. Of course this is a very mastery-oriented thing to do, and acting in such a fashion actually helped her to become more mastery-oriented.

When you first become aware of a negative feeling, rather than immediately assuming that this temporary state of being is "real" and allowing yourself to be swept away by it, simply cultivate your natural curiosity. Begin to ask yourself some questions.

Imagine, for example, that you are having one of those days when, for no apparent reason you suddenly hate your job, your husband, your nose, your weight, your outfit. (Yesterday, of course, these things were just fine, but today your life is totally unacceptable.) Simply say to yourself, "Gee, yesterday I felt just great about my job (or Marvin or whatever), yet, for some reason, today I hate everything. Since nothing has actually happened, nothing has really changed, a thought must have created this feeling in me. Perhaps I have created a story and then believed it." This moment's pause will create a "space," a moment in which you do not immediately *identify* with the negative feeling and get hooked by it, but instead begin a process of observation, detachment, and objectivity.

A fellow writer I met at a writer's support group reports many such experiences. In counseling new writers he says, "Writing is such a long, arduous process that you're bound to have negative feelings. Some days, for example, I think I don't have anything to say, I can't write worth a damn, the book will never get done, and my life will be ruined. On those days I hate writing. It takes an act of God for me to fire up the word processor and stare at the blank screen. The *very next day*, though, my thoughts change. I think, 'Hey, this is really good. I love this metaphor. I am a great writer. Undoubtedly I'm producing a best-seller here.' "

Now, obviously, in "reality" nothing has changed, except his thinking about the task. He is neither a great writer nor a terrible writer. He is both, alternately. But whatever reality or explanatory style he is using that day determines his energy level, his motivation, and his persistence. I have been through this many times myself. Now when I have the bad day, I think, "That's just how you are thinking today. It doesn't make it real. No point in getting depressed." (I do not say this on the good days, however—*those* I choose to believe.)

As you retrace your thoughts and identify which ones led to which feelings, you are exercising power and mastery over your thinking/feeling process. Instead of instantly identifying the feelings created by a negative explanatory style as "real" or being mindlessly swept away in a tide of fear or anxiety, your curiosity creates the detachment that stops the process.*

Over time you will find that regular investigation of the connection between your thoughts and your feelings will enable you to become very specific: to identify certain emotions as products of certain thoughts. Once this happens, you can begin to monitor those thoughts carefully and learn to head one off at the pass before it has the chance to produce the internal response. You'll then begin to respond to risk and change with less gnashing of teeth and greater peace of mind.

Exercise 4: "Affirmations"

Affirmations are another tool for intercepting negative and/or self-deprecating thoughts (before they can manifest into emotions) and replacing them with positive, supportive thoughts. Since many of us received negative messages from our parents or society as children, we never learned *how* to speak kindly or compassionately or encouragingly to ourselves. All we heard were messages of discouragement, such as, "What's the matter with you?" or "What's your problem?" As computer programmers are fond of saying, "Garbage in, garbage out." In other words, these messages eventually became internalized and, like a programmed recording, play over and over whenever we make a mistake or encounter a failure, so that we think to ourselves, "What is the matter with me?"

By the time we are adults, these debilitating tapes, or explanatory styles, have become so habitual that they are no longer available to the *conscious* mind. Affirmations can silence these automatic tapes in two ways: first, by making us aware of precisely what the tapes are saying; and second, by flooding the mind with a positive explanation of events, thereby crowding out the negative, destructive garbage.

Affirmations have become so popular that a lot of misconceptions and ineffective practices have developed around them. Too bad, because they can be a powerful tool if used properly. Here's how.

---

* Meditation teaches the same thing. It helps you train your mind to become aware of this process much more quickly. (It will be discussed in detail in Chapter 10.)

First, and most importantly, affirmations must be written; not typed, not dictated or recited aloud. The process of writing them in longhand, although slow and arduous, becomes an advantage. As one writes, there is time to hear the automatic critical tapes of a negative explanatory style that are so debilitating. The very slowness of the task creates the time and the silence in which to hear the tapes or voices—whatever you wish to call them.

For example, remember my fear of learning how to ski? To confront the fear that was preventing me from trying something new, I began to write an affirmation. "I, Nicky, am perfectly capable of learning to ski. I will fall down, but so does everyone else. I can still learn how to ski." As I wrote, I heard a voice say, "Oh, yeah? What about when you tried to water-ski? Remember what a fool you made of yourself?" I wrote the affirmation again. This time the voice took another tack, "What if you fall down and break your leg?" I wrote the affirmation a third time, so the voice tried a third tack, "What if you fall off the chair lift and they have to stop it? You'll be so humiliated."

Before I had written my affirmation, I was not consciously aware of the kinds of messages I was giving myself. I just knew I was scared. The process of writing in longhand forced me to slow down enough to hear the voice and bring it up to awareness level. Once I heard specifically what it was saying, I understood why it had been so effective at preventing me from going skiing.

The second rule follows from the first: Never try to argue with the voice. It has been a worthy opponent up until now and it will outwit, outargue, and outsmart you every time. In my case, for example, when the threat of physical injury lost its effectiveness, the voice switched to the threat of humiliation. Therefore, rather than trying to win an argument with the voice, simply repeat the affirmation over and over again. Ever so slowly the voice will begin to relinquish its hold on your belief system, and you will be able to gain access to the new belief that you are creating with your affirmation.

Finally, while affirmations should be positive statements, try to keep them believable. Research has shown that an individual's belief system is not changed when she writes daily, "Everyday I am getting lighter and lighter," while the scale indicates heavier and heavier. Therefore tailor your affirmations carefully. For example, suppose you have an important presentation to make. If writing "I am confident and self-assured and fully capable of displaying those traits at the management meeting tomorrow" seems unbelievable, alter it to read, "Even though I feel tense and uncertain, I can prepare well and fake the rest." If you want to go white-water rafting but are frightened and "Every day I am getting braver and braver" seems pretty remote, try "I am scared, but I can do it anyway." If you are trying to lose weight, write, "I am willing to learn to trust my body to tell me when it's really hungry and what it wants to eat. To do this, I must be willing to experience hunger." (At this point, if your mind goes into a panic, fearful of experiencing hunger even for a short period of time, at least you will be able to hear consciously what it is saying to you.)

Finally, if you find yourself feeling slightly hypocritical as you write your affirmation, as in reaching for a cigarette while writing "I, Esmerelda, no longer desire to smoke," don't fret too much. Old mind-sets and old habits do not die easily. Remember, don't argue, simply repeat the affirmation. Have faith that you are cultivating new thought patterns (self-talk) and, *with time* and repetition, new behaviors will emerge to replace old ones. Granted, they will be tentative and fragile. Granted, it will be a slow process. Like little sprouts, they will require a strong support system to keep them thriving, but your affirmations can fulfill that function.

Finally, be specific. Use your name. Give clear directions. Tailor the affirmation to meet your personal needs. Keep the content simple and direct. Remember, you are using affirmations as a method of accomplishing two things:

1. Unmasking and bringing to awareness the negative self-talk of your old, helpless self
2. Giving clear information about the positive new explanatory style and self-talk to be learned

Here are some possible affirmations to get you started:

I, (your name here), am in training as a mastery-oriented individual. Frustration and confusion will be part of my training. I can accept that.

I, _____, understand that everyone experiences fear and doubt. It's okay. That doesn't have to stop me.

I, _____, understand that setbacks are encountered by everyone. They are part of the process. All processes take time.

I, _____, understand that mistakes are a natural part of learning. I do not have to be upset by them.

I, _____, am willing to work at generating many options and paths for reaching my goals. If one doesn't work, I'm willing to try another.

I, _____, am capable of creating the changes I wish to make in my life.

I, _____, am willing to be excited over the prospect of creating a new life for myself.

I, _____, am eager to learn new things.

I, _____, am gradually learning to feel safe in the world.

Here is a lovely prayer that I learned from a friend. Unfortunately I do not know where it came from, but I like to use it as an affirmation. Perhaps you can use it as I do—as a means of opening up to a whole new self-concept.

> I, Nicky, am one link in a golden chain of life and love that sustains the planet. I keep my link bright and strong by joyfully releasing negative thought and by accepting open, happy, and creative thought as my natural state of mind.

Exercise 5: "Bragging Aloud Allowed"

Those with LH accept responsibility for only one-half of the events that befall them—failure—while they continually discount the successes they have had ("Oh, it was nothing"). In other words, they reinforce their lack of belief in self-efficacy with their negative explanatory style. While true humility is a refreshing and rare thing, this refusal to take credit for accomplishments amounts to self-abasement, not humility, and perpetuates the false notion that the individual has not influenced outcomes in her life.

There is an antidote to this toxic point of view, and it is particularly important for women, since we tend to disregard, even disown, our successes. The antidote is to start a bragging-aloud list. Make a written list, every day, in which you take credit for your accomplishments, regardless of how small you think they are, and then read it to someone.

Oh, I know what you are thinking. Most days have no great accomplishments. They are just an endless procession of meaningless tasks and mediocre relationships, and besides, that Pollyanna attitude gives you a pain. Who wants to plaster on a phony smile and blunder through life with blind optimism?

Well, fortunately, phony smiles are optional (although some blundering is probably inevitable). To set positive forces in motion, however, we must be willing to take responsibility for our successes (as men do) and stop discounting them, *no matter how small they seem.* Teaching ourselves to do this on a small scale at first will give us practice in identifying self-efficacy at work. As we begin to see how much we really do influence outcomes, it will be harder and harder to tell ourselves that we don't!

Sometimes (okay, most times) it will be a real stretch to find a success. For example, resisting that third chocolate chip cookie may have been a major accomplishment for you today. Sure, you could use a negative explanatory style to focus on the two cookies you did eat, but the fact that you used to eat the whole bag must be taken into account here. Remember, we are working toward progress, not perfection.

Perhaps just lugging your poor, tired old body out of bed and off to work this morning was a major accomplishment. There are days when this simple act takes on heroic proportions. Perhaps just finding it in your heart to be kind to your children on a day when you yourself required massive infusions of tender loving care was your achievement for the day. These are no small achievements. Although such simple acts often require major sacrifice on the part of the individual, they go largely unrecognized.

As you compile a list of all your small daily accomplishments (or "brag aloud" with friends and co-workers), you begin to see how self-efficacious you truly are. Did you take credit for the two loads of laundry you threw in this morning before you made the mad dash to work? Did you list having made love with your "significant other" last night in spite of your fatigue? Did you include mediating the disagreement between those two co-workers of yours? Did you take credit for organizing your family's social life this weekend? How about when you resisted that second glass of wine at dinner last night? Or the phone call you made to your mother, even though you didn't really feel like talking?

Sometimes I forget to take my own advice. Yesterday, for example, was one of those days. What began as mild confusion soon escalated into total, unmitigated mayhem. Nothing I started got finished. Or so I thought. When, at the end of the day, I made a list of what I had done, I discovered it was not an unproductive day without accomplishments at all, even though it was true that nothing was actually completed. Here is my list:

1. Made two business calls for possible workshops
2. Rummaged through the piles on my desk
3. Jogged and showered
4. Reread two chapters and made notes for revisions
5. Did two loads of laundry, folded one
6. Measured area for new carpet
7. Took dog to vet
8. Looked at calendar
9. Made phone call to financial adviser about interest rates (didn't reach him)
10. Attended meeting
11. Ran dishwasher
12. Balanced checkbook

Now, using a negative explanatory style, a non-self-efficacious point of view, I could say that not one single job was completed. I had intended to reorganize the piles on my desk completely, not just rummage through them; to revise, not just reread, two chapters; to pay the monthly bills in addition to balancing my checkbook. A negative explanatory style would have discounted "looking at my calendar" or "running the dishwasher" or "measuring for new carpet" as too common or small to be considered important. After all, measuring for the new carpet took only about two minutes. Nevertheless, even these small accomplishments eventually contribute to getting things done, to planning for the future, to *outcomes*.

Upon further reflection on my list I discovered that my intentions had been unrealistic. (Aren't they always, when, at seven A.M., we make out our to-do lists with such optimism?) Anyway, once I had actually listed my activities for the day, I realized I did, in fact, accomplish a great deal and had put in a full, productive, *successful* day. Although I had not finished my tasks, nor would any of them qualify as achievements, not being in the category of curing cancer or ending the nuclear arms race, I had made steps toward influencing outcomes in many different areas of my life. I had been self-efficacious.

Overlooking or belittling small daily accomplishments sets up the unbalanced view of LH and reinforces a negative explanatory style. Success or achievement acquires a very narrow definition, such as curing cancer or ending the nuclear arms race. Once that happens, we come to see as self-efficacious only those spectacular achievers who show up on the pages of *People* magazine, certainly not just plain you or me.

In reality, success is the daily completion of seemingly insignificant tasks, of getting up and going to work. Success is the steady accumulation of small victories over time. Success is a process. One thing is sure: When a research scientist finally does discover the cure for cancer, it will be because she got up and went to work every day.

This is so cogent a point for females. Because of our tendency to disown our achievements and claim responsibility only for our failures, we need to make a conscious effort to dwell on our accomplishments, particularly if we are to achieve a belief in self-efficacy. A daily list or "Bragging Aloud Allowed" session with your friends can enhance a positive explanatory style and increase your mastery-oriented potential.

Exercise 6: "The Golden Five"

As an exercise in my seminars I often ask women to list five things they like about themselves *unequivocally*, without disclaimers or qualifying remarks, such as, "Well, I like my legs okay *except . . .*" or, "I think I have a good sense of humor, but . . ." I tell them, "Absolutely no 'buts' or exceptions are allowed. These must be things that are pleasing to you without reservation."

While, in general, the responses are varied and interesting, there is always a fairly large group, perhaps 50 percent, who have trouble thinking of even one, much less five. They unearth very few qualities they can say they approve of unequivocally and point out that even something they think they like is vulnerable to criticism. This exercise often reveals the disturbing degree to which our self-evaluations are dependent on *other* people's opinions.

Try it yourself. Make a list of all the things you like about yourself, regardless of what others may think. If you find yourself unable to come up with at least three, then your beliefs and ideas about yourself are vulnerable to the opinions of others. Ultimately this will influence your ability to take risks and choose learning goals over performance goals because you will fear their criticism should you make a mistake. If even the things you like (the positive aspects of your explanatory style) are vulnerable to outside criticism, then imagine how vulnerable the areas of doubt will be.

Even if you have trouble, do not give up on your list. Start with just one thing. If you can't even think of one, call a good friend. Tell her about the list you are compiling, why you are compiling it, and the difficulties you are encountering. Ask her for help. Ask her to tell you what she likes about you unequivocally. (Actually you will find that your friends *love* you unequivocally.)

Don't be embarrassed. A good friend will enjoy pointing out your positive qualities. (Wouldn't you enjoy doing it for her?) Other people often see things you don't see and can help you discover elements of yourself that may be hidden from your view.

Gradually, as you practice the attitudinal changes offered in this book, your list will grow. Do not be ashamed to let the list expand and develop. It will be an effective weapon when self-doubt or fear of inadequacy or old habits of a negative explanatory style threaten to intrude, as they surely will in the midst of any new undertaking. Don't be stingy. Lavish praise on yourself, especially when things go wrong, as they do for everybody—even the mastery-oriented.

In the past your self-doubts and negative explanatory style (to which you gave free rein) have been dangerous states of mind that have sabotaged your willingness to take risks and reinforced your helplessness. For that reason keep an updated version of the list tucked away in your purse at all times, since you never know where you might be when fears of inadequacy may intrude. When they do, take out your list. Read it and reread it. Demonstrate a mastery orientation by reminding yourself of your positive traits, even in the midst of self-doubt. Especially in the midst of self-doubt.

As you observe the ways in which recognizing your positive traits (mental, physical, emotional, or spiritual) contributes to your feelings of self-efficacy, your list will become a treasure of ever-increasing value, like a savings account whose interest accrues faster with accumulation of deposits. Like money in the bank, your list will be available whenever your immediate resources of self-confidence seem strained. Cash in a little now and then by reading and refurbishing your list.

CHAPTER 9

Who You've Been So Far Doesn't Have to Be Who You Are: Changing Your Self-Concept

---

Until we lose ourselves, there is no hope of finding ourselves.
— HENRY MILLER

In previous chapters you have learned that your old helpless self, with its negative explanatory style, wishes you to believe that if there is something you wish to correct, there must be something "wrong" with you. This overly simplistic and habitually negative style of thinking has kept you stuck in outmoded patterns of self-blame and other debilitating thoughts that do not, have not, and will not serve you.

Similarly, getting stuck in a rigid self-concept, especially if it is a helpless or fearful one, will also prevent the changes necessary for developing mastery behavior and the ability to take risks. The second component of overcoming LH therefore involves changing one's view of self, an idea first introduced in Chapters 5 and 6 on change and the self. This chapter will provide concrete techniques and strategies to help you do just that.

INTRODUCING THE WITNESS

You may remember from Chapter 6 that one way to open up self-concept is to entertain the possibility of the-many-in-the-one. Not only is it an interesting way to look at oneself, it is experientially valid as well.

One of the selves that typically doesn't get much airplay, but whose cool, dispassionate wisdom is critical to developing mastery behavior, is the Witness. She is that self capable of acting as a perennial member of the audience in the drama of life, of standing back away from the action to observe events, the only self with eyes discerning enough to cut through the layers of illusion created by a negative explanatory style and by the many selves jockeying for position.

The best way to think about the Witness is as a superintending awareness that keeps you abreast of developments. She is that self who knows how to observe and correct rather than judge and condemn (the prime territory of another self—the Critic—but more about this character later). Cultivating your witnessing awareness will help you detach from the fear and drama created by a negative explanatory style.

Since we continuously act out our lives in the crucible of theatrical, dramatic events, it may be fun to begin this process of getting acquainted with the Witness by presenting a play. All the characters in this play will probably be quite familiar to most of you, as will the dialogue itself. My invitation to you is to use this play as a way to begin developing the witnessing awareness in yourself so that you can recognize the cacophony of selves within, each explaining reality in a different way, each persuading you that her version is the "right" one, each asking you to believe that she is the "real" you.

As in any good play, we must begin with the dramatis personae—literally translated as the personnel of the drama. In our play the personnel of the drama are entirely internal. They are the voices that play inside the head of the real live woman lying in her bed as the scene opens.

VOICES AT DAWN
Dramatis Personae

Lilgirl	The Critic
The Body	Thespia
The Adventuress	The Witness

The scene opens on a beautiful spring morning, with the sun streaming through the open window of a bedroom. The curtain rustles gently as fresh air drifts through the room and reaches the nostrils of a woman sleeping in a bed. Occasionally she stirs. The action of this drama takes place inside her head.

LILGIRL: Wake up! Wake up! The birds are singing. It's sunny. Let's get going!

BODY: (*yawning*) Hold your horses. I'm not awake yet. Give me a minute. I can't just bound out of bed like you. I'm a lot older than you. Let me get a cup of coffee.

LILGIRL: Why do we always have to drink coffee first?

BODY: Because I can't wake up without it, that's why.

LILGIRL: But I wanna go. Pleeeeease.

ADVENTURESS: I agree. Let's get this show on the road, check out the want ads, start packing. (*to* LILGIRL) Don't worry, you can come with me.

CRITIC: You're always in such a hurry to have fun, but where are you when things get serious? It's time you grew up. You know we have to go over to Mom and Dad's today to break the news. Don't be so careless. Work before play.

LILGIRL: Can we go out and play afterward?

CRITIC: Probably not. You're going to have to learn that there is more to life than playing. Right now for example we have more important things to think about. There are many responsibilities involved in a move like this, and it's not a good idea to go off half-cocked.

LILGIRL: But moving sounds like fun! How long will it take to get there? Where will we sleep? Can we buy new furniture? Who are our new neighbors? Will we be able to make new friends?

ADVENTURESS: Oh, yes! And, there are lots of places we can explore and investigate. As a matter of fact, I was just thinking we could—

CRITIC: It's not good to have fun all the time. Life is not fun. Besides, telling Mom and Dad that we've been transferred to a new town and are moving away is not going to be easy, nor will it be fun. Especially when we tell them we only have two weeks before we have to be on the new job.

LILGIRL: Will they be mad at us?

CRITIC: Probably. They're not going to like this one bit.

THESPIA: Well, at least it'll stir up a little action. Things have been getting pretty dull around here lately.

WITNESS: Another county heard from! I'm sure that telling Mom

and Dad about the move and taking care of all the details will
be enough adventure for us all over the next couple of weeks.

THESPIA: Speak for yourself, darling.

BODY: I don't know about the rest of you, but I smell bad. I'm going
to go take a shower. When I get out, I'll want coffee.

*(At this point we see the woman get out of bed, being careful to
avoid tripping over the boxes and suitcases lying in her path to the
bathroom. She looks at her face closely in the mirror, examining each
profile carefully and studying the bags under her eyes. She sighs and
turns on the hot water. As she steps into the warm womb of the
shower stall, the conversation in her head continues.)*

CRITIC: God, you're getting old. You could use a face-lift.

THESPIA: She's right, darling. You're starting to show your age. On
the other hand, surgery is dangerous. What if we die under
the anesthesia? What if the plastic surgeon's hand slips and we
are permanently disfigured? We would be outcasts, like lepers,
doomed to wander abandoned down lonely streets. . . .

WITNESS: Hold it. You two are like broken records, Critic finding
fault, Thespia dramatizing. You are both distracting us from
the job we have to do today: telling Mom and Dad.

BODY: Let's eat!

CRITIC: We have to be careful what we eat. We shouldn't eat too
much, or we'll get fat. If we get fat, no one will love us. If no
one loves us, we will be alone. If we're alone . . .

WITNESS: About Mom and Dad?

CRITIC: Well, somebody around here has to keep us disciplined.
You're so busy being objective and task-oriented. You give me
a pain. Being fat is the worst thing that could happen to us.
We should—

EVERYONE: (except LILGIRL, who is starting to cry) Shut UP!

ADVENTURESS: Come on, let's get going. No use putting this off.
That won't solve anything. We just have to do it. Besides,
maybe it won't be so bad.

THESPIA: Are you kidding? You know how Mom and Dad are. Mom
is going to go into her 'You're all I've got' routine, and Dad
is going to start harping on how dangerous it is for a single
woman to move to a new town alone. They never change. We
must prepare ourselves for a battle royal.

LILGIRL: I'm scared.

THESPIA: You should be.

LILGIRL: What if Mom and Dad stop speaking to us or what if they die after we leave them? Then it'll be all our fault.

WITNESS: You don't have to be afraid. All the rest of us here are big girls and we'll take care of you. And each other too. We will watch and listen and pay attention and rely on each other. Besides, we don't have to make judgments ahead of time that this is going to be unpleasant.

CRITIC: Not judge it? Have you lost your mind? That's impossible. Besides, it's not a good idea. It doesn't even make sense. We could be making the mistake of our lives. This could ruin everything. We must—

EVERYONE: Shut UP!

THESPIA: For once I agree with the Critic, although I have different reasons. Trying to shield ourselves from the pain is not a good idea. At least pain lets us know we are alive!

ADVENTURESS: There are other ways of feeling alive besides being fearful and in pain, you know.

THESPIA: Oh yeah? Like what?

ADVENTURESS: Like fantasizing about the positive aspects of the move, for one. New surroundings, new friends, a whole new life. Like not overdramatizing the pain part for another. Like creating an approach that will work with Mom and Dad and then thinking up what we'll say if that one doesn't work. I think we can be creative in helping them deal with this move, if we're willing to stop dwelling on the negatives. Besides, change is interesting, if you have the right attitude.

CRITIC: Bully for you. What a trouper. The ol' pioneer spirit. Well, no thank you. I think that's a stupid approach.

WITNESS: But that's it. She's got it. Don't you see? Cultivate curiosity and creativity instead of resistance and fear. It's so much more interesting. Besides, that's reality. We might as well deal with it as positively and as creatively as we can.

BODY: I have to go to the bathroom.

CRITIC: You should be learning to control these impulses.

BODY: I didn't say I couldn't control it. I was just making you all aware of your environment, that's all. It's not a problem right this minute, but if you ignore me, it will be. Either take care of me now or take care of me later. That's how it is when you have a body.

As you can probably tell, this little dramatization is only a scene in a much larger, perhaps epic, play, but you get my drift. Different characters in the internal drama, those different facets of who you are, will dominate depending on the scene that is being played. For those with LH, the Critic may be the star of the show, convincing you that it's all your fault. When a risk presents itself, Lilgirl may suddenly appear, virtually begging to be rescued. When the tedium of life becomes unbearable, the Adventuress may suddenly emerge. When a relationship is in trouble, Thespia may make her grand entrance (and probably refuse to leave the stage). And through it all, the Body will be an ever-present companion, whispering her messages and truths beneath the cacophony of other voices.

It is a waste of your energy to get stuck in the dilemma of trying to figure out which one is the most authentic you. Simply accept that they are all you, variously represented and emerging according to the circumstances. Cultivation of the Witness will render you less vulnerable to all the stories (explanatory styles) created by the various selves. Your witnessing awareness will be able to sort out the stories to determine whose story best suits your needs, serves you in times of crisis, and contributes to your overall growth, development, and mastery-oriented behavior. In other words, you won't have to get stuck identifying with one particular helpless or negative self.

To open up your view of self even further, try something fun. Try seeing yourself *not* as the characters of the drama but rather as the stage on which the drama is enacted. That will disengage you even further from the human tendency to get lost in the drama by identifying with the characters.

Indeed, it is a wondrous capacity of the human brain that it can detach itself at any moment it chooses in order to observe what the play is teaching, to develop the witnessing awareness, and to correct any behavior, belief, or philosophy expounded by some character in the drama whose agenda is to keep you stuck in old, negative explanatory styles or the belief in an unchanging, helpless self. The following exercises are presented to help you develop your witnessing awareness. I invite you to experience this capacity and to use it to ease your way on the journey from helplessness to mastery.

Exercise 1: "Third-Person Narratives"

One of the best exercises for developing the Witness involves speaking about oneself in the third person and conducting a running monologue or narrative describing your activities *as you do them.*

For example, "She's feeling lonely. She's headed for the telephone now. She's thinking about calling her ex-husband. She feels confused. Not sure that this is such a good idea, she decides to wait until the confusion subsides so as to act with greater clarity. She decides to take a relaxing bath instead."

Or how about this one: "She is upset. She is on her way to the cupboard. She is thinking about eating some cookies. Now, gobbling down a cookie, she becomes aware that she is doing so without any pleasure. She is slowing down. She now eats another cookie quite deliberately, taking her time actually to taste it. She now puts the bag back into the cupboard, deciding to call a friend instead."

This running dialogue may strike you as kind of bizarre at first. However, it is really quite useful in teaching oneself simply to observe and correct without involving the critic in the process. The more you practice this, the less strange it will seem and the better you will become at observing your behavior without adding emotional commentaries. This frees you from having to do constant battle with your critic and to correct self-defeating behaviors without the self-flagellation.

It is even possible to engage the Witness when you are interacting with others. For example, "She is sitting across the table from this new co-worker. She is listening to his conversation, nodding and smiling a lot, but she really doesn't feel like it. She wants him to like her because they have to work together, so she is trying to be alert and charming. What she really wants is to go home and go to sleep."

Over time this will not need to be such a conscious act but will evolve into a kind of oceanic awareness of your internal state at any given time. Eventually you may begin to witness at deeper and deeper levels. Since the Witness only observes and corrects, *without judgment*, this highly refined level of awareness results in a mastery-oriented type of consciousness: a self that is able to perceive quickly and clearly when a strategy is not working, change course without interpreting the need to do so as a personal flaw (internalizing blame), and let go of any story (explanatory style) being expounded by a helpless or fearful self desiring rescue.

The most engrossing situations (those with a strong emotional charge) have the greatest potential to drag you into the drama and silence your Witness. They carry the strongest temptation to believe in a negative explanatory version of the unfolding events and they represent the greatest challenge and provide the best practice at keeping the Witness alert. Since situations with a strong emotional charge are the most difficult, however, you should not *actively* seek them out until you have had a lot of practice. (Besides, when we seek out the pain or pleasure of the drama, we are usually acting from the self known as Thespia. She can be an extremely seductive character but is not necessarily a mastery-oriented one.)

Eventually, once you get good at listening and paying attention to the voice of your Witness, these highly charged emotional situations become learning opportunities, helping you to become aware of how you lose and regain the voice of your Witness and how this affects others who are, in turn, relating to *you*. Ultimately, of course, this will help you to develop self-efficacy as you become acclimated to exercising choice over which self you will display and to observing (witnessing) the effect that various selves have on the final outcome of events.

Exercise 2: "The Play's the Thing"

In the play presented earlier in this chapter, the purpose was to witness the many selves inside a particular character, each presenting her philosophy of life and attempting to influence the behavior of the woman lying in bed. By writing your own play (or scene) in which you deal with a particular problem and write the words spoken by the different selves within, you begin to witness the many aspects of your belief system and the behaviors that contribute to continued LH and/or resistance to learning mastery behavior. Plus, writing plays has the extra added attraction of being creative and fun to do.

Simply do what I did. Write a scene from a play. Or better yet, a soap opera, since that is how our lives often seem. You know how soap operas are. It is always perfectly clear to the viewer exactly what the characters should be doing. This is because the viewer, acting in the role of the witnessing awareness, is emotionally detached from the drama. (Also, like affirmations, the slowness of the activity allows for the voices to come up to consciousness.) Granted, the viewer does participate to some extent, but the final outcome of events is unlikely to change the viewer's life, which makes it easier for the viewer to discern what should be done in a given situation.

You know, for example, that Cassandra should not be considering a romantic involvement with Trevor, since, unbeknownst to them, Trevor is Cassandra's biological brother, the product of an artificial insemination donated by a medical student, Cassandra's real father, when her stepmother was in desperate need of money for a sex-change operation. You can see that Cassandra's flirtation will only lead to heartbreak and plot complications. You can see this because you are outside the emotional arena. Cassandra can't see the peril because she is within the emotional arena and also because she (like us) gets only a few pages of the script at a time.

The dramatic situations we see on television are not so vastly different from the ones in which we engage in real life. Once we establish, through the witnessing awareness, some emotional distance from the plot complications in our own real-life dramas, we can be more objective and discriminating about the direction our lives are taking.

Just for fun, start writing your play by imagining the appropriate cast of characters. By appropriate, I mean the real characters who people the story of your *inner* life, not fantasy characters like the Handsome Stranger who arrives just in the nick of time to whisk you away to his condo in Malibu. (This is fun, but save it for something other than problem solving, such as a sexual fantasy before you fall asleep. Besides, because it is more "if only . . ." stuff, it is about rescue, not problem solving.) What follows is a possible list of characters to get you started. Feel free to embellish and expand the list as you go.

The Loving Mother	The Professional Woman
The Wicked Witch	The Lazy Slob
Mother Earth	The Little Girl
The Temptress	The Blessed Saint
The Adventuress	The Critic
The Great Actress	The Competent Adult
The Body	The Witness

Once you have determined the inner cast of characters, begin writing. Some scenes will have many characters. Some may only have one or two. Allow characters (selves) total freedom to speak their minds, without any censorship from you, the playwright. Be alert and sensitive to any new characters who try to emerge as you write. They may have a point of view to express that you hadn't thought of consciously. Be permissive. Allow them, indeed, *welcome* them into the scene, even if you overlooked them initially. They may become the main character, once given a forum in which to speak.

The creative and playful aspect of writing a play does not diminish its potential as an awareness-building exercise. If you allow the scenes to deal specifically with ongoing areas of difficulty in your life or particular risks you shy away from, they can, like the activity of writing affirmations, bring to consciousness thoughts and beliefs you didn't even know you had.

If a play seems too ambitious an undertaking, start with just a single scene. If you regularly write a journal or diary of some kind, allow this scene writing to become part of the journal. The play may develop over quite a long period of time and will teach you to listen to the inner voices of your many selves. Eventually this will enable you to make more conscious choices concerning which of your selves you choose to listen to, building up those voices that serve you in becoming a mastery-oriented risk taker and diminishing those that only perpetuate more LH.

A reminder: always include two important characters—the Witness and the Critic. The Critic will always be around in some form or another, so don't be afraid to call him or her by name. In other words, the Critic, who has no qualms about stealing scenes, may try to pose as other characters in various costumes and guises. Don't be fooled. Simply include the Critic by name in each scene. Also, remember to include the Witness, so that you will be forced to speak for this "self" and develop her into a fully rounded, multidimensional character. The more lines you give her to speak, the more she will be forced to say. Eventually she will begin to speak on her own.

Finally, every now and then review the characters (selves) you are working with and reread the dialogues you have created, asking yourself the following questions:

1. With whom do I identify most strongly? Why?
2. Whom do I like? Whom do I dislike?

3. Whom do I most wish to emulate? What are the specific behaviors, attitudes, beliefs, or points of view of this character that I wish to emulate?
4. To which character (self) am I giving the most lines to speak?
5. Around which character (self) does the play revolve? Does this change from day to day or does it remain the same?
6. Are any new characters (selves) struggling to be heard?
7. Are any of the characters (selves) changing?
8. Is the Witness becoming stronger?
9. What is the Critic up to?

Have a good time and enjoy yourself. This highly creative activity is so much fun that most people do it eagerly and even find themselves daydreaming dialogue for their characters (selves) to speak. Remember, embedded within the lines of dialogue that your many selves speak are clues to your belief system and explanatory style. Use this pleasurable activity to bolster the selves that promote mastery behavior and to diminish those that are helpless.

Exercise 3: "Get an Attitude" (or "Talk Back to Your Inner Critic")

While you're at it, write a scene in which you talk back to the Critic, that rascal who constantly internalizes your failures, but doesn't allow you to take credit for your successes. Since those with LH spend a great deal of time striving to please or avoid the harsh voice of this character, learning to talk back is a healthy, though not always easy, exercise, and therefore you will need practice.

This is because building a case in favor of an inner Critic is easy. After all, some of us jump through some pretty fancy hoops to please the Critic, and the results are not always bad. We earn good grades to please the Critic, we diet to please the Critic, we get promoted to please the Critic. Some of us exercise, get organized, buy clothes, get married, and have nose jobs, breast implants, liposuction, and face-lifts to please the Critic. Some of us even act on our altruistic instincts more to please the Critic than to be truly charitable. The trouble is that we do not necessarily get the approval we sought from all these activities. We just get more criticism.

Because the Critic is a familiar character in the inner drama— for some the *main* character—it is frightfully easy to become accustomed to listening to and believing in the Critic's pronouncements. In order to live a life of less helplessness, in order to change your explanatory style and become a more mastery-oriented risk taker, it is imperative that you silence the Critic's voice and diminish its power to govern your belief system. Here is one woman's story after she did some journal writing.

"Over the years, I jumped through a lot of hoops trying to please this Critic you're talking about," said Simone, a biochemist working in the environmental-protection industry who attended one of my workshops. "I took on more responsibility at work than I should have, making myself sick in the process. I acquired an eating disorder. No matter what I did, though, I couldn't shake the feeling, stuck to me like Saran Wrap, that I had to do still more in order to be acceptable. I had to be perfect just to be okay.

"Writing these scenes has shown me not only how strong a voice the Critic can be but also that you really *can't* please the Critic because the Critic's job is to be critical. I realized this because of the lines he always spoke. It hit me how futile it is to strive to please a character whose sole purpose is *not* to be pleased. It's kind of funny really, except that it made me feel foolish to have tried so hard for so long."

Simone's statement about feeling foolish shows why the Fool has attained such importance in legends, myths, and metaphysical literature. It is often our very foolishness that, *when exposed to well-developed witnessing awareness,* ultimately leads us to wisdom. The Fool, bless his warped little heart, coaxes us down a variety of primrose paths and then cracks the punchline in the cosmic joke by making us laugh at ourselves.

"But even with that new awareness," she continued, "my Critic wasn't done with me."

"What do you mean?"

"Well, I was given no time to enjoy my great, profound insight. My Critic immediately retaliated with, 'How could you have been so stupid not to see that in the first place? Anyone with the IQ of a brussels sprout would have seen the absurdity long ago. You are stupider than I thought.' "

Everyone laughed at this point, identifying in full measure with the situation, for almost all of us have a harsh Critic inside that just won't shut up.

"How did that make you feel?" I asked her.

"It made me laugh. I don't really know why."

Mark Twain, the great humorist-philosopher, said, "Against the assault of laughter, nothing can stand." He understood that humor is a powerful ally against even the greatest of foes. Court jesters, also known as fools, were, after all, powerful satirical voices who were allowed to poke fun at the most serious issues. As Oscar Wilde said, "Life is too important to be taken seriously." We can use our "foolishness" in much the same way, not as a tool of the Critic to make us feel bad but as a tool *against* the Critic to diminish his or her power in our lives.

Therefore, particularly when dealing with a heavy-handed character like the Critic, laughter is a great way to talk back. Laughter is the secret weapon to disarm the Critic's arsenal of abuse, for when we laugh, we open a space within that makes room to love ourselves, to welcome ourselves into our own hearts, to love as much as we can from wherever we are, and to forgive the sweet human flaws that make us so divinely comical.

Simone continued. "The laughter was a great release. It helped me to realize that even though the Critic won't give up so easily, he's nothing but an old blowhard. He doesn't scare me so much anymore. He only has life if I give it to him, and I'm going to unplug his life-support system!"

What a terrific metaphor. Use it. Unplug your Critic's life-support system by laughing at him, talking back, refusing to identify with his cruel and gloomy pronouncements, which will only keep you stuck in old patterns of choosing performance goals over learning goals because you are fearful of the Critic's disapproval should you make a mistake. Remember that the Critic is constantly reinforced by various spokespeople of our society, such as those rascals on Madison Avenue who are hell-bent on making us feel inadequate in order to make sure that we consume their products. We must deliberately undermine this conspiracy and liberate within ourselves a more balanced point of view.

One word of warning: Be aware that you may accidentally involve your Critic in the process of becoming mastery-oriented. Be alert to any voice that puts you down for not being a risk taker. If this happens, use your Witness to speak out and affirm that the purpose of becoming mastery-oriented is to serve *you*, no one else. Your goal in developing mastery behavior is to cope effectively with whatever life presents, not to prove something to your Critic.

You can still be a hard worker if you choose, you can still be disciplined, organized, committed, caring, compassionate, thin, and fit. You can, in fact, be anything you choose *without* the existence of the Critic. Remember, the Critic's only job is to find fault, to humiliate, to make you feel worthless and inadequate. Do yourself a favor and evict him from the premises.

Exercise 4: "The Actress Within"

"All the world's a stage and all the men and women merely players. . . . And one man in his time plays many parts." These immortal words from Shakespeare convey the gossamer line between fantasy and reality and the experiential validity of recognizing the many-in-the-one.

As we have seen from the chapter on "self," this quote from the Bard represents more than just the poetic musings of the world's most gifted playwright. They capture a profoundly subtle truth with hard evidence from social scientists to support it. *We literally construct our identities by the parts we are given or choose to play.* Eventually the parts we play become who we are.

In order to create a role, an actress must relinquish temporarily her notion of a rigid self. Similarly, moving from LH to mastery requires the same willing surrender of an old self-image. The metamorphosis of an actress donning a new role (self) and acting convincingly enough that the audience forgets she is acting so eerily matches the process of changing self-image that one can learn from theater people how to bring one's new character to life.

Therefore experiment with some of the techniques of theater in your life. Be an actress. Take on the role of the person you wish to become. Imagine you are an actress and must prepare for the role of the New You. Here are some techniques used by actresses to get you going:

1. Write the New You into one of your scenes.
2. What are her motivations? How would she explain negative events?
3. Give her lines to say in a variety of different circumstances.
4. What would she wear in a variety of circumstances?
5. How does she walk?

6. What actress or public figure best represents or embodies the New You that you wish to become?
7. Practice your lines (the ones you have given the New You to speak in your scenes) in front of a mirror.
8. Audition the New You in familiar, comfortable settings.

Try the role on for size and see how it fits. You can make adjustments and experiment with various combinations until you hit upon the one you like the best. Remember, the part you choose to play will become the person you are.

Despite how it may appear on the surface, this does not encourage phoniness or hypocrisy. Think of it as "Practice makes perfect." In other words, at first it may seem phony and uncomfortable to act mastery-oriented and confident when you feel helpless and inadequate, but the more you do it, the more comfortable you will become. The more you practice anything, the better you get at it, and mastery-oriented behavior and risk taking are no different. If you practice mastery-oriented behavior long enough, it won't be an act anymore. As they say in the Twelve-Step addiction-rehabilitation programs, "Fake it till you make it."

Exercise 5: "The Warrioress"*

One of the selves that often gets overlooked (and that we can use the actress within to develop) is the brave, courageous warrioress. Men regularly turn to a male version of this self quite often, but we do not.

As women, we have few mythical or fictional heroines to emulate who embody qualities of power, strength, courage, and risk taking. Typically when women are presented as powerful in Western mythology and fiction, it is within a very "feminine" construct—nurturing, seductive, beautiful, and fertile (Venus, Mother Earth, Eve, Cleopatra, Scarlett O'Hara); or young, innocent, and nonthreatening (Persephone, Echo, Juliet, Cinderella). Another type of powerful woman is depicted as saintly, beyond reproach, guardian of all that is pristine and unsullied in life: the Virgin Mary, Athena, Saint Joan, Mother Teresa, Snow White. A third set of powerful mythical or fictional female characters threatens the traditional

---

* For my more fanciful readers. She is my personal favorite.

male-female power structure and so must be depicted as evil—Lady Macbeth, the Wicked Witch, the Evil Stepmother, sometimes even Mother Nature herself (as in "It's not nice to fool Mother Nature").

These personae, though acceptable to our society, are limited and insufficient to mentor us through the full range of experiences that will be presented in our lives, particularly if we are out there taking risks or coping alone without men (or even *with* men, now that I think about it). Anyway, it is strictly to our advantage to give greater attention to the strong and powerful Warrior/Huntress, such as Artemis, also known as Diana, Goddess of the Hunt, and, of course, the great Amazons of myth and legend.* It is time to call forth these myths of the fearless Warrior/Huntress so that we may develop our calmness and our clarity in the face of risk and/or danger.

Let us consider for a moment the nature of a warrioress. Her most salient feature is that she has purpose in the face of danger. She *acts*. She does not cower. She does not wait to be rescued but meets the challenge head-on. She has clarity of vision, for her aim must be true lest her bow tremble as the danger approaches, the arrow miss its mark, and the Huntress be slain. She is therefore utterly present and authentic in the moment, meeting danger and conflict with full awareness and poise.

As with all mythological figures, the Warrioress resides within. She symbolizes one facet of female potential often overlooked, but she is not dead or even sleeping. She is waiting. We can ask for her help as mentor, teacher, protector. We can use her as a role model. We can borrow her shield and her sword until we have our own.

This is not as childish as it may at first seem. Who among us has not, at least unconsciously, called upon the Seductress or the Great Mother within? We unconsciously embody these myths all the time, so why not add another? The trouble is, we are just not accustomed to doing so on the conscious level, so at first it may feel a little silly to practice it more deliberately.

Usually we are in the habit of turning to men to protect us, but lately they seem to be the ones we often need protection from! When we purposefully embody the characteristics of the Great War-

---

* Unfortunately, during the women's movement in the sixties, the Great Warrior/ Huntress became associated with being a man-hater. This is an inaccurate portrayal.

rioress, we honor and enthrone a sleeping archetype—*a female protector of females*, like Jodie Foster in *The Silence of the Lambs* or Susan Sarandon in *Thelma and Louise*.

The next time you face a dangerous or risky situation, call up from within the Great Warrior/Huntress to come to your aid just as you call from within the Great Mother to nurture the ones you love. You will be surprised to discover she actually *does* live within you and will grow stronger and more potent with your commitment to give her life.

Act on that commitment by honoring her spirit within you and within all females. Use the following suggestions to ignite your creative imagination and bring into being your version of the Great Warrior/Huntress:

- Incorporate her as a character into one of your scenes or plays.
- Draw her. Costume her.
- Write a children's story about her for your daughter. (Okay, for your son, too, but especially for your daughter.)
- Do a photographic study of women you see on the street who radiate the qualities of strength, courage, and determination that remind you of her. (I'm doing this one myself.)
- Imagine whom you would cast in the part of the Great Warrior/Huntress if you were making a movie.
- Write a poem about her strength and courage.
- Write a song about her.
- Act the part. Walk like her, talk like her.
- Read myths and legends about her.

By doing these activities, you will begin to give expression to this new self. Gradually learn to see yourself emulating her courage and purposeful action in the face of danger. Cultivate within yourself the qualities of her character you admire the most and gradually embody these qualities in your own life.

CHAPTER 10

If the Buddha Had Been a Shrink: Mastery, Meditation, and the Eastern Half of the Equation

> With all its eyes the creature-world beholds the open. But our eyes, as though reversed, encircle it on every side, like traps set round its unobstructed path to freedom.
>
> We've never, no, not for a single day, pure space before us, such as that which flowers endlessly open into. . . .
> —RAINER MARIA RILKE

We humans are in a strange predicament arising from a condition that is at once unsettling, ironic, and comical. You see, unlike animals, who have awareness in present time only and are therefore capable of existing moment to moment without fear or doubt, we, on the other hand, have awareness of the future, as well as awareness of our awareness. This is just enough awareness to make us paranoid but not enough to liberate us from our fears and helplessness.

The natural human tendency, when faced with fear, doubt, or helplessness is to cling to that which is familiar and resist that which is not. To the Eastern mind the fact that this is a natural tendency does not necessarily make it good. In fact, Eastern philosophies tend to see natural human reactions as somewhat wild, fearful, and aggressive. Fortunately they also see the human mind and its emotions as highly trainable and have developed very effective techniques to train the mind to react with greater clarity and awareness in the face of danger, risk, or change.

Meditation is one of these techniques that, over time, develops calmness, clarity, and vision. In other words, it develops mastery-oriented behavior. If the Buddha had been a shrink, he would have counseled meditation as a means of coping with our fears; opening the concept of a single, unchanging self; developing courageous nonresistance to the flow of change—one more tool in achieving mastery behavior.

Meditation, as a practice to be developed, is highly practical. As you will see in the discussion that follows, meditation teaches the very skills that are demanded in the process of moving from LH to mastery-oriented risk taking. Regular practice of meditation will train you to do the following:

- Witness unfolding events or passing thoughts and emotions without becoming attached to them or fearfully resisting them. In this way your witnessing awareness is developed and you learn to observe and correct, rather than to judge and condemn. Eventually, with practice, one learns to do this not only during formal meditation but in the flow of events in everyday "waking" life.
- Tolerate intense emotions without caving in, backing off, or going numb. This is critical to risk-taking behavior if one is to learn new skills, adapt positively to new environments, cope with unforeseen events, and accept a new self-image.
- Stop the internal chatter of all the voices vying for attention, so that calmness and clarity can be achieved, even in the midst of chaos and confusion.

In other words, meditation is both the means to experiencing inner peace and the desired end itself, so that we may rejoice in that pure space before us, "such as that which flowers endlessly open into," so that we may grow and be taught by our experience instead of fearfully resisting and getting stuck in helpless behavior patterns.

I am well aware that, to some of you, the mere mention of meditation seems like the first step on the road to disseminating Hare Krishna materials at the airport, or conjures up visions of half-starved, naked yogis sitting cross-legged somewhere on the other side of the globe who certainly have nothing to do with you. Furthermore, isn't meditation part of New Age thinking? Isn't New Age thinking responsible for this bizarre world of movie stars who write best-sellers about past lives and journey halfway around the world to meet aliens who drive Jeeps? Of ancient beings with one-word names speaking to large audiences from across the millennia with messages of salvation? Of workshops designed to alter the original birth experience for full-grown adult humans? Of color therapy, sound therapy, aromatherapy, vitamin therapy, rolfing, channeling, and vision quests? It is no wonder that middle America has reacted somewhat suspiciously to what is referred to as New Age thinking.

Personally I think New Age thinking runs the gamut from sophisticated hucksters hawking miracle snake-oil cures to genuine, merciful healers and teachers striving with compassion to lessen the suffering of others. Of course the problem is how to tell the difference. Personally I believe in the test of time.

You should be aware that much of what is called New Age thinking is not new at all. Many concepts being brought to contemporary life in the West, on both a scholarly and a practical level, have been around for a very long time. That, for me, is a recommendation in itself. Meditative techniques that have come to us primarily from the East are not New Age, but rather ageless, are thousands of years old in fact, and are designed to deal with the very real issues of courage and fear, mastery and helplessness, success and failure, life and death. These ancient techniques have been "market-tested" by thousands of individuals over centuries of practice and refined to intellectually rigorous degrees by brilliant and compassionate teachers.

Remember that the Eastern techniques presented here represent only one-half of the equation for overcoming LH: the half that is necessary to metabolize the stress inherent in change and to counter the interpretation that life between the trapezes (risk and change) is frightening and unpleasant. Hopefully you will use the meditative techniques in conjunction with and as complementary to the more traditional Western techniques that are offered as well.

In this way you as a woman-in-transition are provided with the behavioral tools to get from point A (helplessness) to point B (mastery) and the inner equilibrium to undertake the journey.

THE PARADOX OF NONRESISTANCE

Much of meditational technique involves nonresistance. This may seem strange. After all, the admonition to go with flow, to move along with the current of change, to be accepting of whatever your experience is presenting, is advocating a form of passivity, another form of, God forbid, helplessness. Your old helpless self, with its either-or habit of thinking, says, "Well, if it's not this, it must be that; if I am not resisting, I must be acquiescing," as though there were only two options available.

To the Eastern mind nonresistance does not lead to acquiescence, nor does it lead to passivity, lethargy, or apathy. Going with the flow allows an ample degree of latitude in the realm of action, perhaps even more than resisting does. It means continued activity and cheerful striving *within* the context of what *is* rather than what we would like it to be. Besides, we can never get it to be what we would like it to be until we deal with it as it *is*. Now, doesn't that seem mastery-oriented to you?

The martial arts, for example, teach the Eastern approach of going with the natural flow of energy rather than resisting it. The highly skilled practitioner does not resist the energy of his opponent but utilizes it. Now, no one would dare to imply that martial artist Bruce Lee was helpless because he consented to the flow of energy. No one would ever accuse him of acquiescing. No one would even suggest that he was unable to influence the final outcome of events.

Although I speak somewhat facetiously, the point should not be lost. Ironically, the highly skilled martial artist is mastery-oriented (we even call him a master) *because* he has learned nonresistance, learned to use his energy skillfully rather than deplete it by resisting forces stronger than his own. He stays highly attuned to the demands of the situation in which he finds himself and is able to act mindfully and with awareness. The higher the awareness level, the greater the skill of the practitioner.

Like the martial artist, we can become aware and learn to use the energy flow of any situation to sustain us. When we call some flow of energy negative—for example, fear (remember the trapeze act?)—we either try to stop it or become helpless in its grip. Instead we must learn how to use the energy that is there without judging what *kind* it is.

For example, as Thich Nhat Hanh* says, most of us judge the wilting and decay of a bouquet of spring flowers as a bad thing. After all, flowers are lovely and desirable, garbage is ugly and unpleasant. Decay reminds us of mortality. We judge the process of

---

* A Zen monk residing in the United States, an author and speaker who works with Vietnam vets and is active in the peace movement.

decay from flowers to garbage as negative and keep this process hidden from our view.

When we stand back, however, and look at the bigger picture, we discover many things. We see that garbage and flowers are not separate. The seed destined to become the flower will make good use of the garbage. With the passage of time the flower, too, will become garbage, which, when put to use with sunlight and water, will again become a flower. We see that, when treated with equanimity, flowers and garbage are part of the same process of change.

Judging the process with human biases only stops its flow. We don't have to hate the garbage for not being a flower any more than we have to hate the flower for its potential as garbage. We can learn to take them in the flow of time and to let each be in its turn. The flow of energy between flower and garbage is part of a perfect cycle of change, one infinitely larger and more powerful than the narrow demarcations of good or bad, beautiful or ugly, placed upon them by humans with preconceptions and expectations.

When we insist that life be perpetual flowers, we deny the greater reality of process, flow, and change. By resisting situations that do not always fit our expectations or are risky and unpredictable, we miss the opportunity for growth, change, and transformation. Anger, grief, and fear are no more to be resisted than garbage. Like garbage, they are part of a bigger picture and can, over time, produce infinitely beautiful flowers. Anger can be transformed into clarity of action, grief into compassion for self and others, and fear into exhilaration and self-confidence.

That there are forces of risk and change greater than we, forces that are unresponsive to human needs, values, and desires, no one would deny. Some of them are quite destructive, by human standards. A tornado, for example, couldn't care less about my house or my property, my fear or my helplessness. Furthermore, it is simply too omnipotent a force to resist or control. Does that fact, then, render me utterly helpless within the realm of dealing with a tornado? No. I still have power to influence the outcome of events. Although I may be unable to save my property, I can probably save my life by acting skillfully and in accordance with the demands of the situation in which I have found myself, *if* I am aware and mindful (Eastern terms for mastery-oriented).

Mastery-oriented behavior does not ensure that things will always turn out the way you want them to. A spouse, determined to leave, will not likely be persuaded to stay. A corporation, downsizing its work force, will lay off workers. Aging will carry on its relentless process. The garbage will take a certain amount of time to transform into flowers, and a tornado will act like a tornado.

So, if we can't control most events and we can't control most people, what is the purpose of nonresistance to change in order to become mastery-oriented? The purpose is not control. The purpose is transformation. Like the alchemist referred to in the previous chapter, we can transform ourselves, and our perception of and attitude toward risk and change, from the base metal of helplessness to the gold of mastery. We can live more creative and less fearful lives, develop skillful action, turn garbage into flowers, and save our lives in the midst of a tornado.

Paradoxically, then, acceptance of what *is* (nonresistance) provides greater clarity in action and calmness in adversity. Observation and acceptance of the flower-to-garbage process of change enables us to utilize the energy at work for growth and development. Nonresistance to the omnipotence of the tornado enables us to act with greater clarity in its force. Brilliant and compassionate teachers from the East have determined over many thousands of years that meditation is the vehicle that teaches the very difficult process of nonresistance. Nonresistance paradoxically teaches mastery-oriented behavior. Just ask Bruce Lee. Just smell the flowers.

THE TASTE OF BLUEBERRIES

Before a more thorough look at the how-tos of meditation, it is important to mention a few difficulties inherent in this discussion. You see, explaining meditation is a little like trying to explain the taste of fresh blueberries. Some things must be experienced. One can say, "It is like this or like that," but the words do not convey the sensory experience, the multilevels of perception, sensation, and feeling that are activated when one actually takes a bite—the puncture of the delicate, little dumpling and the burst of blue exploding like tart pyrotechnics in your mouth. Using language to describe experience is what the Zen teachers mean when they say, "The finger pointing at the moon is not the moon."

Like experience itself, the nature of the knowing that flows from meditation defies traditional language systems to describe it. Some descriptions of meditation require references and phrases that are metaphorical in nature or can only be apprehended through the skillful application of your own intuitive mind. Therefore, if descriptions of meditation seem vague or confusing, do not be dismayed or try to analyze them logically. Just go with the flow of your intuitive apperception and you will acquire the truth of what is being said. Having said that, it may be useful at this time to explore the nature of meditative awareness.

Each of us has experienced fleeting moments in our lives when we were utterly aware; that is, utterly nonresistant to the flow of experience, utterly present in the moment, and utterly free of self-consciousness. It happened for me one day while practicing the piano. Concentrating on a difficult passage, which I played over and over again, I glanced at the clock, thinking maybe twenty minutes had passed. I was astonished to discover that two hours had gone by! I had been so absorbed in my efforts that time, or my concept of it at any rate, had shifted.

It was a consummate nonresistance to the demands of the pure moment that created this opening during which my usual measurements of reality were allowed to disintegrate. I wasn't thinking about what else I had to do or who around me might resent the two hours of attention I was giving to practicing. But it was not forgetfulness in the negative sense of carelessness or even reverie. The dissolution of conventional reality that happened as a result of my single-pointed concentration was in no way frightening or confusing, but liberating and tranquil.

Such a moment is often referred to as a peak experience, but it can also occur in the realm of the common. Fortunately, it is thoroughly human and easily recognizable: effortlessly swaying to the metered tempo of a favorite song, devoid of thought, allowing the body to feel the rhythm; synchronizing one's movements with the cadence of a galloping horse, merging into a single entity moving through space; skillfully responding without thought during a crisis, expertly dodging the speeding vehicle that has swerved into your lane. The perfect run down the ski slope. The perfect lob on the tennis court. Making love. Giving birth. Allowing the body to do what it already knows how to do.

These moments utterly integrate and unify the nouns and verbs of experience, until there is no separation between me and what I am doing. In other words, it is a type of nonresistance, a type of nonthinking during activity. It is doing rather than thinking. Athletes and musicians may wax rapturous about this experience or just sort of take it for granted as part of their sport or art whenever they perform well. In the words of Yogi Berra, "How can you think and hit at the same time?" Or O. J. Simpson: "Thinking is what gets you caught from behind."

Meditation, then, is the technique that trains the mind to bring this integrated, calm, nonresistant, yet alert and energized state into the waking world, the world of conventional consciousness and ordinary reality. It is the technique that allows the sunlight of clarity so necessary to mastery-oriented behavior to shine through the clouded state of partial awareness created by LH.

Meditation simply teaches one how to be still. It is often referred to as sitting practice and is aptly named, for it is exactly that: One learns how to sit, to do nothing, not even wait. One does not fantasize, problem-solve, worry, or plan. One simply sits. This sitting is not dazed or sleepy but alert, aware, and fully conscious of the uniqueness of each moment that passes before the screen of energized, mirrorlike consciousness. *It teaches us how to let go of the content (drama) of our minds and to observe the process instead.*

This strikes many Westerners as absurd. Why would anyone want to sit and do nothing, not even daydream? Furthermore, we can hardly imagine such a state. It seems zombielike to us. This is because Western culture has no context for, nor do we place value on, learning to be still. Our culture demands that we be doing *something*. "Idle hands are the devil's playground" and all that. (Even prayer is usually another form of making noise wherein we talk to God stating what we need or desire.) Yet it is in stillness that the silence is created in which to *hear* God. Therefore the first thing Westerners must do to cultivate calmness and clarity is to learn to value sitting and doing nothing for a brief period each day. Not planning, not making lists, not rehashing the past or worrying about the future, not replaying content over and over again.

Some meditation instructors suggest the following analogy as a way of understanding the benefit of a totally nonactive, perfectly still period each day: Imagine aliens have landed on our planet. They are very industrious but seem quite exhausted, and you learn that they do not sleep. When you suggest to them that sleep would bring great benefits, they reply, "What? Just lie in one place for eight hours and do nothing? How ridiculous!"

Over time and with practice this capacity to be utterly aware of, present in, and nonresistant to the moment can be brought into even the most stressful of circumstances. It creates the pause in which the correct act, perfectly in sync with the moment, is born; the silence in which the correct word is spoken. It fosters courage in the face of adversity. In short, it enables one, over time, to practice and develop mastery-oriented behavior.

Furthermore, it not only helps one to reach the goal sometime in the future, but it helps relieve the present-time stress created by a changing self-concept. In other words, meditation is both the end and the means to that end. Meditation, then, facilitates change by reducing the stress of change.

When we are nonresistant, there is no self separate from change to protect. We *are* change. In other words, change in circumstances, change in self—they are the same. There is no point in resisting, for since we are *part* of the ever-changing universe, change is the nature of our personal reality as well. It is like the somewhat overused, but perennially pertinent life-as-a-river analogy.

Resisting the flow of a river is exhausting, for the energy of the river is far greater and longer lasting than the energy of the individual. Becoming one with the river (change), however, experiencing no separateness from its flow, allows one to be buoyed up and carried along by its tremendous energy and even improves one's chances of survival. It does not guarantee survival, mind you, just improves the odds. (There are no guarantees.)

It is true that the river may, on occasion, smack you into a tree limb. You may get bruised and battered. However, once you are in the river, which you already are if you're alive, it's too late to resist. Going with its flow is far easier and more mastery-oriented. Sometimes the river may lose depth and momentum and you may find yourself in a stagnant little dried-up tributary awaiting the rising of the river to carry you back into the main current. That doesn't mean you must sit dejectedly by the stream, hating it because it's not a river. You can keep yourself happily occupied by exploring your surroundings, making a comfortable resting-place, and taking care of yourself until the river naturally swells again. You could build a boat for when that time comes or even plan a way to hike out. The point is passivity, lethargy, or depression need not necessarily be the outcomes of nonresistance.

Another prevalent myth is that meditation is always a relaxing and soothing experience. Sometimes it is, sometimes it isn't. Meditation is not always easy, nor is it always bliss. On the one hand, it unquestionably improves the quality or feeling tone of one's life. It helps one attain greater calmness and clarity. As a meditation teacher once told me, "Meditation is about developing strength of mind." On the other hand, it can be a disquieting experience, full of agitation and unusual, possibly transformative revelations. In the words of two masters,

> Meditation is not a matter of trying to achieve ecstasy, spiritual bliss or even tranquillity; nor is it attempting to become a better person. It is simply the creation of a space in which we are able to expose and undo our neurotic games, our self-deceptions, our hidden fears and hopes.
> (CHOGYAM TRUNGPA, *The Myth of Freedom*)

> During zazen [seated meditation] brain and consciousness become pure. It's exactly like muddy water left to stand in a glass. Little by little, the sediment sinks to the bottom and the water becomes pure.
> (TAISEN DESHIMARU, *Questions to a Zen Master*)

Life will continue to be life, of course. The washing machine will still break down the day your entire family arrives for a two-week holiday. The car will still stall on the interstate during rush hour. It will rain on picnic day. It is unrealistic to expect problems to disappear altogether. But with a concerted effort to meditate regularly, over time, you will develop the *clarity of mind* to deal with your problems *as they are*, with greater mastery and with less wear and tear on your nervous system. In the words of yet another master,

> [Meditative] clarity allows you to see the factors that determine your choices from moment to moment. You don't have to think about it to grasp all this. . . . With no effort your response is optimal on all levels, not just mechanically reactive on one.
> (RAM DASS, *Journey of Awakening*)

DIFFICULTIES IN MEDITATION

I feel that it is helpful to point out early the difficulties commonly encountered when an individual first begins a sitting practice. This is because individuals with LH will have a tendency to conclude that any difficulties are a reflection of their own personal inadequacies, whereas in truth all meditators encounter similar difficulties. Those with LH will tend to believe that, for everyone else, meditation is easy and simple. For this reason I have chosen to discuss some of the common frustrations of meditating *before* discussing the actual technique itself.

The first time you sit down to meditate, to be quiet and still inside, not to think or plan, worry or ponder, hope, wish, or dream, you may be surprised at how resistant the mind is to just being quiet, at how quickly your thoughts will career off in a thousand directions, at how incredibly noisy your chattering intellect becomes. Sometimes, for example, your thoughts will feel dangerously out of control, tearing around helter-skelter. Other times they will just quietly meander off down some path, taking you with them, before you realize you are not being still but are unconsciously participating in old-fashioned thinking by planning or remembering or problem solving. Still other times your thoughts will appear to be happily leapfrogging around the pond of ideas just for the heck of it. Most often your chattering intellect will attempt to convince you that you should be trying to "figure things out" instead of just sitting there, quiet and still.

MONKEY MIND

There is a very apt Buddhist description of this resistance to stillness, this tendency of the mind to jump from one subject to another: monkey mind. The mind, like a restless chimp, bounces from one mental spot to another, without apparent direction or goal. The mind has great difficulty settling itself down and keeping still. Like a resistant monkey, it must be trained.

Furthermore, monkey mind pulls you off center, away from awareness with great speed. Monkey mind will inevitably create a lot of noise that causes distraction and confusion. In other words, the difficulty in concentrating on stillness for an extended period of time (a problem encountered by all meditators) turns out to be a characteristic of the human brain. It is simply the nature of ordinary mind to latch on to "things" and to enjoy leapfrogging from one thing to another. It is one way the brain entertains itself.

The first time I ever meditated, I felt bad afterward, acting in an LH manner by blaming myself for what I perceived to be a personal inability to concentrate. My teacher looked at me kindly and said, "How long does it take to get a Ph.D.?"

Not understanding what this had to do with meditation, I gave him a blank look.

He repeated his question, "How many years does it take to get a Ph.D.?"

"I don't know, maybe about eight or nine, all total."

"Right," he responded, "so you wouldn't expect to know everything at the beginning. You would expect to take many years before you understood. It is the same with meditation. Give yourself time to learn."

All that is necessary is thirty minutes and the rest of your life— thirty minutes in which to meditate daily and the rest of your life in which to hone your technique, reap the harvest of your efforts, understand the workings of your mind and how it keeps you trapped in old patterns, beliefs, and self-concepts. As Tom Robbins observes in *Even Cowgirls Get the Blues*, "If little else, the brain is an educational toy but it is a frustrating plaything—one whose finer points recede just when you think you are mastering them." The great truth of his statement must be appreciated in order to develop the willingness to cultivate meditation as a lifelong practice that becomes increasingly refined. It takes many years to become a highly skilled practitioner of nonresistant observation.

While meditation is not a religious practice, it does not have to exist separate from prayer or be in conflict with it. Indeed, many traditional Christian religions now teach a meditative type of prayer, one that involves quieting the mind and communicating with God in a way other than the traditional talking form of prayer. In the past these techniques of receiving God were thought to be an elite aspect of faith, reserved for mystics. As understanding and acceptance of Eastern practices grow, many denominations have incorporated these techniques into their more traditionally Western forms of prayer.

Granted, there are some religions that still view meditation as the work of the devil. Obviously meditation wouldn't be considered by those with such beliefs. It is rather for those who have experienced even just a glimpse of the possibilities welling up from within. Meditation liberates the space that allows this welling up to burst into consciousness.

Fortunately there are those who have persisted in the training of their monkey minds long enough to teach the rest of us how it is done. From these wise and venerable masters come wondrous teachings about how to practice serene, nonresistant awareness, both in the meditative state and in more conventional, ordinary-mind states as well. Some of these techniques are offered below. (For those who wish to pursue a sitting practice, and I heartily encourage you to do so, there are literally thousands of different techniques and many handbooks, guides, and teachers available. The following techniques represent the basics for beginners.)

HOW TO DO IT

All techniques of meditation fall into one of two basic categories: techniques involving *focusing* or *one-pointed concentration* and those involving *letting go* or *clearing*. While there are similarities between the two types, the first one is probably the most commonly practiced and best understood, so we will begin there. For beginning meditators, try the different types and stay with whichever one seems to be the best fit.

Meditation Exercise 1: "Counting and Breathing" (a focused or single-pointed concentration method)

Breath is life. But you already know that. Or do you? In the West we take breathing for granted. We do not think about it or pay attention to it or cultivate it unless something goes wrong. We breathe mindlessly. Furthermore, it seems absurd to take time out to practice something so natural.

In the East, however, breathing is not taken for granted. The breath is honored for its paramount and indisputable importance, its ability to connect mind with body. One learns, then, to breathe mindfully. Time is allotted (in the form of meditation) to become acquainted with the breath and its changing aspects—shallow and rapid in fear, deep and fluid in relaxation, and so on—and to appreciate, on increasingly refined levels, the variation and uniqueness of each breath within every moment. The practice of mindful breathing is both easy and profound—easy because it is so natural and profound because it develops subtlety, sensitivity, discrimination, appreciation, and awareness.

Start by unplugging the phone. Sit upright in a comfortable chair and close your eyes. Do not lie down; if you do, you may fall asleep.

This will probably happen on occasion anyway. Do not criticize yourself for it, but do try to avoid it. If you are extremely tired, you may just need to take a nap. Eventually you will discover that meditation, in itself, will be restful.

Now just gently "follow" your breath as it goes peacefully in and out of your body. Remember, you don't have to *try* to do anything. The body knows how to breathe and does so whether or not you are thinking about it. Your only task is to observe a process that comes naturally to the body.

Count at the end of each full cycle (one inhale, one exhale), until you reach ten full breaths. (Example: Inhale, exhale, one. Inhale, exhale, two. Do not verbalize the words *inhale* and *exhale*, only count inaudibly to yourself.) If your mind wanders, gently begin again. Simple, huh? Now go off and try it. If you are a beginner, sit for about ten minutes. (It's okay to open your eyes to glance at the time.)

How was it?

If you are like most people, you probably encountered the following things. You probably lost track of the numbers and got out of sequence. Your mind probably wandered off down arbitrary paths of fantasy or problem solving, or perhaps it got hyperactive like a scared little monkey and began screeching at you. Perhaps you fell asleep.

Gently avoid berating yourself for these mind meanderings. They are natural and common to all meditators. Remember, you are training monkey mind, and you should simply learn to recognize when monkey mind takes over. You may do this by simply observing and correcting. Observe by saying to yourself, "Thinking," when you catch your thoughts wandering off, and then correct by gently bringing your mind back to the object of your concentration—the breath.

When you label the activity of thinking in your mind, as described above, it is imperative to do so without judgment. Simply observe and correct the behavior *without commentary*. In other words, if you engage in an inner dialogue that goes something like this, "Oh, damn. There I go, I'm thinking again. What's the matter with me? Why can't I stop this? Why am I such a failure at something so easy? All I have to do is breathe, for God's sake. Okay now. I've simply *got* to get better at this. I'm going to force my thoughts to stay on track," you have now spent that much more time locked in conversation with the chattering intellect, conversing with your monkey mind.

Each time you fall into the habit of feeling bad or blaming yourself when your mind wanders, you have taken the bait. But don't criticize yourself for criticizing yourself! This kind of endless mind maze just perpetuates the clouded thinking of LH and will frustrate all efforts to cultivate clarity and serenity. Simply refuse to converse with monkey mind on any level.

When your monkey mind does its thing, just gently but firmly correct it and bring it back to observing the breath. Eventually this habit you are developing, that of observing and correcting, will become more natural, and you will be able to use it in a similar manner when observing and correcting the behaviors of LH, without engaging in endless judgment and blame.

Meditation Exercise 2: "Letting Go" (a clearing exercise)

This exercise begins in much the same way, but this time, instead of counting, simply watch. Watch the breath come in and watch the breath go out. This is more difficult to do, because there is no counting, no assignment to keep you on task, nothing for monkey mind to hang on to. In this exercise the mind tends to wander a little more. When it does, just observe and correct by bringing it back to the breath.

Remember, it's okay. The undisciplined nature of the mind is to wander, and since your mind has not been trained to be still, it will take practice. Again, when you discover yourself down some path of fantasy, emotionality, or intellectuality, just learn to observe it, correct it, and let it go.

Meditation Exercise 3: "Thought Clearing"

This is another exercise of letting go. Try each of the three different meditation exercises over a period of a week or so and see which one you like the best.

Prepare your environment (no phones, etc.). Then simply close your eyes and let go of all thought. There are many ways to do this: Let thought disintegrate into nothingness; or, stare at a blank screen; or, imagine your thoughts to be like steam, dispersing into the air and disappearing; or, like a mirage, watch them disappear the closer you get; or, turn down the volume of the voice chattering away until it cannot be heard.

When a thought comes, as you know it inevitably will, just note to yourself, "Thinking," as before, and then let the thought go. No need to resist it or cling to it. Simply note it and then let it go. Some thoughts, particularly those that are old or carry associations, have the power to grab you by the throat and drag you down the road for long periods of time before you even realize what has happened. You can still just peacefully let them go when you become aware that this happened once again. Remember, it is okay. It happens to everyone and for a long time.

A favorite allusion used to instruct meditators in the art of letting go is that of the ocean and its movement. The surface may seem to be in varying degrees of turmoil, from gently rolling waves to vast, dangerous swells. Beneath the surface, however, in the depths, all is calm and still. During meditation, when unbidden thoughts come, think of them as waves on the surface of your mind. They come in, they go out. No need to hold on to them or resist them. Simply observe them as they come in and observe them as they go out, knowing that you may return to the calm, still, quiet place that resides below the surface turmoil.

This process teaches us how to monitor our thoughts (explanatory style) as if they are waves coming in and going out, without being helplessly swept away in the surface turmoil. In other words, not only does meditation develop the witnessing awareness, but it teaches that life can be lived from this tranquil, fluid place as well. The events of life will continue to roll on the surface, always threatening to make you helpless or fearful. There will be undertows and turmoil, perhaps even tidal waves and raging storms, but the comfort comes from knowing (that is, having had the actual experience rather than the intellectual exercise) that the still, blue, calm place of peace is always available.

This is not detachment in the true sense of the word, but rather it is another place, another perspective, from which to view the situation. You cannot detach from the events of your life any more than the depths of the ocean can detach from the ocean itself, but you can find a different space, a different vantage point, from which to observe it.

The wave analogy is a powerful metaphor for dealing with difficult emotions, such as fear and helplessness, and it teaches us the futility of trying to resist change. Happiness, sadness, anger, joy, fear, grief, love—all are the experiences of human life that will come and go, like waves on the ocean's surface. As assuredly as we experience one, we experience them all. As assuredly as one wave goes out, another will come in. There is always a new experience to take the place of the old. It is the very nature of being. We cannot stop this process, which is the very truth of life. Resisting it is resisting life.

Letting life live you opens you to the joys of mastering change so that you may grow and be taught by your experience, instead of resisting and getting stuck in helpless behavior patterns. Deborah let life live her in Rome, and Janet let life live her in her cabin in winter, and Darla let life live her in the high Himalayas, and all emerged from the process more highly evolved human beings.

Letting life live you allows your experience to form your beliefs rather than the other way around. Letting life live you allows for growth and change. Besides, most of the time you don't really have a choice. Meditating will teach you how to let life live you with less fear, helplessness, and gnashing of teeth.

LAST CHANCE

During that helpless period of my life when Ben went crazy, I was unable to summon the energy, stamina, or determination to do the book tour and go to Europe. I knew I needed help, not only to meet my professional obligations but to get through life. I thought drugs were the answer. I went to a doctor and asked for sleeping pills, pep pills, antidepressants, anything I could think of. He listened to my story and said, "Well, I could write you a bunch of prescriptions, but why don't you try meditating instead? If it doesn't help, you can come back and see me."

I took his advice, enrolled in an introductory class, and learned the art of meditation. It helped. I didn't need to return to the good doctor. He had already healed me.

Therefore, before leaving this section, I want to exploit my last opportunity to encourage you to establish a sitting practice (start with at least twenty minutes every day) to help you overcome LH and the fear of risk taking in whatever area of your life they are manifest. If you only read about meditating but never sit down to do it, it will always remains a fascinating model of intellectual concepts but will never progress to a lived experience—the only place where it can do you any good.

Remember, progressing from LH to mastery behavior is no easy task. There will be much standing in your way trying to persuade you that you are not adequate to the task—your own habits of thinking chiefly among them. Meditation is the most effective, nonviolent, gentle means available to train you to change those habits and to develop your strength of mind. It will ease you through the stress of experimenting with new behavior patterns. It will gently relieve the anxiety of a changing self-concept. Finally it will help you believe you can take risks, master change, and cope effectively with problems that have heretofore seemed overwhelming, and it will do so with greater clarity and less wear and tear on your nervous system.

CHAPTER 11

Tapping Into Creativity

If you want to be happy for a week, fall in love.
If you want to be happy for a year, get married.
If you want to be happy for a lifetime, cultivate a garden.
—OLD CHINESE PROVERB

Developing multiple strategies requires creative thinking. Unfortunately most of us have been taught a variety of myths about creativity that get in our way. These myths become part of our LH belief system and explanatory style. Getting rid of these myths, then, is the first step in developing creativity and the ability to generate multiple strategies.

First, creativity is not some "gift" the mastery-oriented have and you do not. It is natural to the human species and, if unfettered by the negative explanatory styles of LH, will murmur through ordinary human experience. If you doubt the truth of this, simply observe the behavior of children, who, as yet unsocialized to "correct behavior" or a belief in their limitations, think creatively and respond spontaneously.

Natural as creativity is to the human soul, however, its nature is elusive. To understand it, try imagining the flow of a waterway. Like water, creativity will swirl into small eddies of imagination, dive from summits of sudden insight, spill from quiet pools, and murmur through ripples of concentric ideas until even the models we use to describe it are washed away or worn smooth by relentlessly flowing streams of thought.

Though we cannot always control the flow of creativity, we can cup our hands to be nourished and refreshed by its presence. Or perhaps, as the Zen masters playfully suggest, we can go along for the ride, like a ball bobbing on the surface of a river. With this metaphor as our guiding principle, let us press on with the paradox of applying a concrete structure to this watery principle in order to make some sense of how we think and what this has to do with mastery behavior.

Most brain researchers agree that the creative process is a five-step affair, with many meanderings up and down the ladder during the process. The process is as follows:[1]

1. Awareness	There is a problem to be solved or an idea to be expressed or a new strategy to be developed or improved.	
2. Frustration	The usual, conventional ways are not working. Why not? Now what?	
3. Incubation	A silent, unconscious activity during which it seems like nothing is happening.	
4. Illumination	The *Aha!* experience, during which the solution is sent from unconscious mind to conscious mind.	
5. Verification	Testing and modifying the answer, idea, or strategy to make it work in daily life.	

I would like to begin by drawing your attention to steps 2 and 3, which are particularly problematic for those with LH. If you fail to understand their place in the process, that they are a thread in the weave of a fabric, these two steps can easily undermine your persistence.

First, all studies of creativity indicate that frustration (step 2) is an inevitable part of the process and that it emerges quite early. (Obviously if the usual way of dealing with the problem proved adequate, everything would stop right there.) The tricky part is learning to deal with frustration so that you derive maximum benefit from it. You must therefore see it as a signal and a cue—a signal that a creative rather than a conventional solution is required, and a cue to change strategies. The problem for those with LH is that they see it as a signal of their inadequacy and a cue to begin blaming themselves. They personalize what is a much larger, and really quite impersonal, process.

When you first become aware you are feeling frustrated, don't judge it or yourself. Explore it. See how it feels. It's like the visualization we did with the high-flying trapeze act. If you learn to suspend judgment about the actual physical sensation you call frustration long enough to tune in to your body, it is almost certain you will discover that frustration is a highly energized state. As long as you do not label this sensation as negative, you won't suppress it, and the energy will remain available to be alchemized into creativity, persistence, and enthusiasm.

Be mastery-oriented and indulge in some positive self-talk. Remind yourself that frustration is an indispensable part of creativity and really has nothing to do with your individual idiosyncrasies. Don't take it personally. To get yourself going, write the following affirmations:

- My frustration is a companion to my creativity. Everyone experiences it.
- Frustration is a friend, helping me to generate the energy I will need to persist in reaching my goal.
- I am using this energized state to generate ideas and focus my activities.
- I am transforming the energy of frustration into the energy required for persistence.
- I welcome the feelings of frustration as a sign that I am thinking creatively and participating in the process of change and growth.

Next allow me to draw your attention to Step 3, Incubation. This is an entirely unconscious process that evolves over time. It takes place on the right side of the brain and seems like a time during which nothing is happening. As such, this presents problems for those with LH, who again will be likely to explain this seeming lull in mental activity as a personal flaw, failing to acknowledge that it is an utterly predictable and indispensable part of the process.*

As you probably know, the human brain is divided into two

---

* Rainer Maria Rilke, the brilliant German poet quoted in the last chapter, endured an almost indescribable incubation period, which would have driven most of us over the edge. In the winter of 1912, while walking on a rocky beach beneath a castle in Trieste, he heard a voice speak the first line of a poem. He rushed back to the castle to write it down. The first half of his great work *The Duino Elegies* was thus begun. Ten years of distressing silence were to pass before the voice came to him again, giving birth to the second half of this monumental work.

hemispheres, left and right. The left side is the rational, businesslike, serious, logical, sequential, competent manager of your daily affairs. It will have no truck with anything it considers frivolous or unnecessary. The right brain is the intuitive, intricate, pattern-perceiving, metaphor maker. Both—and this is important—are capable of high-level, complex problem solving; both contribute mightily to your survival and to the quality of life itself.

Unfortunately, most of us, due to a cultural bias for left-brain thinking, allow our left brains almost total dominance, pooh-poohing activities designed to access the right brain as silly, stupid, frivolous, childish, and so on. This is a grave mistake, as the left brain is utterly incapable of innovation. It is the right brain, with its rich tapestry of ideas, its complex weave of relationships, its powerful images, and its ability to think metaphorically, from which the creative ideas and the elegant solutions will come.

Therefore, do not be one of those people who licenses your left brain to walk with hobnail boots all over the delicate and intricate patterns of your right brain. Permitting your dominant left brain to judge and eliminate a process it can't even understand is like judging sleep to be bad because you can't see the point in doing nothing for eight hours.

Speaking of sleep, dream time is an example of a state of mind during which your left brain is inactive and at rest while your right brain is quite active. Without the vigilance of the left brain to police the content of the right brain, thinking takes on a free-floating and refreshingly spontaneous aspect, offering up themes, relationships, and characters usually inaccessible to the conscious mind. Dreams, a right-brain activity, have been reported as the source of many inventive breakthroughs, even in the ultra left-brain world of science and technology.

Meditation accomplishes the same thing as sleep, providing time during which the inner self may emerge in an atmosphere refreshingly free of judgments. This is why meditation can be such a boon to creative thinking and strategy development. It trains one how to silence the left brain and suspend judgment long enough for the right brain to take over and reveal its elegant solutions. Perhaps this is why meditation has been called waking sleep.

Finally, remember that creativity will have its own weird timetable, one that will be utterly indifferent to clocks, deadlines, and human schedules. Strategies requiring creative thinking must simmer on the back burners of the mind (in the mysterious recesses of the right brain) before they present themselves to conscious, left-brain mind. Therefore, patience and trust, even when you feel dried up, is of the utmost importance.

WHAT TO DO WHEN FRUSTRATION SETS IN

1. Don't personalize an impersonal process by indulging in self-blame. It happens to everyone.
2. Write affirmations to help you appreciate the energy of frustration and its place in the creative process. (See earlier affirmations on pages 141 and 142 in Chapter 8.)
3. Reread the description of the creative process.
4. Allow the energy of frustration to exist. Don't judge it or resist it. Explore it. Channel it.
5. Meditate daily.
6. If possible, allow plenty of time for strategic planning and creative thinking. Don't expect all the solutions to come immediately.
7. Trust yourself.

Remember, the process of generating multiple strategies will require you to: Break through old boundaries of thought and action, make new associations and see new relationships in old ideas, and utilize the imagery of the creative right brain. Following are some examples of how others have changed their thinking to become more creative.

CREATIVITY EXPLANATION 1: BOUNDARY BREAKING

Over dinner and wine one evening I began discussing this section of the book with two good friends of mine, John and Lenore, both of whom are university professors, she in communications and he in sociology. I was discussing with them ways to present an explanation of boundary breaking in an everyday setting, rather than as a dry, academic sort of treatise. They looked at each other conspiratorially.

Finally Lenore said, "Have we got a couple of stories for you."

"A couple?" John asked, eyebrow raised.

"You know," she answered, "you and the elevator zombies."

"Right," he countered, "but what is the other one?"

"Me and the homicidal matinee maniac," she replied.

"Oh yeah." And they both burst out laughing.

"Um . . . excuse me," I replied, pouring them more wine. "What are you talking about and, more important, can I use it in my book?"

"Sure," Lenore managed to blurt out, between fits of laughter. "You go first," she said to her husband.

John and the Elevator Zombies

"Well," he began, "I had just finished preparing my lecture for my freshman sociology class on norms and norm breaking when I was taken with a fit of rapture, what I thought was an extremely creative assignment. I decided to ask my students first to identify a norm within society and then to go out and break it. Finally they were to use their observations of the reactions of bystanders as a basis for a paper."

"Right," Lenore interrupted, unable to resist embellishing on the story, "but I told him that, although I agreed with him that it was a creative assignment, it was a risky one. So, I challenged him to try it out himself first."

Ever poised to take up the gauntlet, our stalwart professor gave his students a reprieve whilst pondered his choices. He seized an irresistible opportunity that presented itself the very next day.

"I was waiting for an elevator in a downtown office building during lunch hour. It was very busy. When the elevator arrived and the doors opened, I wasn't sure whether the elevator had enough space for another passenger, but everyone was politely shuffling around to make room for me, so I decided to wedge myself in."

Taking a sip of wine, he continued, "When the elevator doors closed, it occurred to me that this was a perfect norm-breaking situation. I mean, what's more of an unwritten social code than elevator behavior?"

"Step inside," I responded, taking my cue, "be quiet, and stare up at the floor numbers. What did you do instead?"

"I decided not to turn around and face the elevator doors, as you said. Instead I just stood there facing everybody—staring into their eyes, rubbing up against their bodies, violating their social space, our noses no farther than six inches away."

"What happened?"

"Well, the first thing I noticed was that the discomfort level in the elevator dramatically increased. Eye contact became agitated, and there was a lot of shuffling, shifting, and giggling."

"He had so much fun," added Lenore, "that now he's developed it into a kind of sociology experiment. He's done it numerous times now, and he's actually categorized people's reactions."

"People seem to fall into three basic types. The first type is just plain ticked off," John continued. "They are in no mood for my shenanigans and give me stern looks of parental disapproval, as if I am a recalcitrant child in need of discipline. Then there is a slightly more hostile subset of this group, who appear to be signaling me to stay out of their faces.

"The second group seems to be insecure. They're not exactly sure how to handle the situation, but their primary reaction is one of embarrassment. They can hardly bring themselves to look at me. They act as if I am an unbelievably naïve bumpkin, oblivious of the fact that I have made some sort of horrible social blunder. They stare at their feet, cough, and periodically glance up at me with quivering, timid smiles. Some even blush."

"They're probably embarrassed *for* you," I suggested.

"The last category of response is the antithesis of the first. This is the group that becomes waggish and frisky, wanting to participate in the little scenario themselves. In other words, they don't seem to care why it's happening or where it's going. They're willing to take a risk and eager to go along for the ride. They smile. They wave. They make funny faces at me and cross their eyes and stick out their tongues. They want to participate in and accelerate the norm-breaking process themselves. They get into creating what is almost like a little impromptu party."

Obviously there is no "right" way to respond. For our purposes, it is far more interesting simply to witness, without judgment, what the various reactions tell us about those involved. Some are vigilant in protecting a carefully constructed and rigid self-image of adult seriousness; some are watchdogs of propriety, avoiding risks and wanting to maintain the etiquette that acts as a social lubricant, promoting tension-free interactions with others; still others are risk takers, alert to opportunity and eager for a new experience.

The most impressive thing for our purposes is the *effect* of this boundary breaking, which really amounts to forced risk taking. It matters not whether the boundary breaking is theirs or someone else's. As their safe world unexpectedly loses its predictability, those involved are compelled (ready or not) to wake up. Everyone suddenly becomes alert and attuned to the zen of the moment, usually without even being aware they have done so.

You see, before our friend John enters the elevator, the passengers are standing there anesthetized, an elevator full of somnambulists, dozing behind their wide-eyed, vacant stares. Suddenly the elevator zombies find themselves in a situation without behavioral guidelines. As the forced risk taking takes over, the adrenaline starts flowing, the animation level becomes more pronounced, and everyone comes alive. Forced to respond in ways that are not predetermined by social sanctions, their reactions are highly individualized, spontaneous, and honest.

Though some readers may find John's behavior kind of silly, its value lies in its potential as a wake-up call. (Besides, *silly* is just the kind of word the left-brain loves to employ in order to dismiss the more lighthearted nature of right-brain activity.) For that brief moment everyone in that elevator is alert, everyone is aware, everyone is fully present in the moment. It is not often that that kind of opportunity is presented in the routine of day-to-day life.

We can create the rare occasion to appreciate and participate in the moment—the only real place where life happens anyway *and* the only real place where we have the genuine opportunity to act with mastery and skill, by being willing to break boundaries of thought and behavior. In this way we not only learn to respond with awareness and alertness in present time, but we add a little zest to the grind of daily living and learn to become mastery-oriented in the process.

"Now tell her your story," John said. Then, turning to me, he added, "I turned the tables on her and challenged her to do the same."

"Did you do it?" I asked Lenore.

"Well, since norms and boundaries of behavior are part of my field too," she said, smiling, "how could I refuse?"

Lenore and the Matinee Maniac

"It was an idle, wintry Tuesday afternoon at about two o'clock," she began. "I was bored and decided to take in a matinee, but I felt guilty about goofing off, since we all know that responsible, hard-working adults are not supposed to take off in the middle of the week to catch a movie.

"Anyway, since I live in a small college town and could easily bump into someone I knew, I decided to wear a hat to hide my identity.

"I got to the theater, purchased my ticket, some popcorn and a soda, and slunk into the movie theater. The movie hadn't started yet, and the theater was completely empty except for one guy seated right in the center. Well, I just couldn't resist."

"You sat right next to him?" I asked breathlessly.

"No, it's worse than that," volunteered her husband. "Guess where she sat. Right in the middle of this empty, cavernous theater, she plunked herself down directly in *front* of him! And with that hat on, no less," he chuckled, obviously taking great delight in his wife's chutzpah.

Now, there's a boundary-breaking risk taker. Here she was, alone in an empty theater with a guy who, in all probability, was con-templating how much time he could get off for good behavior or whether the jury would buy a temporary insanity plea if he strangled her on the spot.

"What did he do?" I asked.

"Well, at first, he just sort of grumbled around in back of me, muttering to himself. Finally, in disgust, he started noisily rear-ranging his things and moved his seat to one down the aisle.

"I just couldn't help myself," she said apologetically. "I grabbed my popcorn and soda and, with hat firmly in place, I also moved down the aisle to sit directly in front of him again."

She stops her story briefly, she and John laughing as I register horror.

"Oh my God, what did he do?"

"This time, of course, he asked, in a less than pleasant fashion, just what I thought I was up to. 'Testing your tolerance for deviant behavior,' I responded politely. He gave me a blank look, so, with a big, silly grin on my face I added, 'This is a joke.'

"I watched his facial expression change as he processed the information. He went from homicidal maniac to, 'Oh, I get it. A joke. Well, okay, then,' and gradually worked himself into a little chuckle. Of course, he never thought it was as funny as I did, but he did allow himself to be amused."

Exercise 1: "Seeing Boundaries"

Entertaining stories, you say, but what has all this to do with mastery behavior?

The ability to strategize, to think creatively, to generate many potential options or avenues of thought and behavior, entails being able to break through old boundaries of thinking and acting—usually our own, but sometimes those of society as well. Either way, personally or socially, breaking boundaries requires the ability to take a risk.

I am fully aware that John and Lenore's behavior could be classified as possibly dangerous and certainly rude, as well as just plain silly. Obviously one must use judgment and not engage in the kind of boundary breaking that could get you killed. (If you live in a large or dangerous city, you may want to use more caution, since provoking strangers may lead to serious encounters.) The value of John and Lenore's stories, however, is that they exemplify ways in which we can all practice taking small risks and observing our own response.

More often than not, being willing to push through comfort zones and break old boundaries of thought and behavior in order to become mastery-oriented is difficult and challenging. But pushing through is important so that our experiences, indeed our very lives, are not circumscribed by old (helpless) concepts *and* so that we learn what it feels like to initiate change. Incorporating play, humor, and a light touch makes it so much less threatening to old, helpless mind, which will always be on guard and anticipating trouble. Learning how to break through boundaries with a light and playful attitude disengages the overly protective ego, prevents us from taking ourselves too seriously, and allows for curiosity and detached observation. By not clinging to old (translate: safe) methods, we liberate ourselves to test new boundaries and still enjoy the experiment.

Maybe some of the strategies you develop will be unorthodox. You may have to face the inevitable naysayers:

"Where did you get a crazy idea like that?"

"That'll never work."

"Oh, we tried that last year."

"There are no procedures for that."

"But you haven't got the money, education, experience, etc."

"But you're too old/young, tall/short, etc."

If you have creatively experimented with boundary breaking in a fun fashion, it will give you the tools to stay strong, even when the going gets more serious. So the next time you are talking with friends or sitting around during a coffee break with your co-workers, tell these stories and then suggest brainstorming the different social and cultural norms that are possible to break without actually being arrested.

This is more than just a silly exercise. First, if we are going to break through the boundaries of our current helpless beliefs and perceptions in order to become more mastery-oriented, we must learn to *see* those boundaries. Most of us live our lives adhering to hundreds, maybe thousands, of unwritten rules and regulations that govern how we perceive, feel, and act. We never think to question them, but then, why would we if we can't even see them?

The value of brainstorming with others about possible norms to break is that it identifies the boundaries that restrict our lives, rule our behavior, and set before us unconscious limitations and useless restrictions. Moreover, when we see the unwritten rules by which we live, we come to live more mindfully, consciously choosing which rules to observe and which rules represent nothing more than a cultural capitulation, one that can blind and bind you, like the helplessness aspect of femininity. After all, refusing to turn around and face the doors in the elevator will not get you arrested.

Finally, brainstorming norms to break is only the first step. It is imperative to go out there and try breaking a few. Though John and Lenore's experiences were not life altering, they provided training that would serve them well if and when it becomes necessary to push beyond old social and cultural comfort zones to reach a goal, change a behavior, or alter a self-image.

Exercise 2: "Pushing Through Boundaries"

First, make a list of some of the boundaries of behavior in your own life. Noodle around for ideas about boundaries you can playfully break. Start simple. Have fun. Remember, no one is forcing you to run right out and be wild and crazy or to alter your life forever (although you may decide to, and that's all right too). Just be curious and see what happens. Here are a few to get you started:

- Keep a set of Groucho Marx glasses in your glovebox. Put them on while driving home from work and wave to people at stoplights.
- Go to a party overdressed or underdressed (whichever makes you more uncomfortable).
- Walk or bicycle to work or the grocery store or take a different route.
- Take a different route *in* the grocery store. (I'll bet you get your cart and always proceed in the same direction.)
- On a slow day at the shopping center, make a statement by parking your car in the opposite direction indicated by those little diagonal lines intended to keep you "in line."
- Give up meat for a week.
- Buy an outfit that feels like a costume, something you would never wear normally. Buy several of them. Try them out in different situations and see how they make you feel.
- Volunteer at an AIDS center.
- Rearrange your furniture.
- Whistle in church.
- Spend some time with a person you would not normally spend time with.
- Roll down a grassy hill.
- Go without makeup for a day. (Or, if you don't normally wear makeup, do the opposite.)
- Steal a tulip from your neighbor's garden.
- Acknowledge a homeless person on the street with a cheery "Hello! How are you?" or, as Mitch Snyder suggested, offer to buy him or her a hot (or cold) drink or a meal.
- Wear mismatched socks or clashing colors.
- Burst out singing your favorite song while walking your dog in a public place.

- Be the clown for a kids' party or volunteer for a clown ministry at your church.
- Do a somersault, cartwheel, or headstand.

Although none of these suggestions will get you arrested (with the possible exception of stealing the tulip, though it's highly unlikely), I'll bet that most of them actually make you quite uncomfortable. That's the whole point.

If all you ever seek is freedom from discomfort or frustration, you will never develop the risk-taking behavior that teaches mastery. You will never be able to access creative thinking and develop the multiple strategies necessary to accomplish your goals. You will be even less likely to act on them. Ultimately, by continually seeking safety and/ or comfort, you take perhaps a greater risk, one that keeps you helpless and stuck in listless, unproductive, perhaps even miserable situations that may eventually preclude all possibility of change.

CREATIVITY EXPLANATION 2: MAKING NEW ASSOCIATIONS, SEEING NEW RELATIONSHIPS

The ability to form connections between formerly disparate entities, reconciling conflicting ideas or reassembling the old elements of a problem in a new way, can produce astounding results.

As an illustration of this approach and an interesting digression, allow me to present a few examples from the worlds of science and art. Johannes Kepler, a German astronomer and mathematician, described the motion of the planets as they revolve around the sun. Galileo, the renowned Italian astronomer, scientist, and contemporary of Kepler, clarified the motion of bodies here on earth. For years the principles thought to govern these two types of motion were regarded as different and separate. Along came Isaac Newton, whose idea that gravity could operate even over immense distances enabled him to see a new relationship, to fuse the theories of Kepler and Galileo and show that bodies in motion, whether in the heavens or on earth, are subject to the same laws.

Even the seemingly disparate worlds of science and art can combine (or recombine) to pioneer new visions. Witness the reaction of the Impressionist painters to a newfangled gadget known as the camera, which could capture the details of reality so much more accurately than the painter himself: They were inspired to relate differently to visual reality by presenting their "impressions" of the world.

This wondrous capacity to make new associations by synthesizing old ones must be consciously encouraged, however, because human minds tend to act like creatures of habit. Unless actively encouraged to synthesize and create change, our minds will continue to do what they have always done, until acted upon by *another force*. In encouraging our minds to make new associations and see new relationships (a critical component of developing multiple strategies), we must create the other force that will act on our perceptions and coax our minds into new streams of thought.

Exercise 3: "The Spider Web"

This technique is the first in a two-step process that coaxes new connection making.[2]

Begin with a circle in the middle of a page. Put the problem to be solved inside the circle. Now free-associate any ideas that come to you that are even remotely related to the problem you have placed in the center. Now is not the time to judge ideas but simply to generate them. When the ideas come, draw a spoke out from the circle and attach the idea so that it looks like this:

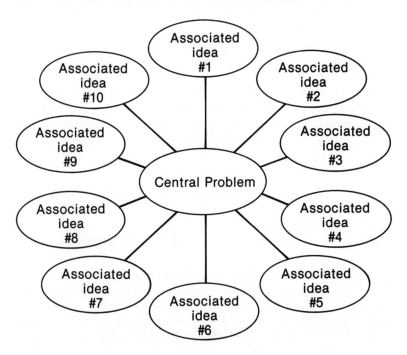

Next take some of your favorite ideas that are on the periphery of the web you have created and place each one, in turn, in the center of a new "spider web." Now free-associate as you did before, like this:

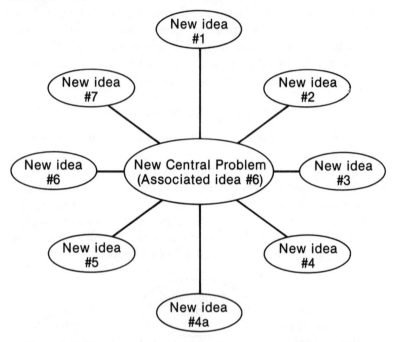

Keep doing this process until you have several spider webs with many connecting and associated ideas. Save all the spider webs you have created. Essentially what you have just done is to brainstorm with yourself—a great technique when there is no one around off of whom to bounce ideas.

Exercise 4: "Making a Mess"

Next cut out all the ideas that you have generated so that you have lots of little pieces of paper with your ideas written on them.*

---

* This is not just idle play. Educators have discovered that there are three primary learning styles: visual learners, auditory learners, and kinesthetic (touch) learners. By cutting your ideas out, playing with and manipulating them, you are giving yourself both a visual and a kinesthetic experience by providing time to "handle" the ideas and turn them over casually in your mind.

Arrange these scraps of paper in front of you in random order. Stare at them. On a separate piece of paper large enough for notes, write down the connections that are suggested by the pattern before you. When you feel you have exhausted the possibilities from that pattern, rearrange them and start all over again, jotting down the new connections that are present within the new pattern.

What you are doing is tricking yourself. By rearranging the ideas you have generated, you automatically create different visual patterns that suggest new connections—ones that might not otherwise have been made by your habit-bound mind. By visually creating new patterns among the pieces of paper, you are digging alternative trenches, so to speak, to carry new streams of thought to different places. With the pieces of paper in front of you, you coerce your mind out of its comfortable rut and coax it into seeing fresh relationships and making new associations.

This forced synthesizing not only activates innovative thinking, it will help you get ideas for developing alternate strategies when old ones cease to work. You can do this as many times as necessary. Remember, the right brain will not necessarily be functioning on a left-brain, nine-to-five schedule or according to falsely imposed deadlines, so give it time to synthesize the ideas and relationships that will help you develop multiple strategies.

CREATIVITY EXPLANATION 3: IMAGERY, THE LANGUAGE OF THE RIGHT BRAIN

One thing we have learned from brain research is that the left and right hemispheres speak different languages. The left brain (the businesslike side) uses traditional language (words) to process, understand, and communicate ideas. The right brain (the creative side) knows nothing of words. It uses an entirely different language system to process, understand, and communicate. It uses pictures.

Imagine, for example, an individual who has been brain damaged on the left side of her brain. If I were to hold up a ballpoint pen, that individual could not identify the object with words, that is, she could not retrieve the word *pen* from her left-brain memory banks. However, if I were to show that individual a series of items, one of which was another ballpoint pen, she could match the two ballpoint pens *and* use them for their intended purpose. This illustrates that the right brain does in fact think and solve problems and utilize elements of the environment to aid the individual in survival; however, its language is one of images and pictures rather than words.

Therefore, to communicate with the right brain and activate its creative potential, we must respect it by making an effort to speak its language. (There are a number of ways to do this, but first, remember the earlier warnings concerning the reluctance of the left brain to engage in these seemingly childish endeavors.)

The most common technique for accessing the images of the right brain is the popular dream journal, in which dreams are recorded upon waking. Without a concentrated effort, most of us lose the sophisticated material coming from our dreams. (As I mentioned earlier, the world of science is full of discoveries and solutions that were presented to a dreaming scientist—the discovery of the benzine ring, the structure of the DNA double helix, and the chemical proof of the mediation of nerve impulses, to name a few.)

Who knows how many solutions have been presented to us via the images in our dreams, only to be filtered out by an overactive left brain busily trivializing the images as unimportant or frivolous or merely as the "stuff dreams are made of" so that the information is never allowed to come to consciousness. When the left brain is literally put to sleep, however, the right brain is liberated to think freely, to present its ideas fresh and unrestrained.

Dream researchers realize, for example, that sometimes a desire for sleep that is not part of your regular nightly regimen, such as the desire for an afternoon nap, can really be a need to dream. Some creative idea trying to emerge from your right brain may be blocked by the "rational thinking" so dearly loved by your left brain. Acknowledge this and allow yourself dream time. It is not laziness or procrastination but sometimes the means through which your right brain is creating the silence to be heard.

Nearly all the creativity experts recommend recording dreams by keeping a notepad by the side of your bed. Personally this has never worked for me, because in a sleepy stupor the last thing I want to do is turn on the light and write something down. By the time I retrieve the pen, which always rolls under the bed, I'm wide awake. So, instead, I would tell myself to make a mental note and remember it in the morning. Of course you know what happens to those ideas.

Finally it occurred to me to place a tape recorder by the bed. Instead, I could vastly simplify things by mumbling something into the recorder in the dark. I play it back in the morning for further elaboration.

Exercise 5: "Draw the Problem"

If you have a problem for which the traditional methods of problem solving have failed to produce results, methods such as talking it over or writing down the pros and cons, it may be time to try something radically different. Try communicating with your right brain instead. Try "dreaming" your way to the solution. Here's how.

Begin by assembling some drawing materials—sketch pad and colored pens, crayons, or chalk. Put them together next to a comfortable spot, such as your bed or the couch. Put on some contemplative instrumental music or, better yet, play ocean-wave tapes, which are very relaxing. (Avoid music with lyrics, as these will engage the word-recognition performance of the left brain.) Unplug the phone. Get comfortable, close your eyes, and begin to talk yourself through relaxing your body from head to toe. (Avoid this exercise when you are already tired, or you may fall fast asleep instead.)

Next just visualize the problem. Suggest to yourself that you wish to "see" the problem. Be receptive. Allow all images to flood in. Reject nothing, cling to nothing. If you have trouble with the judging mind of the left brain (the Critic), tell yourself you will be like a mirror, which reflects all that passes before it without judgment. Allow the images to be whatever they are. Continue this process for a while. Don't rush it. (Remember, you can't push the river.) If your mind wanders, simply bring it gently back to the task at hand—visualizing the problem. Keep your visualization going for at least ten minutes.

When you feel you are done, calmly bring yourself back to conventional consciousness. Now, without speaking or interrupting the right-brain process you have begun, pick up a sketch pad and begin to draw whatever your right brain instructs your hand to do.

There are no formal instructions for drawing. You may find yourself sketching what you visualized, but not necessarily. This is not an art class, and you are not being graded, either for content or for quality. Whatever you produce is absolutely correct. It is immaterial whether what you produce is art. Your goal is to engage and communicate with the right brain, using pictures as the language the right brain understands.

If you produce a conglomeration of weird abstract shapes that appear to have no meaning, fine. If you draw a childlike, concrete representation of reality, no problem. If you are moved to create an extraordinarily detailed and colorful tableau, draw that. If you produce an ultrasimple black-and-white sketch, no problem.

Remember, no judgments. Judging, at this point in the process of creative thinking, is downright destructive. It is a left-brain activity, and we are attempting to communicate solely with the ideas of the right brain.

Each time the left brain insists on interjecting itself into the proceedings, telling you this is childish, silly, and a waste of time, simply reassure it that you will provide time *later* to judge, edit, and eliminate some of the ideas but that for now you are just gathering information. Do this exercise many times.

Finally, do not expect "The Answer" to unfold miraculously before you on the paper. Maybe it will, but then again, it probably won't. It is more likely that it will wake you up at three o'clock in the morning four days later or come to you while putting out the garbage or standing in the shower shaving your legs. Maybe you will have to repeat the exercise numerous times. The idea will present itself when it is ready. The key is to be receptive when the answer does come. And it will.

Above all, pay respect to your right brain by shining the light of awareness on the images it presents. Perform the mental exercises presented in this (and previous chapters) that allow the right brain to be nourished and heard. Coax it to release its visions by quieting the racket of the judgmental left brain. In this way you will enlist the help and active participation of your creative psyche in the development of multiple strategies—a powerful component in the mastery-oriented approach to life.

CHAPTER 12

Taking Your Act on the Road: Developing More Strategies

> The great end of life is not knowledge but action.
> —ALDOUS HUXLEY

Having been a public school teacher, I know that one of the reasons people have difficulty developing multiple strategies (and acquire LH) is that strategic thinking is a *process*, whereas public schools teach *content*. No one ever really teaches us *how* to think. Most of us acquire our thinking skills by osmosis. Ironically, though, it is process and not content that is critical to strategic thinking and mastery-oriented behavior. This chapter is therefore "action-oriented," that is, it deals with process, not content. It deals with verbs not nouns, since the mastery-oriented are those among us who take action.

WHO IS BENJAMIN BLOOM AND WHAT IS HE DOING HERE?

This chapter will explore the verbs (processes) of mastery behavior by looking at the work of a man named Benjamin Bloom who, in 1956, developed what is still the only good model we currently have for delineating the higher-level thinking processes (verbs) so necessary to mastery behavior.

Simply put, Bloom's taxonomy is a hierarchy of thinking skills. It begins with the easiest thinking skill (recall) and moves up the scale through progressively more complex and sophisticated levels to the most difficult level (evaluation).[1] It looks like this:

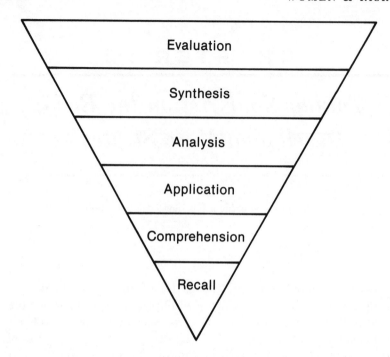

The bottom three levels are those at which public school education is focused and are fairly self-explanatory. The top three will be our focus, because they are the ones neglected in most of our educations and they are the levels of creativity critical to developing the multiple strategies characteristic of mastery-oriented risk takers.

We will look at each level in greater depth, but for now an overview will suffice. Briefly, then, at the level of analysis, the mastery-oriented individual breaks down the problem (idea, belief, behavior, object, or event) into manageable pieces in order to look at the individual constituents. At the next level, synthesis, the constituents filtered out during the analysis phase are put back together in *new* ways, in order to create new solutions (ideas, structures, patterns, inventions, etc.). Synthesis is the level of true creativity (see Chapter 11). Finally, evaluation is the last phase of strategic planning. It is the process of applying a criterion or standard of appraisal to the options that have been identified or the strategies that have been created.

Before discussing each level of thinking (analysis, synthesis, and evaluation), allow me to introduce you to Megan and Ruth, two women from my seminars who worked with the verbs of Bloom's taxonomy to solve their problems. You can track their progress to see ways in which they applied these levels to the solution of real-life dilemmas caused by LH.

Megan and Ruth

Megan is typical of the women in my workshops in that she displays mastery-oriented behavior in many aspects of her life but shows LH in others. A successful director of nursing at a major metropolitan hospital, Megan, a late-born only child of an older couple, felt particularly connected to and responsible for her partially disabled, seventy-five-year-old father. At thirty-four Megan's life revolved around the care and comfort of her dad, whom she adored, respected, and bitterly resented.

"I put in a pretty stressful work week at the hospital, usually over forty hours to meet our combined financial needs," she began. "Then, I spend my nonworking hours, if you call them that, living with and caring for my father. He is becoming less self-reliant each year.

"The bad part is that I have had to sublimate my dreams of travel and adventure to take care of him. I've always wanted to be a gypsy, really, to just pack my bags and see the world. One reason I chose nursing was because I figured it was a job that could travel. But I'm stuck taking care of my father." Then she added with embarrassment, "I feel like I'm waiting for my father's life to end so that mine can begin."

Ruth was an eighteen-year veteran of the public-school wars and was suffering, quite literally, from battle fatigue. She came home every night with a migraine but was dependent on her secure, if underpaid, teacher's salary to maintain the trappings of a middle-class lifestyle and to finance the education of her twin children nearing college age. She was further stymied in her desire to change careers by the belief that she was untrained (therefore unable) to enter any other field.

"I can't do anything but teach," she said with the finality of LH.

"I'm not trained for anything else. I'm getting too old to go back to school."

Ruth had lost her zest for teaching, a loss that was at the root of her feelings of helplessness and her reason for taking the seminar.

"In these last few years there's been no joy in my work," she told the group. "I've started to resent my students, which is a very bad sign. Now they've started to resent me back, our communication is poor, and the sense of purpose I used to get from teaching is gone."

"What about a sabbatical?" I suggested.

"I've already taken one. I don't have another one coming for seven more years. I'll be a basket case by then. I don't want to spend the rest of my work life longing for retirement and being one of those old, weirded-out teachers we all had in high school."

The manifestations of LH are evident in both of these women. Each endures an untenable situation because she believes she is helpless in the face of her particular circumstance. Furthermore, the belief that the problem is beyond her control has short-circuited any attempt at risk-taking or strategizing solutions.

At my urging, each of these women applied the levels of Bloom's model to her individual dilemma to study the problem cognitively. Starting at the level of analysis, we will look at how each woman worked with specific processes (verbs) to move from LH to mastery of her problem.

THE PROCESS OF ANALYSIS

Take apart	Categorize
List	Specify
Classify	Compare/contrast
Distinguish	Outline
Separate by . . .	Arrange
Sort	Organize

Remember, analysis is the level at which the mastery-oriented individual breaks down the issue or problem into manageable pieces in order to examine the parts. As you look closely at the list of verbs above, you will notice that each involves some sort of taking apart or manipulating of discrete, individual, distinct parts of the problem.

Megan began with the *compare* and *contrast* technique of the analysis level to examine her beliefs regarding her father, resulting in the realization that she had been operating with conflicting beliefs.

"When I compared my beliefs about my father and my situation, I discovered they were really in contrast."

"What do you mean?" I prompted her.

"Well, I guess you could say I hold two conflicting beliefs at the same time. On the one hand, I believe that a loving daughter should care for an aging parent, but, on the other hand, I also believe that a loving father would not expect his child to sacrifice her life for his care. Comparing these two beliefs helped me to get a handle on the source of my resentment."

Using another verb in the analysis category, Megan began to *specify* what the word *care* really meant to her. Did caring for her father require living under the same roof? Could she still care for her father with altered living arrangements?

"In other words," I interjected, "through being very specific about the nature of the word *care*, you began to ask the question of whether you could care for your father without sacrificing your life?"

"Yeah, it was working with that verb that helped me to see that perhaps there were other alternatives that could be considered caring. Before, it had seemed like, no matter what I did, I couldn't care for my dad and change the course of my life at the same time."

Of course, it wasn't that easy. Megan would have to deal with her father's feelings of abandonment, which she felt would be inevitable.

Ruth, also beginning with the level of analysis, but working with a different verb, began to *distinguish* the faulty or incomplete logic within her belief ("teaching is all I'm trained for") from the conclusion ("I'll have to continue teaching as I am," which meant teaching elementary school in the public school system).

"When I really looked closely at these two beliefs," she said, "I distinguished a difference. See, it wasn't the teaching side of my belief equation that was out of whack, it was the elementary school side that was no longer fulfilling. Teaching is something I really like."

THE PROCESS OF SYNTHESIS

Imagine	*Revise*
Elaborate	*Add to*
Embellish	*Simplify*
Modify	*Invent*
Rearrange	*Express*
Improve	*Improvise*
Compose	*Design*
Devise	*Integrate*
Predict	*Substitute*
Hypothesize	*Minimize*
	Maximize

Here, the mastery-oriented individual begins to recombine in new ways the pieces of the puzzle that were filtered out during the analysis phase. By recombining or rearranging pieces of the old puzzle, new patterns, ideas, and solutions are generated. This is the level of true creativity, because something new or original is created.

As you know from the last chapter (on tapping into creativity), this is the level at which a great deal of patience and mastery-oriented self-talk is required, because so much of it takes place unconsciously. Even though we can consciously work with these verbs, the answer is not likely to come immediately. Therefore, for those with LH particularly, we must be willing to work patiently with the verbs and to trust that, in time, the right brain will process them to present the elegant solution.

Megan's work at this level was accelerated by a fortuitous event—a job-related opportunity. An international nurses' association to which Megan belonged was offering a work-study program aboard a floating hospital that toured Third World countries offering free medical care—all expenses paid! This was the travel-adventure experience Megan craved, but there were still her father's financial and emotional needs to be dealt with. If the organization absorbed her expenses, she could save enough from her salary when added to her current savings to hire a part-time companion for her dad. If she stressed that her travel was of a very temporary nature, he would feel less abandoned and more secure in her eventual return.

If she openly confided her longing to see something of the world, instead of keeping it concealed like some shameful secret, perhaps he would be less likely to view her choice as a personal rebuke.

Megan began to explore the synthesis level by working with the verbs *hypothesize* and *predict*. Predicting all the possible responses her father could have, she was able to have a tender and loving response ready. This gave her the courage to take the risk and tell her father what she wanted to do. She hoped that a tender, loving, and *well-strategized* conversation would significantly reduce her father's resistance to the changes about to occur in his life.

When Ruth reached the synthesis stage of her strategic plan, she began by imagining a change where she could teach (teaching was something she enjoyed and was good at) outside the public-school environment. For years Ruth's hobby had been gourmet cooking, particularly elegant pastries, and she had even managed an abbreviated course at the renowned Cordon Bleu while spending a summer in France. Very quickly Ruth was imagining herself teaching adults the tender alchemy of food preparation.

Allowing herself the fun of considering all the wild possibilities without restraint, Ruth began to *elaborate* and *embellish* on her budding career goals. She saw herself as head of a successful cooking school, owner of a successful catering business, bakery, or delicatessen, author of a bestselling cookbook, and host of an innovative cooking show on TV.

THE PROCESS OF EVALUATION

Decide	*Prove*
Recommend	*Disprove*
Critique	*Verify*
Validate	*Judge*
Select	*Debate*
Assess	*Suggest*
Justify	*Weigh*

As stated above, the mastery-oriented individual at this level of strategic thinking and planning applies a criterion or standard to what she has generated at the synthesis level. Evaluation is the final phase in the process, not because it is the most difficult, but because, if applied prematurely, it thwarts the creative process and leads to LH.

This is the level at which the Critic becomes active, which is not necessarily a bad thing. We can use the Critic to be discriminating in our choices and to help us apply our ideas in a workable fashion. But be forewarned that in those with LH, the Critic tends to be overstimulated and crosses over the line from discriminating awareness to judgment and abuse.

Megan's carefully laid work-study plans fell apart when, near the time for her departure, her father suffered a stroke, which left him partially paralyzed and more needy than ever. As so often happens, the circumstances of life forced her to reevaluate her original plan.

"I was devastated," she explained. "I was so bitter over having to sacrifice myself once again. Plus, I felt guilty for resenting my father's illness. Here he was suffering and all I could think about was myself. I would think irrational thoughts like, 'This is what you get for being so selfish, for trying to plan a way out.' Talk about my Critic being overstimulated! Anyway, I was on the verge of accepting perpetual care of my dad as my lot in life, when I remembered something you said at the workshop when we got to the evaluation phase: 'If plan A doesn't work, go to plan B.' Well I didn't have a plan B."

Megan had to begin the cognitive process all over again, brainstorming options. This time she hit upon a component she hadn't been able to see previously (the opportunity blindness of LH). Her father had a sister, younger (by twelve years) and healthier, who was living in another state on a meager widow's Social Security pension. Megan devised a proposition for her aunt wherein, in return for moving in with and caring for Megan's father, the aunt would be given title to the father's small house.

Granted, for many this would not be an ideal solution to Megan's problem. She would still need to contribute financially to her dad's living expenses. She would have to live in a tiny apartment and forgo the bulk of her inheritance. But in exchange, Megan would gain the freedom to live her own life in her own space and the satisfaction of knowing she was still caring for her father.

I spoke with Megan some eighteen months after the workshop that initiated her endeavors. "The situation is working out well for my dad," she said. "He and his sister had been close in their youth, and they are enjoying reestablishing their relationship at this late point in their lives."

"And for you?" I queried.

"Well, I'm incredibly broke, but the feeling of freedom is so great, it's worth the price. I can have friends over. I can have a man over. I feel like an adult.

"Also, I can now just love my father, without all the conflicting overlays of guilt and resentment. It's nice."

At the evaluation level, Ruth also had to submit her fantasized options to the harsh light of practicality. She intended to initiate her career change while still in the employ of the school system. She started a part-time catering business, running it in the evenings and on weekends and specializing in elaborate pastries and French hors d'oeuvres. It took much longer to get the business going than she had anticipated (she forgot about all the bookkeeping and paperwork needed), plus she realized she was spending at least half of her time marketing and generating new customers—both things left unaccounted for in her original plan.

In order to find time for these extra, unaccounted-for, but critical tasks, Ruth quickly involved her family in the business: her kids icing napoleons for college money, her husband delivering salmon puffs and lending support to his wife's dreams. In addition, during her summer vacation, Ruth wrote, illustrated, and self-published a handbook on creating fancy pastries. She sold the cookbook through word of mouth and recovered her production costs within fourteen months of publication.

Less than two years after getting started, the time required to run Ruth's business had grown beyond the time allotment she had available. The money earned from her part-time effort had prorated a nest egg big enough to finance an expansion, but not enough to replace her teaching salary.

Ruth was nervous, but she was ready to take that calculated risk. She took a leave of absence from teaching (she didn't quit outright), leased a bakery facility two days a week in an affluent area of town, and entered the retailing phase of her business while continuing the catering service. Again, family provided dependable labor, with a couple of nephews cashiering and delivering. Her customers stopped in for fresh cream puffs or hot stuffed mushrooms, or to plan the menu for an upcoming party. Ruth worked out a side deal with two friends who had started a gift-basket business, including her pâté and cookbook in the baskets. The cookbook promoted the bakery, and the bakery promoted the cookbook.

Ruth and I kept in touch. I spoke with her four years after she had attended my workshop, two years after she had left teaching. Here are her comments:

"The first year was rough and so bad financially that it looked like the twins were going to have to postpone college for a year or so. They didn't like that very much, but on the other hand, they didn't have to watch their mother suffering from constant migraine headaches either. Mostly I was too busy to pay much attention, frankly. I started teaching pastry baking through adult education at night. Every dollar I could earn was spent.

"Then things began to gel. As I made more money, I could hire more people to make more money still. The business is now on solid footing, and the kids have started college.

"As I look back, I feel teaching was, in many ways, easier, but not nearly as gratifying. Also, even though this is stressful, it's a different kind of stress. *I'm* in charge now. I make decisions, and the harder I work, the more I earn, unlike teaching, where you don't make the decisions and you constantly deal with other people's problems over which you have very little control."

At this point, Ruth offered me a bite of a new pastry creation she was working on—a raspberry-swirl brownie.

"I put in a lot of hours now, but I don't intend to work this hard forever. A local entrepreneur and former restaurant owner here in town has proposed a partnership in a tearoom/bookstore next door to the bakery. It may be too soon to think about that kind of expansion, but I believe the business will grow and will be the career I want.

"The things I learned about strategizing options gave me the initiative to stop complaining and do something about my dissatisfaction. Action is stressful, it's absolutely true. But, for me, limbo is worse. I was drained and depressed. I hate to think what I would be like now if I had stayed in teaching. I have far more confidence in my ability to take action, and that confidence spills over to other aspects of my life.

"Also, I want to add one more thing. Tell your readers to remember that stuff you said about things taking time. None of this happened on the timetable I thought it would. It took much longer."

* * *

It is obvious from these two stories that nothing progresses as smoothly as we hope it will. Once exposed to the clarity of evaluation (both theoretical and circumstantial), both women were forced to return to the other levels of thinking and planning again and again. In the process of evaluation and reevaluation they would discover areas of gross neglect or ignorance or simply unforeseen events (like pauses on a rock ledge) and would have to return to the verbs (processes) of analysis and synthesis until they reached their goals.

BRINGING BLOOM TO LIFE

As long as Bloom's taxonomy exists only as a lifeless diagram in a self-help book or a tidy list of verbs on a piece of paper, it will have little value in your life. If these verbs are to have an impact, they must be worked with, *acted upon*, in conjunction with the internal exercises offered in earlier chapters. Like meditation, it is in the doing, the lived experience, rather than the intellectual exercise, that change takes place.

What follows are some ways to apply these verbs in your own life. Certainly these suggestions do not cover all the possibilities. It would be impossible to cover all the verbs in just one chapter, but they are ideas to get you started. Any ideas you have on your own from reading the lists of verbs should be incorporated into your strategic plan as well.

Analysis Level

CLASSIFY, CATEGORIZE, LIST, SORT

Begin simply by *listing* the various beliefs you have about the problem you wish to solve, or list the behaviors you have exhibited in the past. (Remember to keep the Critic out of this exercise. In other words, do not judge; simply list. Here is where the Witness will come in handy.)

Once your list is complete, put the items into *categories*. For example, imagine that you have been enduring an emotionally painful and abusive relationship—no physical violence, but plenty of verbal and emotional mistreatment. For some reason you have been unable to muster up whatever it takes to get yourself out the door. After listing your beliefs and behaviors, you could *sort* them (separately) into a variety of different categories, such as:

212

BELIEFS THAT SUPPORT STAYING	*vs.*	BELIEFS THAT SUPPORT GOING

1. I won't be able to attract another man. I'll be lonely.

2. Maybe he will change.

3. I love him.

1. It's better to be alone than to be with someone who treats me badly.

2. He probably won't change unless I give him a reason to, such as leaving him.

3. I must love me more.

OR

BELIEFS BASED ON THE GLOBAL THINKING OF LH	*vs.*	BELIEFS BASED ON THE SPECIFIC THINKING OF MASTERY

1. I'll be so miserable, I won't be able to work.

2. I can't live without him. He is my whole life—romantically, financially, emotionally.

3. Nothing ever works out right. Why should this?

1. Work will be my saving grace. There I can keep busy and not have to think about him.

2. I'll date other men. I'll get a roommate to help with finances. I'll turn to my friends for emotional support.

3. That was then, this is now. I have more strength now than I did then.

OR

BEHAVIORS THAT INVOLVE TRYING TO CONTROL HIM	*vs.*	BEHAVIORS THAT FOCUS ON CONTROLLING MYSELF

1. Suicide attempts.

2. Coaxing, submitting, pleading, yelling, threatening, etc.

1. Seeing a therapist.

2. Calmly explaining what I will do should he repeat an abusive behavior, and then *doing* it, just as calmly.

3. Trying to please him.   3. Stating what I need.

OR

BEHAVIORS BASED ON PERFORMANCE GOALS	*vs.*	BEHAVIORS BASED ON LEARNING GOALS
1. Staying stuck and repeating the same old arguments I have presented a hundred times before.		1. Packing my bags and moving on.
2. Going on a diet, trying to look good enough to re-spark the interest and kindness he showed me during the early days of our relationship.		2. Packing my bags and moving on.
3. Begging him for the tenth time to go see a therapist with me.		3. Packing my bags and moving on.

Once you have begun to sort, categorize, list, and classify, you are looking at the problem cognitively rather than emotionally. Exercising your mind over your emotions is critical to developing good, sound strategies. Second, listing, sorting, and categorizing brings beliefs and behaviors up to a conscious level where you can actually see them and work with them to make healthier choices concerning those that need to be changed and those that need to be emphasized or expanded. Once you have figured out which beliefs support you, can use them in your affirmations to develop the positive self-talk of the mastery-oriented.

You may discover, for example, that you hold the belief that you are unable to attract another man, so it makes you willing to accept a poor relationship over no relationship. Or perhaps your sorting and reflecting reveals a belief that all men are Neanderthals anyway, so putting up with your particular Neanderthal is no different from putting up with any man. Once you have become aware of these beliefs, they can be worked with, modified, and changed into ones that support you in your growth and risk taking.

Now that you have a somewhat organized list of your beliefs and behaviors, you can *compare* them (see how they are similar) and *contrast* them (see how they are different). For example, staying because you believe you are not pretty enough, sexy enough, smart enough, or whatever enough to attract another man is similar to putting up with a bad relationship because it's better than no relationship. On the other hand, staying because you believe that you do not deserve a good relationship is different from staying because you believe you can ultimately control his behavior and make him love you.

Comparing and contrasting components of a problem is useful in overcoming the global aspect of learned helplessness (the tendency to generalize failure from one area of life into all areas). Comparing and contrasting often reveals enough dissimilarity of events or behaviors to counteract the notion that past failure will determine future failure. On the other hand, if the components of past actions or beliefs are undeniably alike, the process will identify the faulty ones that need adjustment or correction.

DISTINGUISH, SEPARATE

Still at the level of analysis, one could *distinguish* personal behaviors associated with procrastination or failure from behaviors associated with successes. For example, as I mentioned earlier, a high-powered executive woman may be quite mastery-oriented when it comes to risking thousands of corporate dollars in a gamble designed to expand the company, but become weak-kneed and pale at the thought of white-water river rafting. Should she decide she wants to overcome her fear (and subsequent helplessness) in order to go on a trip with her boyfriend, she could begin by distinguishing her self-talk in the two different situations. For example:

WHITE-WATER SELF-TALK	CORPORATE-DOLLARS SELF-TALK
1. I'll probably drown.	1. I could make the company a fortune, get promoted, and make a lot of money.

2. Water is dangerous.

2. Risking money is not fatal.

3. Everybody on the trip will probably be a super athlete, and I would just look like a wimp.

3. I can fake an air of self-confidence if I have to. I have time to get my act together.

Suppose a close friend of this executive is exactly the opposite— an accomplished athlete with few physical fears but utterly terrified of the risk of investing money. Her self-talk in the same situation would reflect a different explanatory style:

1. In the water I have some control. I can save myself.

1. I have no control over what happens to the national economy.

2. At least a river trip is fun.

2. Investing money requires a lot of attention and work. I will have to monitor the ups and downs of the market. It sounds stressful to me.

3. Even if I am injured, I can recover over time.

3. If I make a mistake, I'll lose my job, then I can't pay my bills. I'll lose my car, house, everything.

As we have seen before, neither explanatory style necessarily reflects reality. Nor does either one distort reality. Reality is not even the issue, since it is impossible to tell what will happen. What is reflected above, when we learn to distinguish our beliefs and make them concrete in self-talk, is that different realities are stressed by the two different women. Their explanatory style changes to reinforce whichever area of fear they are avoiding. Using the analysis level to examine these beliefs and explanatory style reveals oneself *to* oneself.

Synthesis Level

IMAGINE, COMPOSE, EXPRESS, INTEGRATE

Begin by *imagining* some alternatives. Forget about whether or not they are practical, just have fun and consider the wild possibilities. Under no circumstances should you limit yourself at this stage. (In the evaluation phase you can make them more realistic if necessary.)

Remember, *imagine* comes from the same root as the word *image*, therefore the more you can use the concrete visualizations of your right brain, the better. For example, one desiring to go into business for herself might begin by "image-ing" herself at her new office, composing the elements she imagines are part of this new position. She should imagine herself dressed the way an individual in this line of work would dress, speaking in a tone that indicates authority, making decisions, hiring and firing, being responsible for outcomes, acting like the competent professional in whatever field of endeavor she has chosen.

Then, and this part is truly mastery-oriented, begin gradually to bring this image into reality, even if only on a small scale at first. Reread the discussion of "The Actress Within" exercise on page 160 to remind yourself of the importance of pretending a behavior until it becomes natural. Just try out the new role, practicing it in some small way at first. Perhaps, at first, it will only be slight, even unnoticeable to others, such as costuming or carrying yourself as you imagine the new, self-confident you would carry herself, but eventually, with time and practice, you will be able to integrate these new characteristics into your view of self, because if you do them long enough, they really are you.

EMBELLISH, ELABORATE

Once you have begun to concretize the image of the new you in your mind's eye and to experiment with it a little in the outside world, continue to visualize but allow yourself free rein to *embellish* and *elaborate* on your visualization and strategies as much as you want. Make them as ornate and interesting and fun as you like. Give yourself permission to consider the wildest of possibilities.

Ruth, the teacher turned entrepreneur, said about this level, "This is the fun part, precisely because you're not supposed to judge it but just get wild and crazy. I realized that sometimes it's the wildest, craziest ideas that, with a little modification, actually work the best!"

How right she is. You may remember that, at this stage, Ruth had herself quite a time embellishing and elaborating on her budding career goals. She saw herself as head of a cooking school, owner of a successful catering business, bakery, and delicatessen, author of a best-selling cookbook, and host of an innovative cooking show. The most important thing about this level is that if you are unable to see yourself in these exciting roles, you will never get there. Seeing them is the first step.

Finally, remember to watch out for the Critic again, since embellishments and elaborations can be negative in nature, as well, which will only reinforce fear and LH. When I was contemplating leaving my job as a teacher to become a full-time writer and speaker, I found myself dwelling on the failed-writer syndrome. I would worry and fret (translate: elaborate and embellish) about my professional demise and eventual homelessness (negative "what-if-ing"). When I would encounter the occasional lost bag lady, I would wonder if she had once fancied herself an artist, if she wasn't some kind of symbol or omen of an inevitable comeuppance for one who would so foolishly and cavalierly turn her back on security.

Just as it did with the redheaded politician in an earlier chapter, this sort of negative embellishment undermined my courage and delayed the fresh breeze of a new self-concept to refresh my life for over a year. Certainly it is important to cover your backside as much as possible, but dwelling only on the negative consequences of your risk taking, without an equal emphasis on the possible rewards, only contributes to and perpetuates LH by making you afraid to act on the strategies you develop.

During this time of negative embellishment I said to my mother, "What if I end up a bag lady?"

My risk-taking, warriorlike mother replied, "What if you get rich and famous?"

Point taken.

Many months later my boyfriend, watching me pack my garment bag for yet another workshop in yet another city, looked at me with an ironic smile and said, "You know what? You actually did end up a bag lady!"

MINIMIZE, MAXIMIZE

This is an interesting set of verbs to work with and one that yields unique results. The goal here is to *minimize* some aspect of the problem (discovered during the analysis phase) that has heretofore received maximum attention and to *maximize* some other aspect that may have seemed trivial, petty, or unimportant, such as the following story told by a woman at a workshop.

"I am thirty-nine and single. I have desperately wanted a child for at least the last ten years.

"More times than I care to count I have scared off a good man because I pushed so hard to get married and start a family. The older I get, the more desperate I get because of the biological-clock bit. Lately I haven't even used good judgment with the men I get involved with, because at this point I just want the man so that I can have my family."

"Why don't you try adoption?" offered one woman.

"Or even artificial insemination," offered another, "after all, it *is* the 1990s."

"Well, see, I knew somebody would say that. But my parents, who are Orthodox Jews, would have a fit. I was raised very traditionally, and in their eyes you build a family by starting with a mother and a father. Period. That's the only way it's done.

"I realize I am maximizing the importance of tradition and pleasing my parents. That part is obvious. But I never really thought about how, by doing that, I am actually minimizing my own needs. I don't like the sound of that. Why am I doing that?"

Chances are there are a number of reasons. One is probably that she, too, like her parents, values (maximizes) tradition. Another reason is probably the result of LH—she is afraid to take a risk. She believes that "no matter what she does" she cannot please her parents and meet her needs at the same time. If that is true, then she must start maximizing her own needs and minimizing tradition and pleasing her parents, since her current predicament is evidence that her old way hasn't been working very well.

The processes of minimizing and maximizing are valuable in helping us see old problems in new ways—a critical step to jogging your old, helpless self out of its helpless ways of thinking.

MODIFY, SIMPLIFY, REVISE, REARRANGE, ADD TO

You may want to *modify* an idea by *simplifying* it or *rearranging* it or *adding to* it. You can have great fun if you let yourself design or revise your various strategies, fantasizing all the ways to improve. You will begin to see how infinite your choices truly are once you have learned the skill of synthesizing, because any strategy can be modified, improved, redesigned, or combined with other strategies until it finally works. Also, it almost goes without saying (but not quite) that, like Megan and Ruth, you will probably be forced to modify and revise your original strategies. Because no one is capable of foreseeing all the changes that will take place over time, learning to revise, improve, modify, and so forth is critical to mastery. There-fore, refer again and again to the list of verbs in the synthesis section as you develop new ways of looking at old problems.

Finally, since synthesis is the level of creativity, review the sug-gestions in Chapter 11 (on tapping into creativity) *and do them* to dig new trenches of thought that will lead to the open sea of mastery behavior.

Evaluation Level

Remember that the main danger at this level is that when old, helpless mind evaluates, it does so out of fear, defensiveness, or insecurity. Its habitual response has been to lead you down paths of avoidance, on the one hand, or internalized blame, on the other—paths that have neither served you in the past nor will con-tribute to your growth in the future. Old mind (self) will continue to resist change. Therefore guard against these deep, habitual grooves of thought. They are ruts, and we all know what happens with ruts: We get stuck in them. As Mark Twain once said, "The only difference between a rut and a grave is the depth."

Second, as you narrow down your choices to decide on an even-tual course of action or strategy or plan, remember not to close off the other options, strategies, and plans that you generated at the synthesis level. The purpose in generating them in the first place, and then generating several more after that, was to become like the mastery-oriented, who develop multiple strategies. They capitalize on the belief that if one strategy fails, others are always available.

When plan A fails, they go to plan B (or C or Z, if necessary). Once you, too, believe this, you can relax more and fret less about whether you chose the "right" course of action or not.

VERIFY, PROVE/DISPROVE, VALIDATE, JUSTIFY

These verbs indicate that evaluation is often simply a matter of testing out your plan, either partially or completely, to see if it worked. If possible, try to test it on a small scale at first to minimize your risk. If your plan doesn't work for some reason, do not become mired down in the fears of inadequacy or performance anxiety so typical of LH. Simply do what the mastery-oriented do: Interpret the problem or failure or obstacle as a cue for you to change or modify your strategy, go back to the analysis and synthesis levels, and begin again.

WEIGH, ASSESS

One can *assess* the various options by actually *weighing* them, assigning numerical values on a variety of scales:

FEASIBILITY:

Totally impractical			Practical but needs modification					Highly Feasible	
1	2	3	4	5	6	7	8	9	10

TIME CONSTRAINTS:

Very Protracted Commitment			Moderate Time Investment				Ready for Immediate Action		
1	2	3	4	5	6	7	8	9	10

MONEY CONSTRAINTS:

Very Expensive			Moderately Expensive				Affordable		
1	2	3	4	5	6	7	8	9	10

PERSONAL PREFERENCE:

I loathe the idea			Well, maybe . . . I can see the possibilities				Can't wait to get started!		
1	2	3	4	5	6	7	8	9	10

CAN THIS DECISION BE CHANGED BACK AGAIN?

Written in stone				Somewhat				No problem!	
1	2	3	4	5	6	7	8	9	10

Obviously these scales can be highly personalized to fit whatever circumstance you are dealing with. For example, your heading might be "My Child's Happiness," or "My Mental Health," or "The Importance of Creative Expression," or "Making a Lot of Money," or whatever you choose. Then you can weigh the categories themselves on another one-to-ten scale, perhaps realizing in the process that making money is more important to you than your mental health. (At which point another evaluation may be in order!)

DECIDE, RECOMMEND, SUGGEST

Remember, very few decisions are written in stone, although some are certainly more adaptable to future reversals or afterthoughts than others. Also, once a decision is made, the process carries on and proceeds. In other words, you will continue to analyze (take things apart and look at them), synthesize (rearrange and recombine ideas and behaviors to refine strategies), and evaluate as you go (what worked, what didn't?).

Obviously, once you are here, you begin to realize that mastery behavior is a lifelong process that you refine and develop at ever-more-sophisticated and elegant levels. You will get better and better at it as you go, although sometimes it may not feel like it because you may be taking bigger risks as you get better at the process. Anyway it's not a race. As Confucius said, "It matters not how slowly you go, only that you do not stop."

Once again, the value of Bloom's taxonomy lies only in its application to real-life circumstances. Work with the levels and their accompanying verbs in conjunction with the other exercises presented throughout this book. In this way you will be developing both the inner woman—the one who will provide the psychic energy—and the outer woman—the one who will take it out into the world.

CHAPTER 13

Zen and the Art of Risk Taking: Making a Masterpiece of Your Life

We cannot put off living until we are ready. The most salient characteristic of life is its coerciveness: it is always urgent, "here and now" without any possible postponement. Life is fired at us point-blank.
—JOSÉ ORTEGA Y GASSET

Every tomorrow ought not to be like every yesterday.
—BERYL MARKHAM

So.

Here we are at the last chapter. If you have read other self-help books, you know that this is the point at which, as the author, it is my responsibility to write soaring, commanding prose of such power and eloquence that you will be inspired, indeed compelled, to go forth, salt-spray in your hair, wind at your back, undaunted by meager means or dark of night, to seek your fortune amid the bustling marketplace of humanity.

Human nature being what it is, however, it is more likely that your life will continue pretty much as it is—an average day in the life of an average adult—predictably nondescript, thankfully devoid of high drama and peacefully mundane. Most of us are grateful for this tranquil uniformity. But if these days of sameness linger indefinitely, stretching into a numbing kind of deadness, they carry with them a different kind of risk, one sheathed in a comforting cocoon of complacency, an anesthetizing belief that we have all the time in the world to dine at life's table, that *tomorrow* would be a great day to accept a challenge, thank you, but for now we would just as soon lie down and take a little nap.

There is for all of us an enormous temptation to allow the forces of inertia to dominate, to sink down into the well-worn grooves of habitual behavior like a pair of comfortable old loafers, to putter around our houses endlessly nesting, reading our books, cooking our meals, opening only familiar doors, passing only familiar hallways. We achieve security (or boredom) at the expense of freedom, growth, and change.

Yet, as Annie Dillard says in *Pilgrim at Tinker Creek*, "The world is wilder than that in all directions, more dangerous and bitter, more extravagant and bright." Personally I know that every risk I have ever taken has taught me the grandness of life, the vitality of each moment, and the limited time I will be given in my one puny lifetime to experience it. When I succumb to fear and helplessness, my world shrivels accordingly into a safe but claustrophobic little cell. When I choose risk (or have been catapulted into it), the world freely offers itself to me, rolling at my feet, teasing me to dance, to play, to flirt, to grow.

Any event in life that coaxes us to reach and stretch must be appreciated for the opportunity it is, not as an annoying burden to be borne. It is the opportunity to learn mastery in the Zen of present time, compelling us to participate fully in our lived experience, to develop our moment-to-moment awareness and our ability to think on our feet, obliging us to reevaluate the "self" we thought we knew. Whether the experience involves forced risk taking (such as an unwanted divorce) or voluntary risk taking (such as participation in a wilderness-survival school), its power to transform our lives can be used as a tool for change. Ultimately, learning to take risks enables us to make a work of art, a masterpiece, of our lives.

You've got the information. You know that LH is a belief system, fueled by a negative explanatory style (stable, global, internal) and solidified by an unchanging view of self. You know that these beliefs result in negative self-talk, decreased effort, lack of persistence (or initiative), and a breakdown in strategic thinking. You even know the complex ways in which these forces interact to reinforce each other. Most importantly, you know that they sabotage any inclinations you may feel to take those risks.

You've got the tools. You know how to begin changing the view of self both at the internal, psychic level and at the external, worldly level. You know how to metabolize the stress caused by internal change and a new self-image—meditation—and you have the left-brain tools to learn how to strategize your way through the rigorous demands posed by the external world.

The question is: Will you do it? I admit this is something of a dare, but then, how much time have you got? How much time has already passed?

Certainly, it is important to plan, to muster one's courage, and to anchor one's resolve. No point in releasing your hold on one trapeze if the other has not been set in motion, particularly if you are working without a net. The danger, however, is that you will spend your whole life planning. At some point you just have to do it.

The only way out is through. It has been hinted at, pointed to, whispered about, and shouted throughout the earlier chapters of this book, but the final paradox inherent in unlearning helplessness is this: Risk taking is what builds mastery, not the other way around. We do not become mastery-oriented and *then* take risks. We take risks and then become mastery-oriented.

I wish there were another way. I am fully cognizant that what I am suggesting is troublesome at best and downright infuriating at worst. That is, in order to acquire faith in yourself (belief in self-efficacy), you must *show* faith in yourself. To learn risk-taking behavior, you must take a risk.

Again, the only way out is through. You can't learn to ski by reading about it. You have to put the boards on your feet and go careening down a mountain. You can't learn to be mastery-oriented by postponing the risk taking in favor of reading a book.

It is okay, however, to start from wherever you are. If you can only muster a little faith in yourself, then take that little bit and go take a little risk (so long as it is something new). Then the self-confidence that you have acquired from that little risk will stand you in good stead to take another, slightly bigger one. Gradually, through this process and through utilizing the information, strategies, and techniques that have been provided throughout this book, you will become a more mastery-oriented risk taker than you were before.

Risk taking, like most other things in life, is relative and exists on a kind of continuum. Thus far I have presented stories that most of us can relate to (with the exception of Snow Leopard Lady)— regular women taking the risks of regular life. But for those of you on the continuum who crave greater excitement, who thrill to stories of female adventure, valor, and derring-do, I must indulge us both and tell of three risk-taking women, tales I want to pass along for the sheer joy of showing how daring women can be. After all, as females, we have so few role models in the realm of high adventure.

I must keep these tales brief, but I encourage you to read these women's stories on your own. They are some of the most glorious risk-adventures ever to have shivered their way up a human spine. These women's autobiographies, in particular, are enlightening for our purposes, because when you read *their* words, you discover that these women are not alien creatures made of entirely different stuff than you or me. They were *not* utterly fearless, utterly brave, Masters of the Universe. Like you and me, they knew fear, loneliness, and helplessness, too, but they overcame, either by choice or by necessity, their fears and self-doubts and became role models for us all.

The stories of these women can help reinforce your belief that you can take those risks, for, embedded in their words you will hear all of the elements of LH versus mastery behavior that have been discussed throughout this book. You will realize that, in fact, even for experienced risk takers, the process remains the same.

BERYL MARKHAM, PILOT

This author, aviator, horse breeder and trainer defies categorization. Perhaps "adventurer" says it best. Beryl flew passengers, mail, and supplies to remote areas of the Sudan, Tanganyika, Kenya, and Rhodesia from 1931 to 1936. She scouted elephant herds by air for rich hunters on safari—an activity so hazardous that the best pilots of her day tried to discourage her. Calling it a release from routine, she did not stop.

In 1936 she was the first person successfully to fly solo from east to west across the Atlantic Ocean. The decision to undertake the journey was not an easy one for Beryl. Her autobiography, *West With the Night*, chronicles some of the fear and self-doubt with which she wrestled:

> I could lie there [in bed] a few moments longer . . . telling myself with senseless repetition, that by tomorrow morning I should either have flown the Atlantic to America—or I should not have flown it.
>
> I stared up at the ceiling of my bedroom in Aldenham . . . feeling less resolute than anxious, much less brave than foolhardy.

I could ask, "Why risk it?" as I have been asked since, and I could answer, "Each to his element." By his nature a sailor must sail, by his nature a flyer must fly.

Ultimately she undertook the journey and survived the crash landing that she had to make in Nova Scotia twenty-one hours and twenty-five minutes after takeoff. In her book she describes the ineffable loneliness as she piloted her tiny plane through the wild night skies above a stormy Atlantic:

> Being alone in an aeroplane for even so short a time as a night and a day, irrevocably alone, with nothing to observe but your instruments and your own hands in the semi-darkness, nothing to contemplate but the size of your small courage, nothing to wonder about but the beliefs, faces and hopes rooted in your mind—such an experience can be as startling as the first awareness of a stranger walking by your side at night. You are the stranger.

After her historic journey and crash landing (which you really must read as a firsthand account), recuperating on a freighter bound for Africa to see her father, and speaking as a true mastery-oriented individual, she says,

> It was the end of a phase that I felt had grown and rounded out and tapered to its full design, inevitably, like a leaf. I might have started from any place on earth, I thought, from any point.[1]

ALEXANDRA DAVID-NEEL, EXPLORER

"Adventure is what I live for," said Alexandra, and if the events of her life are any indication, she lived it well, for she made it to her hundredth birthday.

Eschewing marriage until age thirty-six, vowing she would not "surrender her liberty," the beautiful Alexandra earned her living as an operatic chanteuse in turn-of-the-century Paris. Except for one sojourn to India at the age of twenty-three (about which very little is known), the zeal for exploration, which was to become the theme of Alexandra's life, had not as yet begun to manifest.

Then, in 1911, at the age of forty-three, abandoning a financially secure and comfortable existence with her husband, Philip, she undertook an expedition to Asia, alone, ostensibly to perfect her

Oriental languages. Promising her husband she would be gone only a year, her journey stretched to fourteen years.

This sojourn, begun in midlife, transformed the rest of her life. She left Paris as a student of the East with a strong interest in Buddhist thought. She returned, fourteen years later, as a Tantric adept and world-renowned Buddhist scholar and writer. During this time, she met and fell in love with the prince of Sikkim, who was later stricken with a mysterious illness, which quickly took his life. From 1914 to 1916, she lived as a hermit in a stone hut high in the Himalayas, where, as a student of a revered lama, she meditated daily in sky-high caves and undertook training in the secret and powerful practices of Tibetan Tantric Buddhism. She was granted two interviews with the Dalai Lama.

By this time her husband, keeping the home fires burning back in France, was disgruntled, to say the least. He wanted Alexandra home. Yet, in October 1923, at the age of fifty-five, she began a four-month trek, on foot, over treacherous mountain passes to the holy, forbidden city of Lhasa, Tibet. In February 1924, with her very life in peril both from bandits and from Tibetan officials guarding the city, Alexandra, disguised as a beggar and carrying a pistol, became the first Western woman to enter the great holy city in the Land of Snows.

(I love the mastery-oriented comment made by a close male friend of mine who, upon hearing of her incredible journey, said "Now, *there's* an attitude!")

Returning to the European continent in 1925, she wrote *My Journey to Lhasa; Magic and Mystery; Buddhism;* and *Initiations.* She lectured extensively on women's rights in Belgium and France. Spicing her lectures with spine-tingling stories of the courage and independence of the Tibetan women (who often had more than one husband, were merchants, holy personages, and expert mountaineers), she honored the women of Tibet, whom she deeply respected and at the same time, did her bit for the feminist movement of her day.

Even though she was back in France, Alexandra and her husband did not live together. She bought property in the south of France and set up a meditation retreat, where she lived. Philip then resided in Algeria but made the trip to visit her whenever he could. Undoubtedly this arrangement made it easier for Alexandra to begin considering her next expedition.

In 1937, at the age of sixty-nine, despite the fears and hardships she had borne on her last Asian sojourn, Alexandra, the indefatigable traveler, began yet another journey. Saying, "I have left many times without ever arriving," she traveled once again all over Asia and environs, this time for eight years. Her husband, Philip, died in 1941 during her absence. She was genuinely and deeply grieved. It took her six years, however, to return to France. She journeyed home at the age of seventy-nine, to settle the estate and live out her remaining years.

When she died, on September 8, 1969, one month short of her 101st birthday, much honored as an explorer, field anthropologist, Buddhist scholar, and author of over forty books, she was still writing. Many of her projects were left incomplete at her death.

Alexandra's personal accounts of her travels and travails are not only thrilling and educational, they show that even the great explorer herself, who faced wild beasts, Asian bandits, powerful shamans, disease, malnutrition, and the kind of weather that knows no compassion for human life, also knew fear. From her letters:

> This excursion [to Lhasa], considered rough for a young robust man, was pure madness for a woman my age.
>
> I get chills of fear thinking about what I've done . . . we were so little, so lost in the immensity.

Yet despite the fears, toward the end of her life, in her nineties, when she was living, working, and writing in the south of France, she complained of "a filthy, stupid end in an armchair." She longed to return to the hardships of her beloved Tibet and the steppes of the Central Asian plateau:

> I should have died there, among the immense grassy solitudes close to the Tibetan lakes; for a bed the earth, grass or snow, for a ceiling the canvas of my tent and the great starry sky.[2]

The next time you feel too old to undertake an adventure or cherished project, crack open a book about Alexandra David-Neel, who did not even begin her life as an explorer until she was forty-three years old and began her most perilous journey of all (to Lhasa, Tibet) at the age of fifty-five. The world owes a debt of gratitude to this marvelous woman, precisely because she was able to transcend common fears about aging. The Western world is a richer place for her contribution to our knowledge of Buddhist thought. Were it not for Alexandra's trek to Tibet and her writings about the journey, we would be little acquainted with a Tibet that no longer exists.

FOUR CAMELS, A DOG, AND A ROBYN

The incredible story of Camel Lady, as the press called her, is my personal favorite. Robyn Davidson's trek across 1,700 miles of Australian outback, accompanied only by a dog and four camels, is a dazzling journey of mastery, self-discovery, and transformation.

Like Darla Hillard, nothing in Robyn's background, save for a slightly eclectic taste in her educational choices, would have led one to predict that she would one day make such a journey. She was born in Queensland, Australia, in 1950. As a child she attended a small school of only thirty students before going off to a traditional boarding school in Brisbane. As a young woman she studied biology and music, then later Japanese and philosophy at Queensland University.

Vaguely bored and dissatisfied with her life, what she describes as "half-finished, half-hearted attempts at different jobs and various studies . . . sick of carrying around the self-indulgent negativity . . . of my generation, my sex and my class," she lit upon the idea of acquiring the necessary number of wild camels from the bush, training them to carry her gear, and walking into the Australian outback.

Sure. Why not? Doesn't everybody?

Anyway, without going into detail, suffice it to say that the hardships as well as the ecstasies that she experienced almost defy the boundaries of language. As one reads her magnificent story, one becomes acutely aware of many things, not the least of which is that here was another "dummy" attempting an adventure about which she knew basically nothing. But, like all good mastery-oriented risk takers, she was willing to choose a learning goal and support it with a plan.

Robyn began by finding an experienced camel handler to teach her the nuances of handling these highly intelligent, sensitive, and witty creatures. She worked from sunup to sundown, seven days a week, developing her love for camels, perfecting her camel techniques, and training herself for a trek into the desert wilderness of the Australian outback.

One becomes acutely aware throughout her story of the awareness of process itself. So many things changed, from the activities involved in survival to the woman herself. She discovered how to pare down her gear from a pile that required two and a half hours' loading time to one requiring a mere twenty minutes. And she learned to be blissfully at home in the uncompromisingly hostile and indifferent environment of the vast desert spaces, though she became totally intimidated by the canyons of cement and glass she encountered in New York City upon her return.

One would assume that a woman who could even conjure up such an adventure would already be fearless and mastery-oriented, yet in her account of the trip, as told in her book, *Tracks*, we see her filled with the struggles inherent in overcoming helplessness.

On action, process, and change:

> And it struck me then that the most difficult thing had been the decision to act, the rest had been merely tenacity—and the fears were paper tigers. One really could do anything one had decided to do whether it were changing a job, moving to a new place, divorcing a husband or whatever, one really could act to change and control one's life; and the procedure, the process, was its own reward.

On fear, doubt, and the desire to procrastinate:

> [Upon disembarking the train in Alice Springs, where she began her journey] I experienced that sinking feeling you get when you know you have conned yourself into doing something difficult and there's no going back. It's all very well to set off on a train with no money, telling yourself that you're really quite a brave and adventurous person, and you'll deal capably with things as they happen, but when you actually arrive at the other end . . . with nothing to sustain you but a lunatic idea that even you have no real faith in, it suddenly appears much more attractive to be at home on the kindly Queensland coast, discussing plans and sipping gins on the verandah with friends, making unending lists of lists which get thrown away and reading books about camels.

On the need to take risks:

> We always relax back into the moulds of habit. They are secure, they bind us and keep us contained at the expense of freedom. To break the moulds, to be heedless of the seductions of security is an impossible struggle, but one of the few that count. To be free is to

learn, to test yourself constantly, to gamble. It is not safe. I had learnt to use my fears as stepping stones rather than stumbling blocks.

And finally:

> The trip was easy. It was no more dangerous than crossing the street, or driving to the beach, or eating peanuts. The two important things that I did learn were that you are as powerful and strong as you allow yourself to be, and that the most difficult part of any endeavour is taking the first step, making the first decision. And I knew even then that I would forget time and time again and would have to go back and repeat those words . . . that I would lapse into useless nostalgia. Camel trips, as I suspected all along . . . do not begin or end, they merely change form.[3]

Other dramatic risk takers whom you might want to read about include:

Shirley Muldowney	Race-car driver whose story has been chronicled in the movie *Heart Like a Wheel*—available on videotape.
Susan Butcher	Four-time winner of the Iditarod, an almost 1,200 mile-long dogsled race across the frozen tundra of Alaska.
Ruth Benedict	Field anthropologist and close friend and associate of Margaret Mead who, like Alexandra David-Neel, undertook a journey of great distance and hardship at the age of sixty-nine.
Jeanette Picard	With her husband, piloted a hot-air balloon to an altitude of 57,559 feet, thus being the first woman to reach the stratosphere. In 1974 became one of the first women ordained as a priest in the Episcopal Church.

I must tell you that I wasn't entirely sure whether to relate these stories because, although my purpose was to inspire, I was concerned you might succumb to the tendency to compare yourself with these risk takers and feel that you came up short. I worried that you might turn these stories into inappropriate references and thereby be discouraged, like the young cellist discouraged by the performance of Yo-Yo Ma.

But you do not have to do what these women did. When you *do* want to take a risk, however, it's good to know how. When a challenge presents itself, therefore, or you long to rise to an occasion, remember, whether it involves a life-or-death gamble or just a little ego risk, the elements remain the same: altering one's explanatory style, being willing to believe in the changing nature of self, choosing learning goals over performance goals, practicing positive self-talk, developing strategic thinking, and refusing to compare oneself with others. These are the behaviors that will eventually result in a mastery-oriented approach to life, regardless of the degree of risk involved.

Practicing these skills reminds me a little of the advice given continuously to musicians—"Practice your scales every day"—and to dancers—"Do your exercises daily at the barre." In other words, without perfecting the simplest of their techniques on a daily basis, there will be no executing the more complex ones in a performance situation.

The same holds true for acquiring mastery-oriented behavior. We must perfect the skills at the simplest levels first and we must work on them a little every day. It's like the punchline in the old joke about the tourist in New York, lost in the canyons of the city, who stopped a New Yorker to ask, "How do you get to Carnegie Hall?" The answer is the same: "Practice!"

ENDNOTES

CHAPTER 1

1. Tom Robbins. *Even Cowgirls Get the Blues* (Boston: Houghton Mifflin, 1976), p. 227. I have slightly altered this quote based on the "Author's Note," which appears at the beginning of the book, wherein Robbins offers an apology to any reader offended by the use of third-person pronouns in the masculine gender. Robbins states that at the time of writing there were "no alternatives that did not either create confusion or impede the flow of language." Since Robbins took such pains to make this statement, I feel confident he would not object to my changing his use of the pronouns *him* and *his* in this particular quote to *her* and *hers*.

CHAPTER 2

1. Martin Seligman, *Helplessness* (San Francisco: W. H. Freeman and Co., 1975), p. 27.
2. J. P. Howard, "Pluralism and Professional Development: Minorities, Women and the Psychology of Performance" (Chicago: Brass, Richie and Betts, 1985).

CHAPTER 3

1. A. H. Stein and M. M. Bailey, "The Socialization of Achievement Orientation in Females," *Psychological Bulletin* 80 (1973): 345–66.
2. Carol S. Dweck and B. G. Licht, "Learned Helplessness and Intellectual Achievement," in M. P. Seligman and J. Garber (eds.), *Human Helplessness: Theory and Research* (New York: Academic Press, 1980).

3. B. G. Licht and Carol S. Dweck, "Determinants of Academic Achievement: The Interaction of Children's Achievement Orientations with Skill Area," *Developmental Psychology* 20 (1984): 628–36. Also see, D. J. Stipek and J. Hoffman, "Development of Children's Performance-Related Judgments," *Child Development* 51 (1980): 912–14.

4. Jerome Kagan and Howard Moss. *Birth to Maturity* (New York: Wiley & Sons, 1962).

5. As reported on "The Today Show" and "NBC Nightly News," June 16, 1990.

6. In the service occupations, which we know are underpaid, the percentage of women remains more than twice that of men. To make matters worse, a closer look reveals that women's service jobs are of an entirely different ilk. Women are much more likely than men to be private-household workers (7 percent as compared to 0.5 percent), whereas men are much more likely to be in the protective services—police and firefighters (24 percent as compared to 2 percent). It borders on absurdity to compare a housekeeper's and a firefighter's opportunities for promotion, job security, wages, mobility—in short, all the measures of status.

7. Howard, J. P. "Pluralism and Professional Development: Minorities, Women and the Psychology of Performance."

8. Jean H. Block, "Another Look at Sex Differentiation in the Socialization Behaviors of Mothers and Fathers," in J. A. Sherman and F. L. Denmark (eds.), *Psychology of Women: Future Directions of Research* (New York: Psychological Dimensions, 1979).

9. Jeffrey Z. Rubin, Frank J. Provenzano, and Zella Luria, "The Eye of the Beholder: Parents' Views on Sex of Newborns," *American Journal of Orthopsychiatry* 44: (1974) 512–19.

10. Studies vary from a half hour per day to several hours.

11. M. C. Shaw and J. T. McCuen, "The Onset of Academic Underachievement in Bright Children," *Journal of Educational Psychology* 51 (1960): 103–8. Furthermore, studies as late as 1986 continue to verify this trend. In an Associated Press article by Maud Beelman that appeared in the *Philadelphia Inquirer*, March 6, 1986, a researcher said, "Especially high-achieving girls seem to find status (good grades) inconsistent with having a positive self-view in the seventh grade and they reduce their achievement."

Interested readers are also referred to Eleanor E. Maccoby and Carol N. Jacklin, *The Psychology of Sex Differences* (Stanford: Stanford University Press, 1974), a remarkable compilation of information on psychological differences between the sexes such as independence, anxiety, aggression, etc. It is a valuable resource and contains an annotated bibliography of over fourteen hundred references.

12. Lois Hoffman, "Changes in Family Roles, Socialization and Sex Differences," *American Psychologist* 32: (1977) 649.

13. C. S. Dweck et al., "Sex Differences in Learned Helplessness: II. The Contingencies of Evaluative Feedback in the Classroom and III. An Experimental Analysis," *Developmental Psychology* 14 (1978): 268–76.

14. M. S. Horner, "Toward an Understanding of Achievement-Related Conflicts in Women," *Journal of Social Issues* 28 (1972): 157–75.

15. As reported in the *Washington Post*, March 6, 1990, in an article by Jay Mathews.

16. Norton Dodge, as quoted in Sheila Tobias, *Overcoming Math Anxiety* (New York: W. W. Norton & Co., 1978), p. 89.

17. It is safe to say that, as it stands today, our society simply cannot afford equal pay for women and must regard it as an unaffordable luxury. In 1970 statistics show that equal pay for equal work would have cost employers an additional $96 *billion*, and that was only for part-time help. Today, of course, the costs would be even greater. Elimination of sex discrimination in the workplace today would automatically raise women's salaries about 40 percent. In other words, it "costs" an individual woman about $2,000 to $3,000 a year simply to be female. Therefore if she limits herself only to service-sector jobs typically held by women, known as pink-collar jobs—waitresses, hairdressers, housekeepers, answering-service personnel, day care, etc.—she must resign herself to a job situation that offers few benefits (if any), no chance for advancement, and no union representation to offer any hope for change.

CHAPTER 4

1. Carol S. Dweck, "Motivational Processes Affecting Learning," *American Psychologist* 41 (1986): 1,040–48.

2. J. Kagan and K. Bradway, "Intelligence at Middle Age: A Thirty-eight-year Follow-up," *Developmental Psychology* 5: (1971) 333–37.

3. W. Ickes, M. Layden, "Attributional Styles," in J. H. Harvey, W. Ickes, and R. F. Kidd (eds.), *New Directions in Attributional Research*, vol. 2 (Hillsdale, N.J.: Erlbaum Associates, 1978), pp. 121–47.

4. Linda Gannon, P. Heiser, and S. Knight, "Learned Helplessness Versus Reactance: The Effects of Sex-Role Stereotyping," *Sex Roles* 12 (1985): 791–806.

5. First, abuse tends to creep up on a woman. Progressing from verbal abuse ("At least he doesn't hit me") to full-fledged physical brutalization, it may take many years for the abuser to display his full ferocity.

Second, childhood abuse, particularly sexual abuse, will teach LH with deadly certainty. If, as a child, you were forced to endure sexual victimization, night after night, year after year, at the hands of an all-powerful adult, you probably learned that "no matter what you did," you couldn't stop the brutality. Also, your abuser may have made you believe that you were responsible for his actions, causing you to internalize blame, a critical component in the LH syndrome.

6. Eric Berne, *Games People Play* (New York: Grove Press, 1964).

CHAPTER 5

1. Peter H. Johnson and Peter N. Winograd, "Passive Failure in Reading," *Journal of Reading Behavior* 17 (1985): 290.

CHAPTER 6

1. Interested readers are referred to Morris Rosenberg, *Conceiving the Self* (New York: Basic Books, 1979), from which this material was taken.

2. Interested readers are referred to the fascinating studies on multiple personality disorder done by the National Institute of Mental Health.

3. David K. Reynolds, *Playing Ball on Running Water* (New York: Quill, 1984), p. 41.

4. Joseph Campbell, *The Power of Myth* (New York: Doubleday, 1988), p. 58.

5. Donald H. Baucom and Pamela Danker-Brown, "Sex-Role Identity and Sex-Stereotyped Tasks in the Development of Learned Helplessness in Women," *Journal of Personality and Social Psychology* 46: (1984) 422 –30.

6. Donald H. Baucom, "Sex-Role Identity and the Decision to Regain Control Among Women: A Learned Helplessness Investigation," *Journal of Personality and Social Psychology* 44 (1983): 334–43.

7. Donald H. Baucom and Bahr Weiss, "Peers' Granting of Control to Women With Different Sex-Role Identities: Implications for Depression," *Journal of Personality and Social Psychology* 51 (1986): 1,075–80. Furthermore, this study went on to say, "These findings lend support to the sex role explanation for gender differences in depression." And to the authors' credit, they did not blame the individual women for this tendency toward depression, but rather the society that created the problem: "To the extent that this laboratory analogue reflects decisions made in the everyday world . . . this lack of control on seemingly desirable tasks may contribute to the development of depressive symptoms among these women."

8. E. P. Ray and A. R. Bristow, "Sex Role Identities in Depressed Women." Paper presented at the meeting of the Southwestern Psycho-

logical Association, New Orleans, 1978. Other studies show that depression is often a function of low self-esteem. This is germane to our discussion because females suffer a *decline* in self-esteem and ego strength during adolescence, while males undergo an *increase* in self-esteem and ego strength during the same phase of life—a disturbing fact that has been shown in numerous replicated studies. This decline may be due to society's general devaluation of femininity. Since puberty is the time when females begin to identify more strongly with the feminine aspects of their personalities, that is naturally the time when the decline would manifest.

9. Kristen Yount, "A Theory of Productive Activity: The Relationships Among Self-Concept, Gender, Sex-Role Stereotypes, and Work-Emergent Traits," *Psychology of Women Quarterly* 10 (1986): 63–88.

Chapter 11

1. The five-step process of creativity shown here is a slight variation of a four-step model of creativity advanced by Graham Wallas in 1926 in his book *The Art of Thought*. Wallas's model has been imitated many times, with changes and additions by other researchers, but most of the models presented by other researchers are variations on the same theme. Some researchers have added more steps (up to seven) or have renamed the steps, but the original remains pretty much the norm.

2. Gabriele Lusser Rico, *Writing the Natural Way* (Los Angeles: J. P. Tarcher, Inc., 1983). I have presented a somewhat simplified version of Ms. Rico's Trial Web technique.

Chapter 12

1. Benjamin Bloom, ed. *Taxonomy of Educational Objectives* (New York: David McKay, 1973). By a committee of college and university examiners. Since this edition was printed, it has become common among educators to show the taxonomy as an inverted pyramid to indicate the highest level as the most difficult.

Chapter 13

1. Beryl Markham, *West With the Night* (San Francisco: North Point Press, 1983).

2. Barbara and Michael Foster, *Forbidden Journey: The Life of Alexandra David-Neel* (San Francisco: Harper & Row, 1987).

3. Robyn Davidson, *Tracks* (New York: Pantheon Books, 1980).

BIBLIOGRAPHY

Books

Abramson, Lyn Y. (ed.) *Social Cognition and Clinical Psychology: A Synthesis.* New York: Guilford Press, 1988.

Adams, James L. *Conceptual Blockbusting: A Guide to Better Ideas.* New York: W. W. Norton & Co., 1979.

Almaas, A. H. *Diamond Heart Book Two: The Freedom to Be.* Berkeley: Diamond Books, 1989.

Arieti, Silvano. *Creativity: The Magic Synthesis.* New York: Basic Books, Inc., 1976.

Bass, Ellen; and Laura Davis. *The Courage to Heal.* New York: Harper & Row, 1988.

Berne, Eric. *Games People Play.* New York: Grove Press, 1964.

Block, Jean H. "Another Look at Sex Differentiation in the Socialization Behaviors of Mothers and Fathers." In J. A. Sherman and F. L. Denmark (eds.), *Psychology of Women: Future Directions of Research.* New York: Psychological Dimensions, 1979.

Bloom, Benjamin S. (ed.) *A Taxonomy of Educational Objectives.* New York: David McKay Co., 1956.

Campbell, Joseph. *The Power of Myth.* New York: Doubleday, 1988.

Capra, Fritjof. *The Tao of Physics: An Exploration of the Parallels Between Modern Physics and Eastern Mysticism.* New York: Bantam Books, 1975.

Chivington, Paul K. *Seeing Through Your Illusions.* Denver: G-L Publications, 1983.

Dass, Ram. *Journey of Awakening: A Meditator's Guidebook.* New York: Bantam Books, 1978.

Davidson, Robyn. *Tracks*. New York: Pantheon Books, 1980.

De Bono, Edward. *Lateral Thinking*. New York: Harper & Row, 1970.

Deshimaru, Taisen. *Questions to a Zen Master*. Translated and edited by Nancy Amphoux, 1961. English translation, copyright 1987 by E. P. Dutton.

Dillard, Annie. *Pilgrim at Tinker Creek*. New York: Bantam Books, 1974.

Dweck, Carol S., and E. S. Elliot. "Achievement Motivation." In E. M. Heatherington (ed.), *The Handbook of Child Psychology*: Vol. 4, *Socialization, Personality and Social Development*, 4th ed. New York: Wiley, 1983.

Dweck, Carol S.; and Licht, B. G. "Learned Helplessness and Intellectual Achievement." In M. P. Seligman and J. Garber (eds.), *Human Helplessness: Theory and Research*. New York: Academic Press, 1980.

Edwards, Betty. *Drawing on the Right Side of the Brain*. Los Angeles: J. P. Tarcher, 1979.

Fennema. E. "Girls, Women and Mathematics." In E. Fennema and M. J. Syer (eds.), *Women and Education: Equity or Equality*. Berkeley: McCutchen, 1984.

Foster, Barbara and Michael. *Forbidden Journey: The Life of Alexandra David-Neel*. San Francisco: Harper & Row, 1987.

Frieze, Irene H.; et al. *Women and Sex Roles: A Social, Psychological Perspective*. New York: W. W. Norton & Co., 1978.

Gardner, Herb. *A Thousand Clowns*. New York: Random House, 1962.

Gilligan, Carol. *In a Different Voice: Psychological Theory and Women's Development*. Cambridge: Harvard University Press, 1982.

Gilson, Edith. *Unnecessary Choices: The Hidden Life of the Executive Woman*. New York: William Morrow & Co., 1987.

Hillard, Darla. *Vanishing Tracks: Four Years Among the Snow Leopards of Nepal*. New York: William Morrow & Co., 1989.

Houston, Jean. *The Search for the Beloved: Journeys in Sacred Psychology*. Los Angeles: J. P. Tarcher, 1987.

Ickes, W.; and M. Layden. "Attributional Styles." In J. H. Harvey, W. Ickes, and R. F. Kidd (eds.), *New Directions in Attributional Research*. Hillsdale, N.J.: Lawrence Erlbaum Associates, 1978.

Jeffers, Susan. *Feel the Fear and Do It Anyway*. New York: Ballantine Books, 1987.

Jung, Carl G. *Man and His Symbols*. Garden City, N.Y.: Doubleday, 1964.

Kagan, J.; and H. Moss. *Birth to Maturity*. New York: John Wiley & Sons, 1962.

Keyes, Ken, Jr. *Handbook to Higher Consciousness*. Coos Bay, Ore.; Living Love Center, 1984.

Lerner, Harriet Goldhor. *The Dance of Anger.* New York: Harper & Row, 1985.

Levine, Stephen. *Healing Into Life and Death.* New York: Doubleday, 1987.

Maccoby, Eleanor E.; and Carol N. Jacklin. *The Psychology of Sex Differences.* Stanford: Stanford University Press, 1974.

Marini, Margaret Mooney; and Mary C. Brinton. "Sex Typing in Occupational Socialization." In Barbara F. Reskin, (ed.), *Sex Segregation in the Workplace: Trends, Explanations, Remedies.* Washington, D.C.; National Academy Press, 1984.

Markham, Beryl. *West With the Night.* San Francisco: North Point Press, 1983.

Miller, Luree. *On Top of the World: Five Women Explorers in Tibet.* Seattle: The Mountaineers, 1984.

O'Leary, Virginia E.; et al. *Women, Gender and Social Psychology.* Hillsdale, N.J.: Lawrence Erlbaum Associates, 1985.

Parke, Ross D.; and D. B. Sawin. "The Family in Early Infancy: Social Interactional and Attitudinal Analysis." In F. A. Pederson, (ed.), *The Father-Infant Relationship: Observational Studies in the Family Setting.* New York: Praeger, 1980.

Philosophical Library. *The Wisdom of Freud.* New York: The Philosophical Library, 1950.

Reynolds, David K. *Playing Ball on Running Water.* New York: Quill, 1984.

Rilke, Rainer Maria. *Duino Elegies.* New York: W. W. Norton & Co., 1939.

Rosenberg, Morris. *Conceiving the Self.* New York: Basic Books, 1979.

Roth, Geneen. *Breaking Free From Compulsive Eating.* New York: New American Library, 1984.

Rubin, Lillian Breslow. *Worlds of Pain.* New York: Basic Books, Inc., 1976.

Sanford, Linda Tschirhart; and Mary Ellen Donovan. *Women and Self-esteem.* New York: Viking Penguin, 1984.

Schaef, Anne Wilson. *Women's Reality.* Minneapolis: Winston Press, 1985.

Schenkel, Susan. *Giving Away Success.* New York: Random House, 1991.

Seligman, Martin. *Helplessness: On Depression, Development and Death.*
———. *Learned Optimism.* New York: Random House, 1991.
San Francisco: W. H. Freeman and Company, 1975.

Sinetar, Marsha. *Ordinary People As Monks and Mystics.* New York: Paulist Press, 1986.

Smith, Charles P. (ed.) *Achievement-Related Motives in Children.* New York: Russell Sage Foundation, 1969.

Storr, Anthony. *Solitude: A Return to the Self.* New York: Ballantine Books, 1988.

Tobias, Sheila. *Overcoming Math Anxiety.* New York: W. W. Norton & Co., 1978.

Trungpa, Chogyam. *The Myth of Freedom.* New York: Random House, 1976.

————.*Shambhala: The Sacred Path of the Warrior.* New York: Bantam New Age Books, 1986.

Tulku, Tarthang. *Gesture of Balance: A Guide to Awareness, Self-healing, and Meditation.* Oakland: Dharma Publishing, 1977.

————.*Knowledge of Freedom: Time to Change.* Berkeley: Dharma Publishing, 1984.

Walker, Lenore. *Terrifying Love: Why Battered Women Kill and How Society Responds.* New York: Harper & Row, 1989.

Wallas, Graham. *The Art of Thought.* New York: Harcourt, Brace, 1926.

Watts, Alan W. *The Way of Zen.* New York: Vintage Books, 1957.

Williams, Juanita H. *The Psychology of Women: Behavior in a Biosocial Context.* New York: W. W. Norton & Co., 1977.

Winokur, Jon. *Zen to Go.* New York: New American Library, 1989.

ARTICLES

Abromowitz, Robert H.; Anne C. Petersen; and John E. Schulenberg. "Changes in Self-Image During Adolescence." *New Directions for Mental Health Services* 22 (1984): 19–28.

Anyon, Jean. "Intersections of Gender and Class: Accommodation and Resistance by Working-class and Affluent Females to Contradictory Sex-Role Ideologies." *Journal of Education* 166 (1984): 25–48.

Bailey, William C. "Relation of Sex and Gender Role to Love, Sexual Attitudes, and Self-esteem." *Sex Roles* 16 (1987): 637–48.

Baker, Dale R. "The Influence of Role-Specific Self-Concept and Sex-Role Identity on Career Choices in Science." *Journal of Research in Science Teaching* 24 (1987): 739–56.

Baucom, Donald H., "Sex-Role Identity and the Decision to Regain Control Among Women: A Learned Helplessness Investigation." *Journal of Personality and Social Psychology* 44 (1983): 334–43.

Baucom, Donald H; and Bahr Weiss. "Peers' Granting of Control to Women With Different Sex-Role Identities: Implications for Depression." *Journal of Personality and Social Psychology* 51 (1986): 1,075–80.

Baucom, Donald H.; and Pamela Danker-Brown. "Sex-Role Identity and Sex-Stereotyped Tasks in the Development of Learned Helplessness in Women." *Journal of Personality and Social Psychology* 46 (1984): 422–30.

Benbow, C. P.; and J. C. Stanley. "Sex Differences in Mathematical Reasoning Ability: More Facts." *Science* 222 (1983): 1,029–31.

Dweck, Carol S. "Motivational Processes Affecting Learning." *American Psychologist* 41 (1986): 1,040–48.

Dweck, Carol S.; and C. S. Bush. "Sex Differences in Learned Helplessness: I. Differential Debilitation with Peer and Adult Evaluators." *Developmental Psychology* 12 (1976): 147–56.

Dweck, Carol S.; et al. "Sex Differences in Learned Helplessness: II. The Contingencies of Evaluative Feedback in the Classroom and III. An Experimental Analysis." *Developmental Psychology* 14 (1978): 268–76.

Fetler, Mark. "Sex Differences on the California Statewide Assessment of Computer Literacy." *Sex Roles* 3 (1985): 181–91.

Gannon, Linda; P. Heiser; and S. Knight. "Learned Helplessness Versus Reactance: The Effects of Sex-Role Stereotyping." *Sex Roles* 12 (1985): 791–806.

Gill, Diane L. "Competitiveness Among Females and Males in Physical Activity Classes." *Sex Roles* 15 (1986): 233–47.

Gold, Erica R. "Long-Term Effects of Sexual Victimization in Childhood: An Attributional Approach." *Journal of Consulting and Clinical Psychology* 54 (1986): 471–75.

Hess, Robert D.; and Irene T. Miura. "Gender Differences in Enrollment in Computer Camps and Classes." *Sex Roles* 13 (1985): 193–203.

Hock, Robert A.; and John F. Curry. "Sex Role Identification of Normal Adolescent Males and Females as Related to School Achievement." *Journal of Youth and Adolescence* 12 (1983): 461–70.

Hoffman, Lois. "Changes in Family Roles, Socialization and Sex Differences." *American Psychologist* 32 (1977): 649.

Horner, M. S. "Toward an Understanding of Achievement-Related Conflicts in Women." *Journal of Social Issues* 28 (1972): 157–75.

Howard, J. P. "Pluralism and Professional Development: Minorities, Women and the Psychology of Performance." Chicago: Brass, Richie and Betts, 1985.

Johnson, Peter H.; and Peter N. Winograd. "Passive Failure in Reading." *Journal of Reading Behavior* 17 (1985): 290–97.

Kangan, J.; and K. Bradway. "Intelligence at Middle Age: A Thirty-eight-year Follow-up." *Developmental Psychology* 5 (1971): 333–37.

Lemkau, Jeanne P. "Women in Male-Dominated Professions: Distinguishing Personality and Background Characteristics." *Psychology of Women Quarterly* 8 (1983): 144–65.

Levine, Grace Ferrari. "Learned Helplessness in Local TV News." *Journalism Quarterly* 3 (1987): 12–23.

Licht, B. G.; and C. S. Dweck. "Determinants of Academic Achievement: The Interaction of Children's Achievement Orientations With Skill Area." *Developmental Psychology* 20 (1984): 628–36.

Linn, Marcia C. "Fostering Equitable Consequences From Computer Learning Environments." *Sex Roles* 13 (1985): 229–40.

Lockheed, Marlaine E. "Women, Girls and Computers: A First Look at the Evidence." *Sex Roles* 13 (1985) 115–22.

McCammon, Susan; J. Golden; and K. L. Wuensch. "Predicting Course Performance in Freshman and Sophomore Physics Courses: Women Are More Predictable Than Men." *Journal of Research in Science Teaching* 25 (1988): 501–10.

Mark, Sandra Fay. "To Succeed or Not to Succeed: A Critical Review of Issues in Learned Helplessness." *Contemporary Educational Psychology* 8 (1983): 1–19.

Martin, Ruth E.; and Harriet K. Light. "Sex Role Orientation of University Students." *Psychological Reports* 54 (1984).

Mathews, Jay. "Caltech: Science Needs a Woman's Touch." *Sunday Denver Post*, March 18, 1990, p. 19.

Miller, Arden. "Performance Impairment After Failure: Mechanism and Sex Differences." *Journal of Educational Psychology* 78 (1986): 486–91.

Miller, Thomas W. "Advances in Understanding the Impact of Stressful Life Events on Health." *Hospital and Community Psychiatry* 39 (1988): 615–22.

Murphy, Patrick. "Therapist Helps Others With Fears of Being Afraid." *Boulder Daily Camera*, February 8, 1990 pp. 1B–2B.

Orbach, Israel; and Hadas Ziva. "The Elimination of Learned Helplessness Deficits as a Function of Induced Self-esteem." *Journal of Research in Personality* 16 (1982): 511–23.

Plumb, Pat; and Gloria Cowean. "A Developmental Study of Destereotyping and Androgynous Activity Preference of Tomboys, Nontomboys and Males." *Sex Roles* 10 (1984): 703–12.

Ray, E. P.; and A. R. Bristow. "Sex-Role Identities in Depressed Women." Paper presented at the meeting of the Southwestern Psychological Association, New Orleans, 1978.

Richards, Robert K. "The Declining Status of Women . . . Revisited." *Sociological Focus* 19 (1986): 315–32.

Rubin, Jeffrey Z.; Frank J. Provenzano; and Zella Luria. "The Eye of the Beholder: Parents' Views on Sex of Newborns." *American Journal of Orthopsychiatry* 44 (1974): 512–19.

Shaw, M. C.; and J. T. McCuen. "The Onset of Academic Under-achievement in Bright Children." *Journal of Educational Psychology* 51 (1960): 103–8.

Stein, A. H.; and M. M. Bailey. "The Socialization of Achievement Orientation in Females." *Psychological Bulletin* 80 (1973): 345–66.

Stipek, D. J.; and J. Hoffman. "Development of Children's Performance-Related Judgments." *Child Development* 51 (1980): 912–14.

Wahlberg, H. J. "Physics, Femininity and Creativity." *Developmental Psychology* 1 (1969): 47–54.

Ware, Mary Catherine; and Mary Frances Stuck. "Sex-Role Messages Vis-à-vis Microcomputer Use: A Look at the Pictures." *Sex Roles* 13 (1985): 205–12.

Weintraub, Marsha; et al. "The Development of Sex-Role Stereotypes in the Third Year: Relationships to Gender Labeling, Gender Identity, Sex-typed Preference, and Family Characteristics." *Child Development* 55 (1984): 215–28.

Welch, Renate; M. Gerrard; and Aletha Huston. "Gender-Related Personality Attributes and Reaction to Success/Failure: An Examination of Mediating Variables." *Psychology of Women Quarterly* 10 (1986): 221–33.

Whitley, Bernard E., Jr. "Sex-Role Orientation and Self-esteem—A Critical Meta-Analytic Review." *Journal of Personality and Social Psychology* 44 (1983): 765–78.

Williams, Sue Winkle; and John C. McCullers. "Personal Factors Related to Typicalness of Career and Success in Active Professional Women." *Psychology of Women Quarterly* 7 (1983): 343–56.

Yount, Kristen R. "A Theory of Productive Activity: The Relationships Among Self-Concept, Gender, Sex-Role Stereotypes, and Work-Emergent Traits." *Psychology of Women Quarterly* 10 (1986): 63–88.

INDEX